# Revisiting Institutionalism in Sociology

There may not be a concept so central to sociology, yet so vaguely defined in its contemporary usages, than institution. In *Revisiting Institutionalism in Sociology*, Abrutyn takes an in-depth look at what institutions are by returning to some of the insights of classical theorists like Max Weber and Herbert Spencer, the functionalisms of Talcott Parsons and S.N. Eisenstadt, and the more recent evolutionary institutionalisms of Gerhard Lenski and Jonathan Turner. Returning to the idea that various levels of social reality shape societies, Abrutyn argues that institutions are macro-level structural and cultural spheres of action, exchange, and communication. They have emergent properties and dynamics that are not reducible to other levels of social reality. Rather than fall back on old functionalist solutions, Abrutyn offers an original and synthetic theory of institutions like religion or economy; the process by which they become autonomous, or distinct cultural spaces that shape the color and texture of action, exchange, and communication embedded within them; and how they gain or lose autonomy by theorizing about institutional entrepreneurship. Finally, Abrutyn lays bare the inner workings of institutions, including their ecology, the way structure and culture shape lower-levels of social reality, and how they develop unique patterns of stratification and inequality founded on their ecology, structure, and culture. Ultimately, Abrutyn offers a refreshing take on macrosociology that brings functionalist, conflict, and cultural sociologies together, while painting a new picture of how the seemingly invisible macro-world influences the choices humans make and the goals we set.

**Seth Abrutyn** is Assistant Professor of Sociology at the University of Memphis.

## Routledge Advances in Sociology

*For a full list of titles in this series, please visit www.routledge.com.*

**85 Youth, Arts and Education**
Reassembling Subjectivity through Affect
*Anna Hickey-Moody*

**86 The Capitalist Personality**
Face-to-Face Sociality and Economic Change in the Post-Communist World
*Christopher S. Swader*

**87 The Culture of Enterprise in Neoliberalism**
Specters of Entrepreneurship
*Tomas Marttila*

**88 Islamophobia in the West**
Measuring and Explaining Individual Attitudes
*Marc Helbling*

**89 The Challenges of Being a Rural Gay Man**
Coping with Stigma
*Deborah Bray Preston and Anthony R. D'Augelli*

**90 Global Justice Activism and Policy Reform in Europe**
Understanding When Change Happens
*Edited by Peter Utting, Mario Pianta and Anne Ellersiek*

**91 Sociology of the Visual Sphere**
*Edited by Regev Nathansohn and Dennis Zuev*

**92 Solidarity in Individualized Societies**
Recognition, Justice and Good Judgement
*Søren Juul*

**93 Heritage in the Digital Era**
Cinematic Tourism and the Activist Cause
*Rodanthi Tzanelli*

**94 Generation, Discourse, and Social Change**
*Karen R. Foster*

**95 Sustainable Practices**
Social Theory and Climate Change
*Elizabeth Shove and Nicola Spurling*

**96 The Transformative Capacity of New Technologies**
A Theory of Sociotechnical Change
*Ulrich Dolata*

**97 Consuming Families**
Buying, Making, Producing Family Life in the 21st Century
*Jo Lindsay and JaneMaree Maher*

**98 Migrant Marginality**
A Transnational Perspective
*Edited by Philip Kretsedemas, Jorge Capetillo-Ponce and Glenn Jacobs*

99 **Changing Gay Male Identities**
*Andrew Cooper*

100 **Perspectives on Genetic Discrimination**
*Thomas Lemke*

101 **Social Sustainability**
A Multilevel Approach to Social Inclusion
*Edited by Veronica Dujon, Jesse Dillard, and Eileen M. Brennan*

102 **Capitalism**
A Companion to Marx's Economy Critique
*Johan Fornäs*

103 **Understanding European Movements**
New Social Movements, Global Justice Struggles, Anti-Austerity Protest
*Edited by Cristina Flesher Fominaya and Laurence Cox*

104 **Applying Ibn Khaldūn**
The Recovery of a Lost Tradition in Sociology
*Syed Farid Alatas*

105 **Children in Crisis**
Ethnographic Studies in International Contexts
*Edited by Manata Hashemi and Martín Sánchez-Jankowski*

106 **The Digital Divide**
The Internet and Social Inequality in International Perspective
*Edited by Massimo Ragnedda and Glenn W. Muschert*

107 **Emotion and Social Structures**
The Affective Foundations of Social Order
*Christian von Scheve*

108 **Social Capital and Its Institutional Contingency**
A Study of the United States, China and Taiwan
*Edited by Nan Lin, Yang-chih Fu and Chih-jou Jay Chen*

109 **The Longings and Limits of Global Citizenship Education**
The Moral Pedagogy of Schooling in a Cosmopolitan Age
*Jeffrey S. Dill*

110 **Irish Insanity 1800–2000**
*Damien Brennan*

111 **Cities of Culture**
A Global Perspective
*Deborah Stevenson*

112 **Racism, Governance, and Public Policy**
Beyond Human Rights
*Katy Sian, Ian Law and S. Sayyid*

113 **Understanding Aging and Diversity**
Theories and Concepts
*Patricia Kolb*

114 **Hybrid Media Culture**
Sensing Place in a World of Flows
*Edited by Simon Lindgren*

115 **Centers and Peripheries in Knowledge Production**
*Leandro Rodriguez Medina*

116 **Revisiting Institutionalism in Sociology**
Putting the "Institution" Back in Institutional Analysis
*Seth Abrutyn*

# Revisiting Institutionalism in Sociology

## Putting the "Institution" Back in Institutional Analysis

**Seth Abrutyn**

LONDON AND NEW YORK

First published 2014
by Routledge

Published 2016 by Routledge
711 Third Avenue, New York, NY 10017, USA

Simultaneously published in the UK
by Routledge
2 Park Square, Milton Park, Abingdon, Oxon OX14 4RN

*Routledge is an imprint of the Taylor & Francis Group, an informa business*

First issued in paperback 2015



*Library of Congress Cataloging-in-Publication Data*

Abrutyn, Seth.
Revisiting institutionalism in sociology : putting the "institution" back in institutional analysis / by Seth Abrutyn. — 1st Edition.
pages cm. — (Routledge advances in sociology ; 116)
Includes bibliographical references and index.
1. Sociology. 2. Economics--Social aspects. 3. Social institutions. 4. Financial institutions. 5. Social change. I. Title.
HM585.A287 2013
301—dc23
2013015909

ISBN 978-0-415-70276-8 (hbk)
ISBN 978-1-138-63967-6 (pbk)
ISBN 978-0-203-79535-4 (ebk)

Typeset in Sabon
by IBT Global.

**To my loving and patient wife, Danielle. Without you, this book would have been an arduous task.**

# Contents

# Figures and Tables

## FIGURES



## TABLES

# Acknowledgments

First and foremost, I would like to thank my mentor, adviser, teacher, colleague, and friend Jonathan Turner for giving me the space to grow as an academic and theorist; for trusting me to stretch my legs with no discernible fear I would fail; and for reading and commenting on far too many drafts of my papers to count.

I would also like to thank those professors at UC Riverside who have been instrumental in my development as a theorist, sociologist . . . and person: Steven Brint for keeping my flights of fancy anchored in reality and for taking me seriously; Chris Chase-Dunn for treating me as a peer even when I was just a student and for challenging me to think big; Eugene Anderson for numerous coffee breaks, editorial commentary, and intellectual discourse; Peter Burke and Jan Stets for allowing me into your lab, providing an encouraging, growth-inducing, student-centric environment, and for your contributions in instilling an intense work ethic; Alexandra Maryanski for being a great mentor and for teaching me that academia should not just be rigorous but also intellectually inspiring, thought provoking, and creative; and, finally, Stephen Sanderson—I know we don't always get along, but your work and quest for the Truth left an indelible impression on me.

Two other mentors were essential to my growth as a scholar. Robert Wait, whose course on the Sociology of Emotions led me "astray" from psychology and into the arms of sociology. If you hadn't asked me to come to your office I probably would have never gone to graduate school or wrote this book. And, in *memoriam*, George Kirkpatrick was my first theory mentor, and a true friend who taught me theory was the best medicine for the soul.

Along the way, I have had the fortune of having considerate and thoughtful colleagues who have read drafts of this book and papers closely related to this book, or have been central to the development of these ideas, even in their earliest stages. Thus, a warm thank you is in order for Michael Carter, Paul Froese, Tim Gutierrez, Barbara Kuchler, Kirk Lawrence, and Isaac Ariail Reed. In addition, my newfound colleagues at the University of Memphis have been welcoming, encouraging, and supportive, and have given me the room to grow into the job and write this book. Though each faculty member has been instrumental, I cannot help but thank Marty Levin for "protecting" us junior colleagues, Wes James for listening to my random harangues, and Anna Mueller, who has become a great collaborator and colleague willing to entertain my theoretical flights of fancy.

To be sure, I would be nowhere (literally and figuratively) without my parents Ali, Eric, Jon, and Jane. They have supported every endeavor, whether successful or not; they have celebrated every success, no matter how big or how small; and they have let me be me, unconditionally, and with pleasure. I also must thank my brother Russell and his wife Emily who have been unbelievably supportive and their daughters Tessa and Hadley, who have been both inspirations to and pleasant distractions from my work. And, for their unlimited support and generosity, and love, I thank Fred, Susan, and Helana. Finally, both of my grandmothers, Pauline and Martha, motivate me to work harder and smarter everyday with their love and their strength. A special acknowledgement, in memoriam, goes to both of my grandfathers Herman Klonsky and Milton Abrutyn; not a day goes by that I do not think of you.

Last, but absolutely not least, I must ask where I would be without my wonderful, caring, and understanding wife Danielle Morad Abrutyn. You've seen me grow as an academic from nearly the beginning, you stuck with me even in the worst moments as I wrote a dissertation that was probably too long or sweated out a tense job market, and you have supported my work and drive through everything.

# Introduction

> While all see the immediate function of our chief social institutions as the securing of an orderly social life by making these conditions imperative, very few see that their further function and in one sense more important function, is that of fitting men to fulfill these conditions spontaneously
>
> —Herbert Spencer

## WHY A BOOK ON INSTITUTIONS?

Why write a book on institutions, when there are so many books on them? To answer this question with a question may seem strange, but what are institutions? The concept seems so important to sociology that Durkheim once declared that "sociology can be defined as a science of institutions, their genesis and functioning" (1895 [1982]:45). I cannot, however, think of a concept so central to the sociological endeavor more poorly defined, ambiguously used, and colloquially understood in contemporary sociology. For classical theorists like Herbert Spencer and Max Weber, institutions were ubiquitous macro-level spheres of social organization that came to coordinate and control the actions and attitudes of members of a population. Institutions varied across time and space in terms of their level of differentiation and rationalization, yet every society had a kinship, political, religious, economic, and, perhaps, legal sphere of social reality. And these spheres were important axes upon which fruitful historical-comparative methods could be applied. Their interest, to be sure, was different. For Spencer (1897), institutional evolution was central to understanding how societies evolved, as well as how societies dealt with complexity, whereas Weber (1922, 1967, 1978) saw institutions, or macrosocial orders, as he tended to call them, as contested arenas in which different societies could arrive at similar points through divergent trajectories, how these trajectories could be stymied by the outcome of these struggles, and how the tendency toward rationalization led to some highly universal properties regardless of time or place. Despite their divergent interests, Spencer and Weber saw institutions as macro-level phenomena, distinct in their own right.

In fact, a review of the classical sociologists reveals a loosely coupled set of scholars studying the "general characteristics of 'society' or social order," "the comparative analysis of various types of societies and institutional complexes," and "the explanation of such variabilities in terms of social or 'natural' forces or mechanisms" (Eisenstadt 1977:60). The British anthropologists focused on preliterate societies, concluding that they differed from other configurations because kinship, as a macro-level structural and cultural milieu, was the principal institutional domain in which people and groups acted, exchanged, and communicated (Malinowski 1922; Radcliffe-Brown 1965). The point, ultimately, was that problems like biological and cultural reproduction were the most salient concerns humans had to deal with, and it was through solutions centered on descent and marriage in which they were resolved. But what is most fascinating about these ethnographies is that they reveal the existence of other institutions, not yet structural differentiated or culturally autonomous from kinship, but that were able to make their presence felt physically, temporally, and socially. Institutions like law (Malinowski 1959), religion (Radin 1937 [1957]), or polity (Gluckman 1965) were discernible, even if they were not clearly differentiated institutional spheres.

Sociologists, of course, have long been interested in the perplexing rise of the west. Institutional analyses, in the classical tradition, were not focused on societies where kinship dominated, but conversely, in societies where kinship was but one institution among many differentiated and autonomous institutions. The question, of course, has long been why the west developed highly complex institutional complexes—or the total arrangement/relationships of a society's institutional domains—when the west was far more advanced. And, more importantly, what consequences the west's institutional evolution meant for human organization, action, and so forth (Marx 1845–6 [1972]; Veblen 1899 [1998]; Sumner and Keller 1927). What is notable in these studies, and the sociological institutionalism that followed over the last century, was the limited list of institutions a diverse body of scholars identified: kinship, polity, religion, economy, law, and education in addition to the tacit agreement about what each institution does.

One might clumsily classify this tradition of loosely coupled scholars historical or old institutionalism.[1] The tradition, for better or for worse, found its most prominent standard bearer in Talcott Parsons, who reinvented the term institutions by calling them subsystems (Parsons 1951; Parsons and Shils 1951) and bridged the classics with contemporary historical institutionalists. Parsons, like Weber and Spencer, was interested in polity, economy, law, kinship, and religion, but was too interested in theory building to elucidate why they were really important, what made them evolve, and what their evolution's consequences were for society. His interest in sociocultural evolution, as the process of institutional and societal change, came too late to be taken seriously by most sociologists; and today, neo-evolutionary sociologists considered it a primitive and poorly thought-out evolutionism harkening back to 19th-century fallacious arguments (Sanderson 2007). The marginalization of Parsons, which was understandable for numerous reasons, was also the marginalization of the institutionalism of Spencer and Weber, despite the chasm between Parsonsian functionalism and classical institutionalism.

In the vacuum left by Parsons, institutionalisms of various types have sprouted, mostly focused on cultural explanations, meso-level phenomena, and taken-for-granted institutions (Powell and DiMaggio 1991; Nee 2005; Greenwood et al. 2008). Hence the need for a book like this. Although the new institutionalisms have been successful in drawing attention to organizations, and have generated too many insights to catalog here, the idea that the macro-level of social reality exists and is distinct from the meso-level has been lost in the mainstream of sociology. Replaced by organizational analysis, institutions have become "catch-all" environments that are treated like exogenous variables in a structural equation model: they exist, but it is not important to explain them, detail their dynamics, or conceptualize them apart from organizations. Yet, institutions remain as central today as when Durkheim was asserting they are central to the study of society. To be sure, there have been numerous advances in the historical institutionalist tradition: Luhmann's (1982, 1995, 2012) rehabilitation of Parsons through the integration of symbolic interactionism, dramaturgy, and phenomenological insights; Eisenstadt's (1964b, 1965a, 1971a, 1980) dynamic reinterpretation of Weberian historical institutionalism; Lenski's (1970, 2005) models of sociocultural evolution; Turner's (2003, 2010a) evolutionary-institutionalism; and my own (2009a, 2012, 2013) work on institutional autonomy and ecology. My guess, however, is that these advances are lost in the "cacophony" of institutionalisms and the tendency to use the term in its colloquial sense. Again, there is a pressing need for a book that makes the case that institutions are things worth studying and that this argument does not need to be functionalist—even though it can draw from Parsons or Spencer—vis-à-vis the inclusion of conflict and change, or that it need be overly cultural or material.

Perhaps I can be accused of overstating the situation, but there was a time when sociologists in general *discerned* a macro-level of reality *distinct* from other levels of reality—especially meso-levels, or the organizational level of societies. And although some general theorists like Luhmann (2012) or Jonathan Turner (2010) continue to argue that there are there are distinguishable levels of reality, both analytically and empirically, sociology since the 1970s has worked to rectify the things structural functionalism ignored—for example, the micro-, the cultural, and stratification/power, all of which were necessary adjustments and inclusions. But, with the rise of the Marxist cultural program (Baudrillard 1972 [1981]; Giddens 1975; Bourdieu 1977) coinciding with the microsociological turn toward cognition, which emphasized language (Saussure 1959) and phenomenological (Schutz 1967)/ethnomethodological (Garfinkel 1964) epistemology, scripts, cognitive schemata, and the like (Knorr-Cetina 1981), the important aspects like material reality, structuralism, and the macroview of human societies were extricated . . . or, maybe more fairly, relegated to a corner. The macro-level was suddenly reducible to micro-aggregations or simply taken for granted, and the material/structural dimensions of social life were eschewed or given secondary status in favor of cultural explanations. The normative, once the dominant theoretical solution to commitment and social control, was tossed aside for a relatively radical interpretation of Weber that rested on legitimation, taken for grantedness, and traditional authority that somehow found the agent as a creative embedded actor capable of recreating the social universe or creating it within his or her bounded rationality (Berger and Luckmann 1966; for a critique, see Emirbayer and Mische 1998; Colomy 1998); even Marx's interest in the coercive regulation imposed by real groups was replaced by the cultural emphasis on technological and consumptive alienation, and language (Marcuse 1964; Habermas 1985; Adorno 1991). Concepts central to sociology since its advent, for example, the division of labor, were turned aside, in favor of culture—as if culture was somehow distinguishable from the division of labor! Or, as Fuchs has more cogently argued,

> Microsocial reality is held to be somehow "more real" and "more empirical than macrosocial reality; and thus all sociological knowledge depends on microsociological observations for its "ultimate empirical validation." In fact, while macrosociological concepts such as "state" or "organization" can only be reified constructs lacking true empirical referents, microsociological concepts such as "interaction" and "situation" have privileged experiential access to the only objective reality there is . . . Strictly speaking, however, there *are no such things as "individuals," "interactions," or "situations" either* . . . [and they] are in no sense less "reified" and "more empirical" than, say, the constructs of "state," "revolution," or the Watson-Crick model of DNA . . . Thus, we could just as well propose that it is not individuals, but the brain in cooperation with the body that "acts"; and that we therefore must "reduce" or "translate" intentional or rational explanations into neurophysiological explanations. (1989:177–8)

In the vacuum left by the marginalization of functionalism, the mysterious disappearance of economic sociology, and the cultural-cognitive turn, a new form of organizational analysis emerged under the guise "new institutionalism." What differentiated this tradition from previous macro theories was its emphasis on the "cultural-cognitive pillar of social control," as Richard Scott (2001, 2008) terms it, and the shift from the organization to clusters of organizations as organizational environments. The institution became a broader, but vaguer, environment often composed of scripts or cultural myths (Meyer and Rowan 1977) that constrained the forms available to organizations by legitimating some forms over others. The language has varied, but the conceptual apparatus remains the same: organizations are affected by the organizations in their environment, and by murky institutional forces like mimetic isomorphisms (DiMaggio and Powell 1983) or "rules of the game" (Giddens 1984; Bourdieu 1990; North 1990). The few lists of institutions tends to favor all things, no matter how different, that endure over time including roles, organizations, ideologies, rituals, and so forth (Jepperson 1991:144–5).

The decision to write the book, and its need, is ironically supported by the recent flux of institutionalisms meant to supplement (Turner 2003, 2010; Thornton, Ocasio, and Lounsbury 2012) or supplant (Fligstein and McAdam 2011, 2012; Boltanski and Thévenot 1991 [2006]) the "new" institutionalisms. In other words, the new institutionalisms have become untenable to some degree. Thus, I do not reject microsociology—actually, I make quite a bit of use of the three decades of advances—or cultural-cognitive explanations. Rather, the ultimate goal of this book is to *put the institution back into institutional analysis*, not supplant the last 40 years of sociological inquiry. I do not think re-introducing macro-level structural and cultural formations into contemporary sociological discourse can or should threaten well-established traditions or fields, but rather supplement them by bringing in something lost with the exorcism of Parsons. In fact, if there are any lessons learned over the last four decades it's that false dichotomies are good for polemical arguments, but not good explanations of real life; there is no reason to presuppose a cultural or material, agency or structure, normative or cultural-cognitive supremacy in theory building. The theory advanced within, then, draws from Weber and Spencer, Parsons and his colleagues, new institutionalisms and their recent critics (e.g., strategic action fields); it learns from the mistakes of the functionalists, but chooses not to throw out the proverbial baby with the bathwater; and it considers the neo-evolutionary schools advances as useful for constructing a robust theory of institutional change (e.g., Turner 1995, 2003, 2010a; Chase-Dunn and Hall 1997; Sanderson 1999; Lenski 2005; Nolan and Lenski 2009; Turner and Maryanski 2008, 2009).

This, then, is a book about macrosociology and what Durkheim considered the central component for a science of society: *institutions*. Questions that have been central to sociological inquiry since the 19th century will be revisited through a fresh, contemporary analysis of institutions and their relevance. Moreover, the descriptive and explanatory theory building is rooted in three questions: How can we return macrohistorical sociology to its former position in the discipline, where ambition was rewarded instead of shunned, and where generalizable, abstract theory motivated research questions? How can we build a frame of analysis that allows macrosociologists to be comfortable studying *all* human societies and not just those with nation-states or post–World War II societies? And, finally, how can we bring functionalism, whose central question remains interesting even if previous answers were often problematic, back into the sociological conversation? The goal, again, is to return the *institution* to *institutional analysis*. In essence, the theory offered throughout this book offers a more satisfying way of talking about macrosociology, institutions, and historical analyses, while supplementing the invaluable insights and conclusions organizational scholars have been researching since the 1970s. Our first step is determining, precisely, what institutions are and what they are not.

## THE CACAPHONY OF INSTITUTIONALISMS

### The Catchalls

For most sociologists, the concept institution is not even problematized. Generally, it is used in two different, yet similar ways: as a name for any force, mechanism, or phenomenon that endures for an indefinite period of time. We use it quite unknowingly this way, referring to a professor in our department who has been there, seemingly, forever or the university we work at. Others have taken a narrower path that identifies mechanisms that confer duties, rights, and responsibilities like marriage and property rights (Hughes 1942; Burgess and Locke 1945). In essence, there is little systematic consideration of institutions because the term can be used whenever one needs to label something enduring. The question, though, is am I making much ado about nothing?

Well, consider this: if someone provided you with a list of institutions that included a diverse array of social phenomena that included organizations, the handshake, the presidency, sexism, and so on (Jepperson 1991:144–5), would you know what an institution was? That is, are institutions so broadly defined that the differences between collectives, patterned action, role positions, and ideologies are less important than their similarities? If the answer to this is yes, then can we also define "ice cream," "scotch tape," and "rock and roll" as institutions? Ultimately, should a concept, declared central to sociology by Durkheim, be used in a colloquial, catchall manner? This book answers definitely no! I do not take this argument lightly, nor do I intend this to be polemical. Rather, it is imperative that sociology mature as a science, which begins with some clear definitions and classifications that allow us to distinguish between the things we find interesting and worth studying.

#### *New Institutionalisms*

The most pervasive contemporary form of institutional analysis is termed new institutionalism (Meyer and Rowan 1977; Powell and DiMaggio 1991; Nee 2005; Greenwood et al. 2008).[2] In the gap left by the bizarre demise of economic sociology in the 1960s, the new institutionalists emerged to study organizations and organizational dynamics—in particular, formal economic organizations (Aldrich and Ruef 2006). This tradition tends to use the term institution in two contradictory ways. First, institutions are the environments (Edelman and Suchman 1997; W. Scott 2001, 2008) that shape and constrain organizational interaction and exchange. In one sense, this usage parallels the older forms of institutionalism, as it will be maintained throughout the book that institutions are constituted by collectives, among other things. What differs, however, is that this book begins with the institution as the unit of analysis, and rather than take for granted what institutions are or overemphasize one aspect over all others, it lays out a compelling theoretical framework that describes institutions; identifies and explains their most important, emergent properties and dynamics; and tries to link this to organizational analyses. The two perspectives are not contradictory, but rather complementary.

The second usage is processual: institutions are myths (Meyer and Rowan 1977), isomorphic forces (DiMaggio and Powell 1983), rules of the game (North 1990), and so on. The emphasis is on the limits placed on organizations, and institutions remain environmental variables but exogenous to their models. In actuality, what matters most for these new institutionalists are the other types of organizations in the environment that perpetuate legitimated forms. The institutional student cannot help but wonder, then, what institutions really are. The confusion is made worse when some scholars, like Meyer and Rowan (1977), insist that organizations can become institutions.

Perhaps I am being unfair to the new institutionalists who have been quite successful in providing a wealth of empirically verified insights into contemporary organizational behavior. Yet, in spite of their success myriad perspectives have emerged challenging and criticizing new institutionalism and its perceived weaknesses. In particular, new institutionalists have generally ignored divergent patterns in favor of convergent forms (Kraatz and Zajac 1996; D'Aunno, Succi, and Alexander 2000; Fligstein and McAdam 2011), reduced agency to either unintentional script following or utilitarian models (Leca and Naccache 2006), remained historically bound to the post–World War II west (Abrutyn and Turner 2011), and have favored cultural-cognitive mechanisms over analyses of power or normativity. Their hold on the concept *institution* is simply untenable, and would be better served being used to describe the macro-level of social reality. That being said, the theoretical framework posited throughout this book is not opposed to new institutionalisms, but rather looks to supplement them with a more historical, richer, and robust theory of the environments they find their object of analyses embedded. But what about these new challenges? Might we find a better use for *institution*?

## Strategic Action Fields

Fligstein and McAdam (2011, 2012) have recently blended some insights from the new institutionalists and those of the social movements' literature. Their emphasis has shifted the focus from fields (DiMaggio and Powell 1983; Bourdieu 1992, 1993), economic sectors (W. Scott and Meyer 1983), or markets (Fligstein 1996) as centers of reproduction, to strategic action fields (SAFs) as contested spaces in which incumbents struggle to preserve their control over the rules of the game and interpretive frames actors use within the field and challengers who seek to usurp their position and/or alter the cultural space. The advance from new institutionalism is clear and important: (1) SAFs are not closed systems, but exist within a series of higher- and lower-level SAFs both horizontally (e.g., temporally) and vertically (e.g., hierarchically); (2) understanding outcomes requires consideration of "exogenous shocks" or contingencies beyond the SAF that reverberate throughout it; and (3) power is a major variable to consider in all SAFs.

This perspective provides much to like. We can build on it through a more coherent macro-level theory. First, elucidating the larger spheres of social reality in which a series of SAFs begin and end in, more clarity as to what rules are likely to exist, how power is likely to be distributed, the types of resources potentially mobilized by both incumbents and challengers, and the variation we would expect across SAFs. Moreover, institutional boundaries sketch clearer outlines that seem to be invisible in Fligstein and McAdam's work, which suggests fields exist within fields which exist within fields, *ad infinitum*. Third, we can eschew the vague term *exogenous shocks* in favor of macro-level forces, exogenous *and* endogenous exigencies, selection pressures, and so forth. The types of things altering the course of SAFs can be expanded and given greater depth by revisiting the old institutionalism and its current manifestations. Fourth, though Fligstein and McAdam bring power and conflict into a new institutionalist framework, there are still questions of integration, solidarity, and the like that are missing. What links SAFs to each other? What allows or prevents communication? What holds coalitions together and breaks them apart? What is being struggled over? Fifth and final, despite the advance, the structural and material dimensions of SAFs go largely ignored. The fight is over rules and meanings, and power positions. Where are the divisions of labor, and material resources? What happened to structure, and how are fields structured apart from each other and structurally linked to each other? These questions are not impossible to answer, and their answer lies in the various discussions (in particular, Chapters 3 and 5) of macro-level institutions.

## Institutional Logics

Recently, a "new" perspective labeled *institutional logics* has emerged from the work of new institutionalists Friedland and Alford (1991). Like the general theory of SAFs, this new perspective emerged in the face of the growing chorus of criticisms facing new institutionalists—primarily the lack of attention to the macro-world and the general disregard for material/structural dimensions of social reality. Institutional logics have been defined as socially constructed, historically contingent patterns of symbols and practices, as well as the explanations and justification surrounding symbols and practices, that ultimately provide "meaning to [actors'] daily activity, organize time and space, and reproduce their lives and experiences" (Thornton, Ocasio, and Lounsbury 2012:2). As such, logics seem very close to Luhmann's (1982, 1995, 2012) *thematization*, Parsons' (1951, 1971) cybernetic model and his emphasis on value orientations, and to this book's discussion of *intra*-institutional culture and, in particular, *generalized symbolic* media

(Chapter 5; cf. Abrutyn and Turner 2011; Turner 2011). What is interesting, however, is their shift from the meso-level clusters of collectives new institutionalists favor to what they term *institutional orders*—for examle, the state, the market, Christian religions (cf. Thornton et al. 2012:52). Institutional orders are important because each "institution" generates a different logic that is translated into distinct types of practices and "institutional work" (Lounsbury 2007; Marquis and Lounsbury 2007; Thornton and Ocasio 2008). To be sure, this is not that radical of a premise, and in many ways offers some clear overlaps with the theoretical material we will be working with.

Hence, while there is much to like about this perspective, gaps remain that could be supplemented by the proposed theoretical framework of this book. For one, *logic* has been used by numerous scholars and by this particular institutionalism in very vague, catchall terminology (Fligstein and McAdam 2011, 2012). It almost seems an empty concept that deserves greater precision. When we get to our discussion of generalized symbolic media, I believe we could replace or overlay the more concrete circulation of media with the idea of logic. In addition to this criticism, the definition of logic includes both *symbols* and *practices*, but seems to remain stuck in new institutionalisms emphasis on culture and cognition. There is little regard for structure or truly material elements of social life—for example, the division of labor (Eisenstadt 1977; Rueschemeyer 1977), despite their insistence to the contrary. The cultural turn in sociology, besides perhaps that of neofunctionalism (Alexander 1988b; Alexander and Colomy 1990), has basically abandoned the material side of social life, thus robbing institutions and macrosociology of an essential force or mechanism.

More problematic is the use of the term institution that remains deeply indebted to the new institutional school. Institutions are lodged in a specific historical period (e.g., "modernity"), lack generalizability, take on an air of essentialism, and, ultimately, conflate the macro-level (institutions) with meso-level phenomena (the state or the family), networks found within institutions (markets), and entire cultural systems (Christian religions) (cf. Thornton, et al. 2012:52–7). The polity and kinship are more than just the state or a family, and the economy is more than just markets. Furthermore, the point has been made that these types of things, states and families, have tended to vary across time and space in ways that reduce their comparability, whereas polities and kinship have discrete generic properties and dynamics regardless of time and space. Nevertheless, there is much to be gleaned from institutional logic's insights, and as we shall see especially in Chapter 5, we will integrate their work into a robust theory of institutional culture.

## The Mythos of Bourdieuian Sociology

Bourdieu's sociology is both inspirational and a bane to macrosociologists. He is ambiguous and elusive. Yet, a concept like *habitus* in some way captures something uniquely sociological in a way that "role-status position" does not. That being said, *habitus*, like nearly every other Bourdieuian concept, is purposefully *protean*: to avoid being objectivist or subjectivist, favoring structure or agency, Bourdieu's definitions shift ever so slightly from chapter to chapter, book to book. In spite of this, or perhaps because of it, Bourdieu (1990a, 1992, 1993) has become an epochal figure in macrosociology, whose concept *field* has largely been considered a suitable alternative to macro-structural analyses like the institutionalism advocated in this book. Like new institutionalists, Bourdieu's fields appear to be meso-level, and closed, and, in many ways, sites of reproduction (see Swartz 1997); however, like Fligstein and McAdam, there is a sort of embedding of fields within fields within fields with almost no regard to how this happens, what mechanism or mechanisms facilitate integration, and why some fields would not fit into others. Finally, Bourdieu's implicit Marxian approach leads him to deduce, in spite of historical evidence to the contrary, that fields consist of struggles over economic and cultural capital, the latter of which is always reducible to the former.

There is also a lack of historical consciousness, as Bourdieu adopts the Marxist assumption that each epoch is unique (Calhoun 1993). His lack of historicity is further compounded by his missing theory of social change (e.g., 1990a, 1996). He pushes a critical theory of cultural reproduction, yet offers no way out and seems resigned to the ubiquity of distinction and domination. Indeed, as a loyal Marxist he implicitly assumes the rule of the game remain in place unless there is a major revolution, which, short of that, mobility occurs within the strictures of the extant "game" (Swartz 1997). I realize many sociologists will disagree on this point, but the myth surrounding Bourdieu is far greater than his contribution to macrosociology, historical analysis, or social change. The problem with Bourdieu transcends his theoretical framework and lands squarely on his purposeful intent on obfuscating his theoretical concepts lest they take the form of the type of theory he (1990b) abhorred most: positivist theory. Using concepts like *structuring structures* and *structured structures* (Bourdieu 1989, 1991) allowed him to play semantic games and provided his adherents with a blank, malleable canvas to paint whatever sociology they liked, while proving an elusive foil for his critics.

And although this may appear strange, his work on symbolic power and capital can actually be integrated neatly into a discussion on generalized symbolic media. As an enterprise, theory building should not ignore useful contributions. Bourdieu's vagueness, then, will prove helpful as we can take literary license in using them how I interpret Bourdieu and in how they seem to fit and enhance the theoretical framework posited here; admittedly, this is an occupational hazard of a discipline intent on celebrating a theorist's work that is consciously obscure, abstract, and inconsistent.

## WHY SHOULD WE REVISIT HISTORICAL INSTITUTIONALISM?

### Institutional Domains—Getting It Right

By no means does this book assume to be a grand theoretical scheme. It is about institutions. That being said, it offers the reader a definitive theoretical framework for thinking about macro-institutional space, their genesis and functioning. Institutions, from here on out, are conceptualized as *macro-level structural and cultural spheres composed of individual, collective, and clusters of collective actors whose action, exchanges, and communication are facilitated and constrained by their integration into divisions of labor and through the circulation of generalized symbolic media, regulated by the distribution of (material and symbolic) resources and authority, and given a sense of shared meaning through the linkages, pursuit of resources, and the legitimated vision of reality espoused by those actors with the greatest share of the resources.* They are structural and cultural insofar as they physically and cognitively "cut" the physical, temporal, social, and symbolic worlds into smaller, more manageable pieces. They are macro in that while they are constituted by individuals occupying role positions, collectives embedded within horizontal (functional) and vertical (hierarchical) divisions of labor, they possess emergent properties and dynamics that "flow" downward across all lower-level social units. That is, the structure and culture prescribe and proscribe action/interaction, exchange, and communication. Finally, institutions are tenuous, but real, adaptive solutions to the problem of trust and solidarity, to the distribution of power and the control/coordination (or regulation) of various social units, and to the legitimation of order and provision of, at the very least, a baseline shared reality and meaning.[3]

There are a finite number of institutions; though we offer a list, it should not be taken as a closed one given the fact that new institutions emerge from within older ones from time to time. Mesopotamians could not have dreamed of a distinct artistic or medical sphere of social reality (van de Mieroop 2004), yet today both are relatively autonomous milieu for artistic and medical denizens. The finite number and type of institutions is purely a function of the finite number of human problems that are ubiquitous at any given period of time, which is a constrained by ecology/environment, biology, neuroanatomy, and demography. Thus, historical institutionalists generally recognize five, or maybe six, universal institutions (Turner 1997, 2003; cf. Luhmann 1982, 2004; Nolan and Lenski 2009): kinship (J. H. Turner and Maryanski 2009), polity (Johnson and Earle 2000), religion (Stark 2007), economy (Sanderson 1999), law (Hoebel 1973), and, in some cases, education (Maryanski and Turner 1992).[4] By universal, I mean physical, temporal, social, and symbolic traces of each sphere can be found in even the most "simple" societies. Even where they are difficult to discern, the basic concerns they deal with are distinguishable: law, for instance, is about *justice* and *conflict resolution* (Black 1998). In hunter-gatherer groups, kinship often becomes the conduit through which *conflict resolution* occurs, preliterate people can talk about law and crime as distinct from customs and conventions (Malinowski 1959), and in many cases we find conflicts that often require temporary authorization of third parties to make binding decisions (Barton 1919; Redfield 1967). This should not be all that surprising considering the biological basis of *justice* (Gospic et al. 2011; Proctor et al. 2013) that leads to this concern being a potentially salient concern for most humans. The more important question is how salient it is and for how many people. As both of these increase, the pressure for a semi-permanent or full-time body of legal entrepreneurs is heightened (Weber 1967), and by way of entrepreneurship, so is the possibility of a distinct legal institution in space and time, social and symbolic reality (Abrutyn 2009a),

Four advantages are derived from putting the "institution" back into institutional analysis. First, a clearer vision of social reality can be offered. That is, the macro-meso-micro levels must be precisely labeled in order to describe and explain institutional dynamics. Second, the integration of a Weberian-Eisenstadtian institutionalism with a rehabilitated functionalist institutionalism allows us to bring back some of the useful structural elements of Parsons while also taking seriously the insights gleaned from conflict and cultural sociologies. If new institutionalists introduced cultural sociology to organizational analysis because it had been lacking previously, they went too far and omitted the structural-material side. Thus, structure-culture, solidarity-power, material-symbolic elements are all reconcilable. Third, by identifying institutions as polities or law, economies, or religion, a satisfying historical toolkit is offered that does not rely on ahistorical units of analysis like "capitalism" or the "state." And fourth, this framework offers a comparative perspective designed to generate cumulative knowledge regarding human societies.

### *Clarity in Levels of Analysis*

A physicist would not conflate an atom and a molecule, so why should a sociologist conflate an organization with an institution? I realize it is customary to call Yale or Harvard institutions in the sense that they are seemingly permanent physical and symbolic icons in their communities and in the broader American higher educational system; I also understand the term rolls off the tongue when describing a faculty member who seemingly has been in the department forever. Though, if sociologists make a fuss about other concepts like race, power, or status despite the colloquial uses of these terms, then I feel confident that institutions should also be precisely used. Hence, if Yale, the presidency, an individual like Ted Kennedy, an ideology like sexism or patriarchy, a patterned ritual like marriage, or, more mundanely, the handshake are all institutions, then why even use the word as it has no meaning. Institutions are composed of all of these things, but *they aren't any one of these things.*

Polities are more than governments and economies more than clusters of corporations arranged in niches, fields, or markets. The state or government may be the principal organizational unit within the polity, but it is divided into smaller parts, and it exists within a sphere of action, exchange, and communication in which numerous other political actors exist—for example, parties, lobbyists, citizens; non-political actors may also enter the polity, seeking goods and services offered only by political actors. In addition, polities are more than just actors. They are physical spaces that have symbolic meaning beyond the actual collectives; polities are the "factories" and "warehouses" in which *power* is produced, stored, distributed, employed as a language, manifest in externally "real" referents or objects, and comes to demarcate physical, temporal, social, and symbolic space. When a polity has achieved some degree of autonomy, it *exchanges power* in the form of *franchised authority* to other institutional domains for things like *loyalty*, *money* (in the form of taxes), *conflict resolution* (in the form of an independent judiciary that legitimates legal-rational authority), and so forth. We can only conclude that the economy or polity is not simply a bunch of economic or political organizations interaction and adapting to each other, but rather a somewhat coherent set of structural and cultural patterns that facilitate and constrain interaction, exchange, and communication between various types of intra- and inter-institutional actors. And although some patterns vary in terms of the mode of production or the system of governance, polities and economies have some "eternal" qualities that make them recognizable across time and space.

### *Power, Culture, and the Material Bases of Social Life*

Since the 1970s, sociology has embraced conflict and cultural sociologies as one plausible solution to the hegemony of structural functionalism (Eisenstadt and Curelaru 1976; Eisenstadt 1987). The goal of this book is not to offer *apologia* for Parsons or functionalism, but rather to draw what is useful from all sociological sources—including Parsons—to craft the most robust theory of institutions possible. Hence the Weberian-Spencerian axis upon which the foundations of this book lay. Again, both scholars—besides Spencer's less palatable social commentary—were political economists, who saw the distribution of power as relevant to understanding the structure of social life, as well as the perils a society might face. Weber, of course, was far more cultural in his analysis than Spencer, but Spencer was by no means naïve to the way variations in culture across societies led to more tightly organized and integrated groups vis-à-vis less "fit" groups that would likely collapse or be conquered due to their cultural maladaptions (Turner 1985). Thus, our analysis remains steadfast in a material base of social life, with the division of labor and social differentiation being relevant to our analysis. Yet, power, conflict, and culture are equally important dimensions of institutional life. In Chapter 6, for instance, how autonomous institutional domains develop their own system of domination that sometimes overlaps, contradicts, or complements the more global, society-wide systems of stratification is examined. Or, in Chapter 5, the intra-institutional culture of autonomous institutions is explicated as a necessary aspect of any meso- or micro-level analysis of institutional life.

Historicity and Evolutionary Divergence

A powerful theory of institutions must be historically aware and have an engine of change. The scholars who have theoretically informed this book, like Spencer, Eisenstadt, and Luhmann, were all historically conscious and all took serious evolutionary change; even Weber did, although he rejected a stage-model, nomothetic approach. Contemporary sociology has come to revere the classical theorists, yet rarely extend their analyses beyond post–World War II, and, in the case of Bourdieu (1977, 1984) the post-17th-century west is conceptualized as completely different from the apparently "pre-modern" world. The former strategy ignores the fact that "modernity" or whatever one chooses to call it has only been around for a short period of time relative to human sociocultural evolution. And although it is important for sociology to be able to explain how contemporary organizations operate, it is also imperative that we compare and contrast social organization across time and space. Moreover, new institutionalists have generally focused on the economic firm to build its theories—organizations that make up but a sliver of the myriad organizations throughout the world, including kinship and religious organizations; Aldrich and Ruef (2006) estimate that publicly traded formal economic organizations compose about 7% of all organizations in the world, yet are disproportionally studied by new institutionalists out of convenience sampling. It remains an open question how *generalizable* the new institutionalism is beyond the economic sphere. Bourdieu's strategy, on the other hand, conveniently ignores the overwhelming evidence that suggests much of what we see in the form of political domination in the nation-state was extant at lower, regional levels pre-Westphalia. The inversion of Marx, from a focus on the material aspects of social life to the domination of culture and technologies, has led to a calibrated misreading of history that romanticizes village life while demonizing urban life (Marcuse 1964). And whereas the nation-state does have unique features, and political domination expands in size and scale inviting new problems and solutions, it closes off historical analysis by artificially imposing a disjunction.

Perhaps more importantly, historical institutionalism offers sociology a theory of institutional change, something new institutionalism and Bourdieu have been criticized as lacking (Calhoun 1993; Colomy 1998; Fligstein and McAdam 2011, 2012). New institutionalists become fond of explaining change by referring to entrepreneurship (DiMaggio 1988; Endres and Woods 2006; Hardy and Maguire 2008). In their story, entrepreneurs emerge when the opportunities are ripe and the costs are low. This approach, however, has been criticized as visualizing bounded actors somehow disembedding themselves from the macro-level reality that leads to otherwise unintentional script following. This has been attacked as the "abstract voluntarism of rational choice theory" (Emirbayer and Mische 1998:938; Leca and Naccache 2006). As Weber (1978) argued, however, action is rarely purely rational, and beyond the economic sphere we might expect different types of motives and dynamics in entrepreneurship. Not surprisingly, instrumental-rational action is not the only reason for trying to change systems (Rueschemeyer 1977; Colomy and Kertzmann 1995). Moreover, the type of change new institutionalists are interested in is quantitative in nature, and thus the potential for radically different forms of organization is missing.

We use the term *entrepreneur* (see Chapter 2) in a different way. Drawing from Eisenstadt (1964b, 1980, 1990), *institutional* entrepreneurs are the source of variation in the process of sociocultural evolution. They may be responsible for quantitative growth, as they attempt to adjust the institution to its environment, reconfigure the structure and culture of the institution for perceived advantage, or other possible reasons; they may also be the source of *qualitative* transformation (Sanderson 1999; Abrutyn and Lawrence 2010), in which they identify a ubiquitous human concern, innovate to resolve it, articulate why their solutions are better vis-à-vis extant solutions, and, when successful, gain independence such that they can begin to carve out autonomous institutional space. They are the force of institutional evolution (Weber 1968; Abrutyn 2009a). By revisiting Eisenstadt's entrepreneurs, and drawing on recent discussions by Colomy (1985, 1998) and myself (2009a, 2013), a more cogent link between the macro- and meso-levels of social reality can be drawn up. Furthermore, the taken-for-granted process of differentiation, which often seems to just unfold progressively, is replaced with a definite mechanism (social selection), sources of variation (entrepreneurs), and the conditions requisite for selection to be set into motion, as well as the constraints on selection and variation.

### *An Empirical, Comparative, Interdisciplinary Endeavor*

In sum, historical institutionalism pushes institutional analysis to be empirically and historically grounded, comparative in perspective, and, ultimately, interdisciplinary when possible. It is a theoretical framework meant to underscore some of the most essential questions sociological theory has been seeking to deal with, while updating, revisiting, and synthesizing a more robust and efficacious theory then Parsons' cumbersome version of historical institutionalism was capable of. This is not the only theory one would need to know, as it is focused principally on institutions even if it cannot help but delve into larger theoretical questions concerning stratification, the link between meso- and macro-levels of social reality, and other aspects of society. But it is meant to be comprehensive and definitive—a supplement to the organizational analyses of new institutionalists, a discourse for macrohistorical sociologists, and coherent top-down starting point for thinking about the micro-macro link that has consumed metatheoretical work for nearly three decades. Arguably, a book such as this has been long overdue; I wish I could claim that everything in here is original and groundbreaking, but I think that writers who claim that are disingenuous. My project revolves around explicitly integrating Jonathan Turner's work with Niklas Luhmann's, S. N. Eisenstadt's, a wealth of other scholars who have offered bits and pieces of useful thinking on institutions throughout the germination of this book, and my own evolving ideas. To be sure, there are some radically different takes espoused throughout.

## Answering the Big Questions

Each chapter, in essence, asks a "big" question that must be answered to have a clear and robust institutional theory. First, what are institutions and what makes them relevant to sociologists? In Chapter 1, I layout a theory of institutional autonomy, a concept "borrowed" from Luhmann (2004), but uniquely developed within my conceptualization of institutional analysis (see Abrutyn 2009a, 2012, 2013). For Luhmann, autonomy meant system closure such that texts and communication became self-reflexive. Although I agree that autonomy means the creation of discrete life-worlds, it is difficult for me to believe they are closed purely self-reflexive systems; nor do I see the theoretical, empirical, or evolutionary advantage to systems being closed from each other. Quite the contrary, institutional autonomy varies in degree, which sets up unique institutional dynamics as autonomy is rarely complete or even, but rather is a process, a struggle, and a tenuous "state" of institutional being if that is even the case. In essence, autonomy is what makes institutions interesting: it allows us to compare them across time and space; it is what makes them real in their consequences across different levels of analysis; it produces emergent dynamics that vary according to the level of autonomy and, thereby, vary in terms of their ramifications for individuals, groups, and clusters of groups; and, finally, it is what accounts for the variation within and across a set of institutions. At the end of Chapter 1, I examine more closely each institutional domain and briefly elucidate some of the core aspects of them.

In Chapter 2, we turn to the following question: if autonomy is the "master" process, then who or what is responsible for institutions gaining *or losing* autonomy? Turning to Weber and Eisenstadt, a model of institutional evolution is posited that takes as its core *explanas* the concept *institutional entrepreneurs*. Entrepreneurs are what lend the theory dynamism, agency, and contingency, and allow us to consider how power, conflict, and struggle can be synthesized with old functionalist models. Indeed, entrepreneurs become the lynchpin in institutional change and stability, as it is their successes and failures, ambitions and motivations that drive potential institutional change. Yet, their efforts, or *institutional projects* (Colomy 1985, 1998; Colomy and Rhodes 1994), can only be understood within the sociocultural and historical context in which they are undertaken. A theory of institutional entrepreneurs is posited.

Chapter 3 begins to shift the focus from what institutions are and how they are made autonomous, to an overarching question: what properties are most important to understanding institutional dynamics? In Chapter 3, this question is approached by delineating a theory of institutional ecology. Because institutions differentiate physical, temporal, social, and symbolic space, emergent ecological dynamics become central to understanding how trust, power, and meaning are resolved within the domains, as well as why variation in commitment, control, and shared understanding occurs across actors distributed throughout the institutional space. This discussion naturally leads to descriptive and explanatory analyses of the structural (Chapter 4) and cultural (Chapter 5) foundations of intra-institutional space. Structure is conceptualized as a series of horizontal and vertical linkages that connect constellations of individuals, collectives, and even clusters of collectives; these linkages serve as the circuits or conduits along which material and symbolic resources travel, while also signifying the distribution of social resources like power or prestige, and denoting human resource flows or mobility.

As institutional domains grow increasingly autonomous, however, one resource becomes vital to an entrepreneur's ability to impose a vision of reality on a significant proportion of the population, as well as potentially gain the right to help 'steer' society: *generalized symbolic media*. In Chapter 5, we examine this old functionalist concept to better explain and understand *intra-institutional* culture. The vague treatment it received by Parsons (1963a, 1963b) and Luhmann (1976, 2012), gives us a relatively blank canvas upon which we can construct a theory of media that offers a dynamic cultural institutionalism. An ambitious effort, media and the entrepreneurs who monopolize its production and distribution become the axes upon which culture and structure intersect, the material and symbolic worlds collide, and cultural variation predicated on ecological distribution and patterns of stratification emerges and become ramified. Media are symbolic bundles that are *parcelized* into smaller, more ontologically secure parcels of symbols; they provide actors with a specialized institutional language that shapes the direction and texture of discourse and thematize physical, temporal, and social space; they travel along the structural conduits which imply uneven or inequitable distribution based on ecological position; and, finally, they manifest themselves, externally, in important ways that create value and status through objects, practices/dispositions, and ritualized paths.

In Chapter 6, we ask a key question: how are stratification and institutions related? The most important contribution made is the delineation between global and institutional stratification. That is, intra-institutional stratification emerges around the distribution of the indigenous generalized symbolic medium; it is thematized, given meaning, and obfuscated by the symbolic bundle. To be sure, power, prestige, and wealth remain essential to any discussion of inequality, but they are not the only resources desired by people and scarcely distributed. And, thus, the texture of economic stratification looks and feels differently than religious or artistic, even if they share some commonalities. This analysis remains sensitive to the effects global stratification has on institutions, and considers how the two systems intersect or affect each other. Finally, we examine how institutional stratification systems can be grafted onto the global system in ways that sharpen old patterns, add new ones, or reconfigure stratification in positive directions.

In the final chapter, we explore the consequences the theory has for various traditions and literatures at different levels of social reality. The goal in this chapter is to draw out some implicit connections, examine how one might go about using this theory to frame their own work, and to deepen the potential impact institutions have on areas as disparate as identity theory or evolutionary sociology. Admittedly, this discussion is far briefer than it might otherwise deserve, but the principal focus of this book is the development of the theory, whereas these final sketches are meant to invite discourse, integrative efforts, and new lines of research. By the end of the book, the reader should have a robust conceptualization of institutions. Not the old or new view of institutions, but an entirely fresh, revivified understanding of what institutions are, an explanation of how they work, and a deeper respect for the macro-level of social reality. This book, as is, offers a definitive, yet admittedly unfinished view on institutions: theory does not exist in a vacuum, and I suspect others will find this or that useful, and it will evolve as a result. Nevertheless, it is presented as a finished product, the culmination of five or six years of reading, writing, discussing, and contemplating what institutions were. The discussion necessarily begins in the first chapter by describing what institutions are, and then moves quickly from there to explanatory theoretical discourse.

# 1 Institutional Autonomy

> Those who would renegotiate the boundaries between church and state must therefore answer a difficult question: why would we trade a system that has served us so well for one that has served others so poorly?
>
> —Sandra Day O'Conner

## INTRODUCTION

If institutions were nothing more than some vague cultural forces or taken-for-granted environments in which organizational dynamics took precedent, then a book like this would be unnecessary. Institutions do vary in structure and culture, and it is ultimately their propensity to grow more or less differentiated from each other and to evolve into autonomous sociocultural realities that immediately draws our attention. If institutions are *macro-level structural and cultural spheres composed of individual, collective, and clusters of collective actors whose action, exchanges, and communication are facilitated and constrained by their integration into divisions of labor and through the circulation of generalized symbolic media, regulated by the distribution of (material and symbolic) resources and authority, and given a sense of shared meaning through the linkages, pursuit of resources, and the legitimated vision of reality espoused by those actors with the greatest share of the resources*, then it is the degree to which their actors are distinct, their divisions of labor and media bounded, their authority and resources restricted, and their meanings relatively provincial that gives us a baseline for a theory of institutions. We would, of course, want to know why institutions gain or lose autonomy, as well as the consequences that autonomy brings with it. But before we can examine these issues more closely, we must start by thoroughly reconceptualizing what institutions are and what it means for them to gain autonomy.

In essence, institutions are the fundamental spheres of social action, exchange, and communication. They are "macro" in the sense that they encompass the whole population of a given society. Thus, one can look at any society and find a kinship sphere alongside, even in preliterate societies, the rudimentary outlines of polity, economy, religion, law, and perhaps education. Functionalists long argued that sociocultural evolution was akin to the growing differentiation in structure and function of these spheres. While differentiation remains a useful concept, a more flexible and coherent comparative-historical institutionalism can be built around the process of institutional autonomy and not differentiation. Assuredly, the assertion is not mere semantics.. Structural differentiation remains quite common (R. Turner 2001; J. Turner 2010a; Blau 1970) in most societies besides hunter-gatherers. As populations grow larger, new tasks are developed, and an interlocking division of functional labor emerges. Chiefs, for instance, are a perfect example of the differentiation of political roles and political structures (Earle 1991). With the emergence of chiefs comes also the differentiation of physical, temporal, social, and symbolic space. In many societies, huts are organized in concentric circles around the chief's hut, with relative distance from the main hut indicative of relative kinship distance; temporally, chiefs are able to "cut" time up in which political action or goals can be discernible from kinship ones; socially, "chief" becomes a legitimate role *differentiated from* kinship roles; symbolically, chiefs monopolize prestige or luxury goods that signify social distance and authority.

Polity, however, is not autonomous in these societies (Eisenstadt 1963; Adams 1966; Flannery 1972; Johnson and Earle 2000; Abrutyn 2013b), because political action, exchange, and communication are not discrete in meaningful ways. Put another way, polity has not become a social sphere distinct from kinship, but rather the two are deeply embedded in complex ways. To be sure, there are characteristics of autonomy found in these societies, but it is not until the first states formed 5,000 years ago that political autonomy is even conceivable. Thus, differentiation is a necessary condition for autonomy, but not sufficient; and institutions can be differentiated, but not autonomous.

Again, differentiation remains important, but the process of autonomy is relatively undertheorized and, thus, is a blank canvas upon which we can paint a better theoretical framework. Differentiation, unfortunately, is a loaded concept rife with sociologists' biases for or against functionalism. Shifting to a more "hollow" concept allows us to rehabilitate functionalism in light of cultural and conflict sociologies. That is, it gives us an opportunity to build a more inclusive and empirically satisfying theory. Institutional autonomy cannot be divorced from cultural considerations, and hence, the insights of other institutionalisms and the strategic action field theory, and even Bourdieu, will help shape the contours of the theory. But staying rooted in functionalism and Weberian institutionalism (Weber 1968; Eisenstadt 1971) will reintroduce a structural sociology with muscle—one that complements and not contradicts the cultural traditions. Furthermore, it is through the hollowness of autonomy that this book seeks a balance between structure-agency, material-symbolic, and other false dichotomies. By bringing macrostructural theory into dialogue with Weberian institutionalism, a sense of agency through entrepreneurship can be synthesized with a sense of the preset rules entrepreneurs must contend with.

This balance, however, is a two-way street. That is, institutions cannot exist without the people in them, yet it is about time mainstream sociology remembered that there are levels of social reality irreducible to each other; that these levels do constrain humans and are external and *sui generis*; and that revering the classical theorists should not just be a pastime but also one in which we take seriously their macrosociology. It will become apparent throughout that studying identity or bureaucracy requires considering how autonomous an institution is relative to other institutions, especially those that come to dominate a given society's institutional *complex*—or the arrangement of each institution relative to each other in a society Once one has discerned the autonomy of an institution vis-à-vis its counterparts, one must also consider the position of the unit of interest—for example, identity, encounter, organization. How can one speak of identity verification (Burke 1991) without considering a person's location in the institutional complex? Or, how can one build a general theory of organizational dynamics based principally on economic firms in post–World War II America (Meyer and Rowan 1977)? The point should not be taken as polemical, but rather as a reminder that levels of social reality are embedded within each other and divorcing one from the others cannot provide a robust enough analysis.

## A SOCIOLOGY OF INSTITUTIONAL AUTONOMY

Consider, for a moment, living among a small group of 25 people; all 25 people are family, extended family, or fictive kin. Every day of every month of every year of your life is defined by the *familial relationships* your daily interactions occur within. Every building in your environment is defined only by the kinship activities that occur or have occurred; every sacred day is an affirmation of one's place in their family and their family's place in the universe; and the vocabulary one has access to is defined by kinship terminology. There are no "producer-consumer" roles, no subject, citizen, ruler, politician roles, or, for that matter, congregant, priest, or other religious roles *clearly distinguishable* in mind or in body from kinship organization and culture. No matter how hard the reader tries, it is probably impossible to grasp the phenomenological significance of what it would be like to be a hunter-gatherer as it is so far from the reality we are all socialized within. In hunter-gatherer societies,, kinship, in the terminology developed herein, is the sole *autonomous institution*, and though all other domains, including polity and religion, economy and law are extant, they remain deeply embedded in the logic of kinship organization and action. Autonomy, of course, is not a state but a process, and thus those other institutions have some (but very little) autonomy. In essence, then, institutional autonomy is the process by which macro-level structural and cultural spheres *become constituted by distinct actors, divisions of labor, generalized media, systems of authority governed by a relatively discrete and bounded cultural system*. Autonomy, of course, does not unfold on its own, but is a function of the efforts and struggles of entrepreneurs pursuing some independence and mobility. The more autonomous an institution, the more discrete its cultural system is. Although an institution can never be totally autonomous, it would not be incorrect to assert that autonomous institutions seem legitimately different from their counterparts. Thus, in the example above, kinship autonomy dominates reality such that purely political action, economic exchanges, or legal communication is nearly unimaginable outside of the kinship framework that they occur within.

In addition, we have no choice but to conclude that institutions are real things. In our hunter-gatherer example, we can identify four dimensions of space that provide us with the outlines of these macro-level milieus: physical, temporal, social, and symbolic (Abrutyn 2009a, 2012). In preliterate societies, nearly all space is monopolized by kinship as societies are migratory, and thus few buildings or symbols emerge apart from the daily rounds of subsistence (Levi-Strauss 1969; Service 1971; Turner 2003; Nolan and Lenski 2009; Turner and Maryanski 2009). Again, this is not to say there is no polity or law. Just the opposite seems to be true: among the Trobriander Islanders—a preliterate fishing society in Papua New Guinea—"civil law . . . [was] extremely well developed, and that it rules all aspects of social organization. We also found that it is clearly distinguishable, and distinguished by natives, from the other types of norm, whether moral or manners, rules of art or commands of religion" (Malinowski 1959:73–4). That is, law is differentiated from kinship and religious mechanisms of control like customs or norms. It lacks, however, autonomy as law "represents . . . an aspect of their tribal life, one side of their structure, [rather] than any independent, self-contained social arrangements" (ibid. 59; cf. Redfield 1967; Hoebel 1973). In many ways, the four dimensions of legal space are only discernible in certain ephemeral moments, and they require cognitive work as they must temporarily "transform" kinship spaces into legal spaces. Even in societies where the same person is called on as a third-party arbiter, most of his daily life is spent not as a legal actor, but as a kinship actor (for a concrete example, see Barton 1919); his decisions are not made at a courthouse during legal hours, but rather in his own domicile during typical kinship hours, which are temporarily suspended. The world is kin based, because the other institutions lack autonomy.Now, contrast this example with your own life. In the U.S. economy and polity are highly autonomous, but so are law, religion, science, and, to a lesser extent, sport, art, medicine, and parts of education. We often take this for granted, as many humans are adept at compartmentalizing and because the physical-temporal-social spaces are drenched in symbolic cues meant to reduce the complexity of role-status shifts. Yet, this taken for grantedness should not belie the fact that the macro-level of social reality shapes the meso-level (or the diversity and number of collectivities one can be a member of and the number of categories in which a person may fall that distinguishes her from others) and micro-level (or the types of roles available for people to play, the resources that define the status positions of these roles, and the symbolic medium or media of exchange and communication). As a rule, we can conclude that the greater the autonomy of an institution, the greater the degree to which some goals, preferential arrangement of these goals, means/strategies to pursuing these goals, and value-orientations, ideologies, and norms making sense of action, exchange, and communication become institutionally specific. And the more autonomous institutions a society holds, the greater the diversity in (1) types of goals people believe are worth pursuing; (2) the preferential arrangement of these goals; (3) the type, and preferential arrangement, of means to pursuing these goals; and (4) the value-orientations, ideologies, and norms shaping the relationships between means and ends (e.g., both visions of reality (Bourdieu 1977) and strategies of action (Swidler 1986). There are no rules saying that one institution's content must complement another, or that persons located in two or more institutions easily reconcile conflicts in goals or preferences. Quite the opposite is generally true, as institutional domains become realms with competing interests and views (Weber 1946b). The picture is even more complex than this discussion lets on, because conflicts arise not only due to the fact that two institutional cultural systems may contradict each other, but differences in levels of autonomy shape societal beliefs about the relative importance and weight of one institution's reality vis-à-vis another's.

## Describing Institutions

Thus far we have established the fact that institutions are real things in that they differentiate four dimensions of space that become qualitatively meaningful as the institution becomes more or less autonomous. Institutions are constituted by several things that are also affected by the process of autonomy. Institution-specific roles, collectives, and clusters of collectives grow more differentiated in function and culture concomitant to institutional autonomy. In a hunter-gatherer society, the family was also the basic economic unit, but today one would be hard-pressed to conflate a family with an economic firm. They share neither the same function or structure, nor the same underlying institutional logic (Thornton et al. 2012:52–7)—e.g., kinship exchanges rest of very different assumptions and motives, in most cases, than economic exchanges. Additionally, the divisions of labor that link one family to all other families in a community are very different from the divisions of labor that link businesses to each other; likewise, the divisions of labor *within* a family are different from that of a corporate hierarchy—that is, different in structure and in meaning. The physical distinctions are palpable, as are the socioemotional, psychological, and symbolic. To be sure, it is possible that a family becomes a business, or a business takes on qualities of a family. But, in writing that sentence, I had to use language that indicated a distinction between the two realms that is collapsed only in exceptions to the rule. The macro-level is what gives color and texture to these differences.

Institutions are not just real on the cultural-cognitive level of reality, as as the institutional logics perspective implicitly argues (Friedland and

Alford 1991; Thornton and Ocasio 2008).Because the macro-level is difficult to discern with our eyes, it has been common to believe the difference between the macro and the micro is analogous to the difference between the cultural and the material. . Yet, institutions are constellations of actors held together by functional and social divisions of labor that are *real*. They are material constraints on reality. To be sure, they serve as conduits or paths along which cultural travels and also affect reality. But families do not just reproduce the macro-level structure; they are embedded within the macro-level structure. Moral density, as Durkheim would call it, is a real, pulsing, bodily force. Organizations, then, cannot be institutions because they are merely slivers of the larger reality that they find themselves controlled by. Even expanding analyses to clusters of organizations, a familiar practice of the new institutionalisms, leads to fallacies of conflation. You can pump organizations full of intellectual steroids to make them institutions, but at best all you end up doing is studying a sets of organizations as opposed to the broader material and cultural conditions. Economies, then, are not merely corporations, markets, networks, or sectors, just as polities are not limited to governments. Institutions comprise actors *and* linkages like *domination* or *exchange* (Abrutyn and Turner 2011; Turner 2011), as well as structured patterns, values, ideologies, and norms. Furthermore, organizations orient themselves toward real goals, whereas institutions are organized by and around universal human concerns.

Although debates remain, consensus induced from the historical, archaeological, and ethnographic record point to five or six universal institutions: kinship, polity, economy, religion, law, and education (Turner 2003; Nolan and Lenski 2009). Keep in mind, they are ubiquitous insofar as they deal with universal concerns potentially salient in all societies, but whether or not they appear in temporal or social space depends on specific conditions. For instance, the potential for conflict resolution to be a salient problem exists everywhere and at anytime. However, conflicts actually have to occur or be perceived as needing resolution in order for law to be an active organizing sphere of action, exchange, and communication. In addition to this list, at least five "secondary" or newly autonomous institutions have been identified as present in modernity (Abrutyn 2009b): science, medicine, art, media, and sport. Far less attention has been paid these institutions, in part, because most functionalists have ignored their importance and also because autonomy has not always been a process of interest. But their emergence is fascinating as it points to new research questions: when and why did universal concerns previously unproblematic or assumed to be handled well by existing institutions became salient forces pushing entrepreneurship and innovations culminating in autonomous institutional space?. Their emergence also raises interesting questions about how many institutions can be autonomous in a given space, what the consequences for greater numbers of autonomous institutions might be, and whether or not more autonomy is a good or bad thing for society?

To summarize thus far, we can make a couple of generalizations. First, institutions are real spheres of reality that vary in terms of their autonomy vis-à-vis each other. Although Luhmann (1982, 1995, 2004) intended the term autonomy to imply closed, self-reflexive systems, we see institutions as being deeply related to each other, if only because generalized symbolic media circulate across institutional boundaries (see Chapter 5, this volume). Second, institutions occupy four dimensions of space. With greater autonomy come greater demarcated boundaries. Third, because they are real, and because they occupy real space, institutions have both material and symbolic dimensions. Face-to-face social relationships in which action, exchange, and communication occur are just as rooted in a physical-temporal reality as they are in a symbolic-cultural space. Fourth, institutions are organized around universal human concerns and past solutions assumed to work in the present. The question is not whether they deal with these concerns well or for all people, but whether people believe and trust that the institution, by way of its agents and resources, meets these concerns.

## Dimensions of Autonomy

All institutions are constructed out of smaller structural and symbolic elements: roles, organizations, value-orientations, norms, and so on. As institutional domains become autonomous, these elements become distinct from other elements like them in other institutional spaces. Roles, which are bundles of behavioral repertoires, expectations, and obligations, and indicative of status positions (R. Turner 2001), become deeply embedded within the physical, temporal, social, and symbolic reality of the institution and act as vehicles of distinct institutional structure and culture. Quite literally, Mead (1934) saw role-playing as a process of internalizing the symbolic gestures necessary to interact with and call out certain meanings in counter-roles. A child could play "mother," but without a child of her own, the deep performances could not be accomplished, as the gestures lacked significance and the language of kinship was only weakly understood. For Mead, roles were vehicles of social structure and culture as the mature self was complete when the person had internalized the *generalized other*, or the group's normative order, such that a wide array of symbolic gestures made sense and could be imagined by the person. The role, thus, was the gateway into social reality.

As institutions become more autonomous social space, or the constellation of roles linked together through expectations, functionality, and domination become the vehicles of institutional structure and culture. A mother–child relationship makes little sense *outside the boundaries of kinship*. That is, it is one of the most salient role relationships in the physical space of kinship—for example, the household; temporal space of kinship—for example, "family time"; and symbolic space—for example, some of the earliest figurines in human history are of the pregnant "Earth" mother.

Outside of the physical, temporal, and symbolic space, people can easily identify mother–child role performances in public, and it becomes a central narrative in the modern women's attempt to enter other institutional domains (e.g., balancing work–family commitments). Similar to Mead's generalized other, autonomous institutions develop *generalized roles* that are notable in that (1) they share some characteristics with a diverse list of other roles, (2) they have real physical and temporal boundaries that inextricably link them to one institutional domain, and (3) they generally are indicative of a power-dependency relationship, in which entrepreneurs—or institutional elites—control knowledge, practices, access to generalized media, and solutions to basic human concerns and their counter-roles, whose membership criteria is often quite simple, are subordinate, consumer-like role positions (e.g., Ben-David 1965; Eisenstadt and Roniger 1980). Autonomy depends on distinct generalized roles, because the struggle to maintain autonomy requires a significant proportion of people *believing* or legitimating the institution and its entrepreneurs existence and autonomy; it is a necessary, but by no means sufficient, condition.

A second dimension of autonomy is the ecological construction of the space. All institutional domains, if they are autonomous, have one or more institutional cores that are resource niches in which entrepreneurs produce and distribute the most valued resources of an institution. These physical and cognitive spaces are like beacons that draw the attention of other actors, cue certain roles, and thereby orient them toward the institution. Cores, of course, vary in terms of how discrete their boundaries are vis-à-vis other institutions. In addition, as institutions grow more autonomous, they become environments marked by internal differentiation. Myriad organizations and groups emerge who, like the generalized roles, exist primarily within the reality of the institutional domain. The institutional environment, then, is constituted by clusters of collectives, linked together through structural mechanisms like the divisions of labor and cultural ones like generalized symbolic media. Some clusters of note are niches, or resource spaces that house numerous collectives that look similar and compete for the same base of resources; fields, or a series of niches that are arranged horizontally and vertically, and are characterized by cultural equivalencies but structural inequalities; and networks, or resource flows that link collectives in one niche to another niche, or one niche in an institution to another niche in a different institution. In addition to these smaller social units, variation occurs in terms of a collective's, or cluster of collectives', relative distance from the core. Actors located near the core are like mid-level managers (Michels 1911 [1962]); as *secondary* entrepreneurs (Eisenstadt 1965a, 1971a) or *subsidiary* actor (DiMaggio 1988), these actors are oriented directly toward the core and are often powerful simply because they are gatekeepers and generally provide support for the entrepreneurial class (Abrutyn 2012). There are other classes of actors, like the *liaisons* who emerge within the overlapping environments of numerous institutions and "translate" the special language of one institutional domain into another for the sake of inter-institutional communication—for example, like law firms (Luhmann 2004).

Although the formation of generalized roles and a set of internal ecological dynamics points to structural dimensions, there are two important cultural dimensions that also capture institutional autonomy. The first refers to the emergence of a discrete *generalized* cultural system, and the second elaborates the idea of "universal human concerns," or the underlying logic or premises of an institution's autonomy and its entrepreneur's claims.

### *The Generalization of Culture*

Institutional autonomy coincides with the emergence of discrete generalized symbolic systems of exchange and communication. Human action, whether it is substantive or instrumental, is guided by broader cultural principles such as values, ideologies, norms, and so forth. Symbolic elements become concretized in the process of actually acting or exchanging, which tends to obfuscate the abstract, general qualities of the cultural system, yet society would be *impossible* were it not for some tacit acceptance of a basic normative system of exchange and communication (Durkheim 1912; Goffman 1959, 1967; Eisenstadt 1971a; Luhmann 1995, 2012; Collins 1975, 2004; Turner 2010a, b). Without generalized exchange and communication, individuals would attribute positive rewards and emotions to each other only, and not to the larger system or collective (Lawler, Thye, and Yoon 2009; Ekeh 1974; Gillmore 1987; Lawler 2001, 2006); trust and solidarity would be impossible in a heterogeneous society, and things we take for granted like a university or a mall would just not exist because of everyday tensions and distrust (Goffman 1963a). That is, successfully erecting a generalized system of exchange "helps establish the conditions of basic trust and solidarity" as "the mechanisms of generalized exchange perform functions of *security* or *insurance against risks and uncertainties*" (Eisenstadt and Roniger 1980:52). In turn, generalized systems of exchange seem to be inextricably linked to the generalized patterns of actions (Parsons and Shils 1951), including the structuring of intermediate means and ends (Parsons 1990) as well as generalized role-status positions (Parsons 1964b). Others have pointed to the generalization of communication, as themes of discourse and texts reflecting these themes become constraints on oral and written communication (Goffman 1963a; Luhmann 1995, 2004, 2008; Abrutyn 2009a). The theory posited herein sees both types of generalized interaction as relevant to understanding institutional autonomy, and considers both a product of the production and circulation of a generalized symbolic medium unique to the institutional domain's cultural system (Simmel 1907; Parsons 1963a, b; Luhmann 1976; Vandenberge 2007; Abrutyn and Turner 2010c, 2011; see also Chapter 5, this volume).

Generalized systems of exchange provide the key link between non-utilitarian motives, often hidden within the taken for granted and normative structure of generalized exchanges—and, especially, the use of media of exchange, and the obvious, oft-instrumentally oriented motives of specific, "intermediate" exchanges (Parsons 1990). Generalized exchanges are highly structured, and are where institutionalized produce "limitations to the *free exchange of resources in social interaction*, and the concomitant structuring of the flow of resources and social relations in ways that differ from 'free' (market or power) exchange. *Such structuring stands in contrast to the purely conditional, instrumental, or mostly adaptive activities that characterize simple or specific exchange*" (Eisenstadt and Roniger 1980:52, emphasis added). Yet, every individual exchange, as potential unit of analysis, is not bereft of self-interest or instrumentality; it is within the limitations set by the normative and organizational framework of generalized exchange that makes impossible *pure* rational choice. It is also within a generalized system of exchange that power relations can be hidden, as imbalanced exchanges often go unnoticed because both participants are being rewarded, and as Lawler (2001) notes, exchange partners rarely associate the other partner with either rewards or costs because relationships are not necessarily direct or reciprocal, but instead indirect and mediated through various media of exchange and communication.

Ultimately, generalized systems of exchange and communication provide the cultural link between the macro and the meso/micro; traveling along the circuits provided by structural linkages like the division of labor, generalized media penetrate the myriad ecological spaces distributed throughout an institution and, through networks, across institutional boundaries. As collectives and individuals within these spaces pursue and acquire, use and exchange these media in the various manifestations (see Chapter 5, this volume for a detailed discussion), culture is internalized, norms are accepted, authority and social order are legitimated, and action and attitudes regulated. Media act as

> conveyer belts that link the global system to the local life-worlds, they are the ideal tools to construct systematic linkages between . . . social positions and ideas on the one hand, and interpersonal or intergroup relations on the other . . . [They] allow people and groups that are not physically co-present . . . to enter into contact and communication. (Vandenberghe 2007:307)

The efficacy of these systems is less important to our general analysis, than the very fact that trust, meaning, and power are problems that entrepreneurs look to resolve if they are to sustain their privileges, the stability of institutional resource flows, exchanges, and communication, and if people are to continue to believe the institution is autonomous and a place worth devoting time, energy, and other resources towards.

## The Existential Foundations of Institutional Autonomy

The concept *universal human concerns* has been used throughout the discussion above, yet has not been clearly defined or examined closely. Drawing from Weber (1978), Parsons (1990) argued that institutions were undergirded by one or more substantive or *ultimate* ends—for example, *justice*, *salvation*, and the like. What he meant, it would appear, is that all structural/cultural constraints on action had to be undergirded by some existential goal. To be sure, the goal or end, as Weber understood them to be, was unattainable, intangible, and rooted in something eminently human, yet transcendent from the mundane aspects of social life (see Eisenstadt's introduction to Weber 1968). What mattered was that people accepted the constraints, often unconsciously, because they came to believe or took for granted that the immediate (or, in Parsons' terminology, intermediate) means-ends relationship was part of a longer chain of means-ends action units oriented toward the ultimate goal. In other words, everyday decisions were, within reason, self-interested and not destructive to the moral order because they (1) were collectively-oriented in the grand scheme or long run; (2) were not really choices in a rational sense, but part of the scripts and norms facilitating generalized action; and (3) were embedded within cultural systems through which values and ideologies from the institutional core reached actors throughout the domain and gave meaning to their actions, even when these meanings explained and justified them as self-interested and beneficial. To be sure, actors could pursue naked, self-interest to the detriment of the system or people around them; after all, school shootings and other things that shake the moral order occur sporadically and spontaneously. The marvel, of course, is that most people most of the time act in stereotypical fashion, which is what makes these other events so earth shaking.

For the purposes of our discussion, and to purge this theory of any unfortunate remnants of functionalist fallacies, the idea of needs or requisites will be abandoned in favor of *universal human concerns*. These are the *ultimate ends*, or substantive goals, that come to constitute the phenomenological and ontological foundations of institutional cores, and what allow entrepreneurs to claim their authority, vision of reality, and goals "come into contact with the very essence of being, to go to the very roots of existence, of cosmic, social, and cultural order, to what is seen as sacred and fundamental" (Eisenstadt in Weber 1968:xix). Universal concerns are universal in the sense that all people, by way of our biology and neuroanatomy, are *capable* of perceiving them as salient concerns (see Table 1.1 for a list of concerns and the institutions often built on their resolution), even though (1) not every concern is salient all of the time or for all of the population, (2) the resolution of a concern is not historically or socioculturally obvious (or guaranteed in short or long run), and (3) extant power structures or sociocultural conditions can prevent one or more concerns from being salient while making others priorities. Justice, for instance, has biological roots (Gospic et al. 2011) that make it a universal concern. Its salience, however, may not be frequent or intense in some societies or among some groups for various historical and sociocultural factors. However, when conflicts begin to multiply and become increasingly real for a greater proportion of the population, then the structural window of opportunity for entrepreneurship will emerge as some actors will try to resolve the problem through organizational and symbolic innovations (Black 1998; Yoffee 2000); if they are successful in solving, or being perceived to have solved the problem, and if they are likewise successful in monopolizing the solution, they can potentially reconfigure the social landscape in qualitative ways (Barth 1963; Eisesntadt 1964a; Colomy 1985; Abrutyn 2009a). The inverse, that is, if they fail, then the problems continue to exist, pressures for distingration become amplified, challenges to legitimacy and norms increase, and the social order is dramatically weakened; collapse may or may not be eminent, but societies that cannot resolve these types of crises eventually wither away, collapse rapidly, or are conquered from outside.

In essence, then, the key to this theoretical advance is the simple fact that there are no guarantees that people will (1) perceive concerns as salient or will be able to resolve them in a manner deemed by others as efficacious or "cost-effective"; (2) solutions will work in the long, or even short,

*Table 1.1* Ubiquitous Human Concerns and Their Respective Institutions

| | |
|---|---|
| Biological Reproduction | Kinship, Polity |
| Cultural Reproduction | Kinship, Education, Polity, Religion, Science |
| Security | Polity, Kinship |
| Communication with the Supranatural | Religion, Polity, Art |
| Conflict Resolution/Justice/Fairness | Law, Kinship, Polity |
| Knowledge of The Biotic/Social World | Science, Education, Religion, Polity, Economy, Art |
| Subsistence | Economy, Polity, Kinship, Science, Medicine |
| Transportation/Communication Tech. | Polity, Economy, Science, Media |
| Distinction/Status | Polity, Economy, Sport, Religion, Art, Education |
| Moral Order | Kinship, Religion, Law, Polity |
| Socioemotional Anchorage | Kinship, Religion, Art |
| Immortality | Medicine, Kinship, Religion |

*Note*: This list is not definitive, but rather suggestive. Other concerns can become salient and, therefore, ubiquitous.

term; or that (3) power structures will permit or favor efforts to deal with new concerns. Societies and parts of societies collapse. However, humans are still alive, and autonomous institutions reflect the adaptive efforts to deal with concerns. Of course, institutions are living things in the sense that they reflect both past adaptive efforts and the present interpretations of these past solutions, adjustments to environmental changes, and the ambitions and skills of current entrepreneurs and institutional actors. Just because an autonomous legal institution is believed to be the factory and warehouse of *justice*, and its entrepreneurs are accorded legitimacy, independence, and power-dependency advantages, does not mean *justice* is distributed fairly, evenly, or even effectively. Autonomy is a process by which domains become distinct organizing spheres of action, exchange, and communication. The older fallacious ideas of "fitness" or "functioning" have to be eschewed for contingencies and uneven efficacy, and of course, the reality of stratification.

## AN INSTITUTIONAL INVENTORY

The remainder of this chapter will briefly take inventory of the six universal institutions as well as some of the newer or more recently autonomous. The list is not definitive, as some debate surrounds the inclusion of large spheres like the military (Mann 1986), whereas newer institutions like sport or media point to the unpredictability of the emergence of newly autonomous institutions.

### Kinship

In all likelihood, the kinship institution was the most prominent and autonomous institutional domain for much of human sociocultural evolution (Service 1962; Turner and Maryanski 2009). In part, this is because it historically has dealt with the most basic problem: producing and reproducing (human) life (Fox 1967)—both biologically *and* culturally (Turner and Maryanski 2009). In the earliest societies, hunter and gatherer economies, polities, law, religion, and education were "folded" into kinship. Recall the example above of Trobriander law: although "observers, as well as the indigenous people, can distinguish law from other types of norms, law itself represents . . . an *aspect* of their tribal life . . . [rather] than any independent self-contained social arrangements" (Malinowski 1959:59). Therefore, some aspects of law, especially temporal and symbolic ones, are differentiated from kinship in even some of the simplest societies, but kinship continued to be the overarching sphere of action, exchange, and communication. Indeed, there were few pressures for greater institutional differentiation or autonomy, as these societies could handle most human concerns through kinship solutions or, in the rare case, by inventing novel fixes (Johnson and Earle 2000). Things changed, however, about 12,000 years ago as the climate shifted (Fagan 2004), sedentary settlements began to emerge in certain circumscribed locations (Carneiro 1970), and the urban revolution changed human societies for good (Sanderson 1999).

Regardless of time or place, or the other concerns it may deal with, kinship as an institutional domain organizes individuals and groups according to rules governing biological and cultural reproduction. That is, kinship domains coordinate actors and resources in ways that give answers to questions typically unasked: who is allowed to reproduce with whom; why is this so; when is reproduction acceptable; where; how many children is normal; what type of sex is preferred; whether—and if so, how—unions can be dissolved; and so forth. Where kinship is the only truly autonomous domain, it also deals with questions that other institutional domains become interested in: descent, inheritance, the division of labor, the distribution of power and authority, residence patterns, and others.

In the earliest societies, its autonomy was characterized by nearly all physical, temporal, social, and symbolic distinctions being kin based—for example, the family was the basic organizational unit for kinship *and* for economic production/reproduction/distribution. Today, its autonomy is predicated on its fierce resistance to "colonization" from without: clusters of families called neighborhoods and communities try to guard the boundaries of what are called "residential" zones from the invasion of potentially harmful or corrupting foreign invaders—for example, industrial corporate actors or illegitimate religious actors. These zones are distinguished by their most prominent types of buildings (homes and apartments), and stereotyped architecture and landscape; temporality is thrown in sharp relief more so by its negation: work, school, church, and other times are salient non-familial moments of life; the social space, that is, familial relationships are quite obvious.

In particular, the symbolic dimension of space deserves closer attention, as it is what links the larger structure to the everyday reality of its denizens. Kinship, historically, has been drenched in the symbolic meanings of *loyalty* (Levi-Strauss 1969; Paige 1974) and *love* (Luhmann 2010). There has been considerable debate about whether "love," in the romantic modern sense, is a new invention predicated on the democratization of mate selection (Goody 1998), but I would argue this is a needless game of semantics. It is clear to most ethnographers who have spent time with those remaining preliterate people that what we call love is present in kin relationships, as well as fictive kin relationships. The "hotness" of *love/loyalty*, that is, its strong particularistic, moral meanings anchored in socioemotional moorings, makes it very incompatible with other cooler, universalistic media and their respective institutions—for example, *money* (economy) or *power* (polity). These symbolic realities set up some of the most important "dramas" and "narratives" for most people: where do the boundaries of parental authority begin and end, how much penetration should the state have in familial decisions, or choosing work life or family life?

That kinship entrepreneurs work so hard to protect their boundaries rather than expand them speaks to both its greatest strength and weakness in modern societies. Its autonomy is predicated on strong socioemotional anchorages, ideologies that the hearth is shelter from the storm, and the common experience of familial life before all other types of social interactions. Kinship actors are especially sensitive of efforts to penetrate the kinship cocoon from foreign media and pervert the meaning of *love* and the price of *loyalty*. On the other hand, the instinct is to turn inward, and so like trench warfare, kinship action is rarely on offense but rather against encroachment. As such, we are reminded that autonomy does not mean independence, and in modernity kinship is routinely penetrated from outside. Polities regulate and *franchise* kinship authority; economies need workers; law circumscribes rights, duties, and obligations; education re-socializes children into larger, more generalized and impersonal systems; and on and on. Even its most fundamental concern, biological reproduction, is a concern for other domains such as polity, religion, and science.

## Polity

From kinship, we move to polity because, historically speaking, it was the first autonomous institutional domain to emerge from the kinship domain (Eisenstadt 1963; Adams 1966; Yoffee 2005; Abrutyn 2013b). Polities appear in the face of selection pressures for greater control and coordination of populations that have grown heterogeneous (Johnson and Earle 2000; Abrutyn and Lawrence 2010). If kinship deals with the problems of biological reproduction, then polity deals with control and coordination and is thus about *power* (Parsons 1963b; Coleman 1970), and *power*, according to Michael Mann (1986), emerges in two forms—social and distributive. Both types of power are predicated on control and coordination problems associated with heterogeneity, managing risk, and coordinating divisions of labor. Some have emphasized the evolution of the polity because of its ability to meet growing societal needs by marshaling social power at previously unimagined levels (Parsons 1963b; Service 1975). Social power allows groups to do things that individuals alone could never do: public works projects like irrigation (Adams 1966); facilitation of "long-distance" trade with other bands or tribes (Johnson and Earle 2000); defense against external hostile threats (Abrutyn and Lawrence 2010); centralization of economic surplus, its storage, and its redistribution (Earle 1991); and the arbitration between two different kinship units who's customs do not bind the other group (Yoffee 2000).

On the other hand, conflict theorists like Morton Fried (1967) have followed a Marxian approach and argued that the first supra-kinship organization was likely rooted not so much in providing services to the entire population, but rather providing services to the growing propertied classes vis-à-vis protecting their interests against the larger proportion of small farmers, landless people, and, eventually, slave population (see also Lipinski 1979). Power, in this sense, becomes distributive, though still tied to social power: building public monuments that reinforce a king's claims to legitimacy, conscripting armies for plunder and venture capitalism that expands the elite's access to prestige goods, facilitating long-distance prestige markets that are meant to firmly entrench a king's lofty position, using force to quell rebellions, and so forth. It is very likely that both perspectives co-evolve because both types of power are only analytically distinct and not so much in real cases.

As *control and coordination of social units and resources*, as well as *security* and *conflict resolution*, are the primary problems polities emerge to deal with, we should expect *power* to define the contours of political action, exchange, and communication. And, indeed, it does. The evolution of autonomous polities occurs in ecological spaces in which groups cannot easily segment and disperse (Carneiro 1970), which leads to the amplification of numerous problems founded on population size/density and resource scarcity (Spencer 1897; Durkheim 1893). As these groups became increasingly heterogeneous—for example, occupational and social divisions of labor—supra-kinship roles, organizations, and mechanisms of control, coordination, and conflict resolution emerged as potentially successful solutions (Yoffee 2005; Turner and Maryanski 2009; Nolan and Lenski 2009). When a certain threshold in selection pressures was surpassed (see Abrutyn and Lawrence 2010 for a discussion of political evolution and thresholds), the conditions emerged for political entrepreneurship in the form of monopolizing the legitimate right to use force, centralizing the flow of resources to the center for selective redistribution, organizing and controlling long-distance trade, and coordinating economic units, as well as military units (Abrutyn 2013b)). A new generalized system of exchange and communication, centering on the medium of *power* (Parsons 1963b; Baldwin 1971; Luhmann 1979), became possible as political entrepreneurs faced massive second-order problems related to legitimating their claims to *power*, delegitimizing the claims of kinship entrepreneurs, and finding efficacious ways of controlling and coordinating ever greater amounts of resources, swaths of territory, and disparate populations (Eisenstadt, Abitol, and Chazan 1987).

Finally, like kinship, polity exists in real physical, temporal, social, and symbolic space (Postgate 1977; Potts 1997; Joyce 2000; Abrutyn 2013b). Palaces, parliaments, downtown federal "districts" defined by federal buildings, courthouses, jails, and so on, are physical realities. Annual public rituals, like national holidays and voting periods, temporally slice up social reality and are meant to elicit collective rituals of solidarity. Socially, the links again are far less intimate and personal, as king-subject, president-citizen are only realized in very distinct settings and circumstances, but one should not underestimate the imperative that the ruled, occasionally, activate these role/counter-role sets: presidencies are won and lost based on the "warmth" and personal charisma of the candidates (e.g., recall, most people that met Bill Clinton would report feeling as if they were the only person in the room). Finally, these three dimensions of space are drenched in the symbolic essence of *power*. Presidents exude power; the seals, flags, anthems, and other unifying political equipment are rooted in nationalist power; the stories and narratives we use to understand politics are power-based—for example, King Solomon used his power wisely; Nero was a fool and thus drunk with power.

## Religion

There may be no institutional domain more complex than religion. There is rarely agreement over the definition of religion (Spiro 1966), and because most common definitions include the sacred and the supranatural, religions tend to be far more elusive than their material counterpart institutions. Rather than wade into these sticky disagreements, we propose that (1) religion is *the* institutional domain organized around the conception of and communication with the *supra*-natural, which appears to be universal (Radin 1937 [1957]; Swanson 1966; Stark 2007; Abrutyn 2013a); (2) autonomous religious domains create generalized systems of action, exchange, and communication between religious actors as well as between religious actors and the supranatural (Stark 2007; Luhmann 2013); (3) although religious actors pursue technological and rational goods/services—for example, rain or healing through hexes or prayer (Wallace 1966)—three basic problems all religions deal with are existential and ontological: death/immortality, suffering, and evil (Geertz 1966; Eliade 1978), hence Weber's (1922, 1946c) interest in soteriologies and eschatology. In addition, (4) religion is the second major institutional domain to become autonomous, most likely occurring around the Axial Age (Schwartz 1975; Eisenstadt 1986a; Bellah and Joas 2012).

As such, religious autonomy emerges when communication with the *supranatural* is a salient and efficacious solution to problems of death, suffering, evil, and other tangible needs. As we would expect, then, the Axial Age (*c*. 900–100 BCE) is a period of tumult founded on political empires reaching their zenith in size and population (Taagepera 1978, 1979), and their nadir in terms of existing integrative and legitimating mechanisms' efficacy (Abrutyn 2013a). Religious entrepreneurs emerge to underscore the chasm between the mundane and transmundane (Eisenstadt 1986a), as they make salient the existential/metaphysical crises stemming from the intersection of distant political controls combined with excessive coercive measures (Eisenstadt 1971b). In addition, their universalisitic symbolic solutions that emphasized ethical imperatives, moral paths, and religious checks on political authority was fueled by the intensification of brutal warfare and horror borne of iron age weapons and ruthless imperialism (Armstrong 2006), heterogeneity and cultural clashes spurred on by urbanization and improved transportation/ communication technologies, and, finally, a host of political, economic, and sociocultural factors (Eisenstadt 1986b; Bellah 2011), and the fierce competitions between religious entrepreneurs for human and material resources (Eisenstadt 1984).

Autonomous religious institutions, of course, are also founded on the physical, temporal, and social spaces being differentiated and drenched in a symbolic system characterized by *sacredness/piety*, or the generalized symbolic media of religion (Abrutyn and Turner 2011; cf. Luhmann 2012:138–50, 2013). Houses of worship, cemeteries, and sites of importance related to mythical deities, theophanies, or the birthplaces of real prophets and virtuosi are the foci of *sacredness* and, often, *piety*. Temporality is fully defined by holy-days, fasts, feasts, the Sabbath, pilgrimages, and other important events. Social relationships become, more often than not, shrouded in the language of kinship, but with a *sacred* and *pious* dimension: moral communities become a "brotherhood" and "sisterhood" of the faithful; gods are imagined as strict, forgiving, or lenient fathers; cosmologies refer to the sky as father and the earth as mother. But, these relationships transcend blood, and thus it is the *sacred* bond that links fictive brothers together. Symbolically, then, *sacredness/piety* come to drench the entire religious space where it becomes autonomous. It also becomes a relevant and, in the oldest agrarian states necessary (Eisenstadt 1963), force of legitimation and currency outside of the religious sphere. Through filial piety and ancestor worship, heads of patrilines derive supra-kin authority, whereas kings either assumed central religious functions as the Priest-Kings or, in some cases, were the divine incarnate (Chandler 1976). Even today presidents are sworn in through an oath over the Bible.

## Economy

The evolution of political autonomy may have been the first significant "break" in human sociocultural evolution as it was both cause and consequence for the agrarian and urban revolutions some 5,000 years ago (Childe 1936). In the last millennia, however, the institution of economy has become an equal, if not greater, driving force behind sociocultural evolution as well as in shaping the structure and culture of numerous societies (Wallerstein 1974; Braudel 1979-84; McNeill 1982; Collins 1990; Turner 2004). The economy is the central locus of actors organized in the pursuit of "gathering resources from the environment, converting them into usable commodities through production, and distributing these usable commodities" ( Turner 1997:9); it deals with the basic concerns of subsistence, adaptation to the environment, and in contemporary societies, with creating distinctions between actors.[1] Like other institutions, the economy was inextricably embedded within the kinship realm for most of human evolution (Polanyi 1957); with the rise of autonomous polities, the economy itself grew more autonomous, but was still heavily controlled by political entrepreneurs until the rise of the European city-states in Italy (Weber 1927 [2002]; Braudel 1979–84). The production and distribution of subsistence goods, and then prestige or luxury goods and services, was central to both kinship and political entrepreneurs. The former type of goods allowed small groups to survive and was part of their daily rounds (Sahlins 1972), whereas subsistence goods were vital for the existence and expansion of urban societies where food production could not occur in the political center (Adams 1966). Prestige and luxury goods emerge with long-distance trade networks between chiefs, and the polity explodes with the rise of an aristocracy and a political class (Earle 2002); these are purely goods and services of distinction that symbolically come to reflect the social distance between categoric units (Richards and Van Buren 2000). Ironically, the engine that eventually drives economic entrepreneurs to struggle for their own independence comes from political entrepreneurial needs for free resources—that is, free from kinship, ascriptive, and territorial collectives' control—to realize their personal and political goals (Eisenstadt 1980). As they break the hold kinship has over economy, and move the workshop out of the home and the farm out of the control of the small farmer, they create an economic and social division of labor that can become cognizant of its own interests and, eventually in Europe beginning around the 12th or 13th centuries, a true entrepreneurial unit struggling for independence and autonomy.

Although sociologists often attribute Weber's sociology to an historiography in which the Protestant ethic gives rise to western rational capitalism, and autonomous economy in which market principles and pure economic values shape economic action, exchange, and attitudes, Weber was more nuanced than his critics and adherents give him credit. In his *General Economic History*, Weber (1927 [2002]) argues that the "march" toward the peculiar form of western capitalism, and in our terms economic autonomy, began in the unique construction of European cities. These cities were homes to an economic class protected by charters given by either the prince and/or the church (Lopez 1971); the cities' inhabitants were integrated through the local church, which was often located in the center of the community and was deeply involved in the construction of day-to-day reality (Southern 1970); because of the freedom accorded to the urban denizens through the charters, they created western ideas of citizenship and participatory democracy hitherto unseen except, perhaps, in ancient Greece (Ullmann 1975). Implicitly, Weber saw this as the beginning of the end of traditional authority, or traditionalism, and the rise of a legal-rationalism that would become a bifurcation or axial point in human evolution (Unger 1976). All that was left was for the guilds to fall as they were no more rational than the Indian caste systems for a free labor market and for the church to schism during the Protestant Reformation, as a centralized hierocracy that relied on magic and mediation between God and his subjects could not produce a rational religious ethic that could mesh with an equally rational economic ethic (Collins 1997; Swedberg 1998).

Although numerous accounts explaining the rise of the west exist (e.g., Wallerstein 1974; Chirot 1985; Hall 1985; Sanderson 1999), it is argued here that it happened because of the rare configuration of Europe's institutional complexes. On the one hand, you had a series of decentralized polities struggling against each other and unable to create what China, for instance, was able to create: a centralized bureaucratic polity. On the other hand, you had the most centralized and organized religious organization in human history in the Catholic Church. Thus, Europe was a huge territory held together not by a generalized system of political action, exchange, and communication, and thus the circulation of *power* as a currency, but rather by one of religious action, exchange, and communication where *sacredness/piety* was the force of integration, legitimation, and regulation. Psychic violence brought together a civilization instead of physical violence, which remained local or regional and directed towards other polities more often than the general population. It is in this struggle, especially after Pope Gregory VII's reforms, the investiture conflict, and the religious spheres rare victory over the political sphere (Jellenbach 1945; Clagett, Post and Reynolds 1966), that we see the structural holes for economic, legal, educational, and scientific entrepreneurship that could never have happened in other civilizations. Weber and most sociologists seem blind to this part of the story. His excuses are obvious: he was Protestant in a Protestant region that hated Catholicism; his theory relied on demystification and rationalization, and Catholicism's doctrines and dogmas appeared too magical to usher in rational capitalism; and, he was far more interested in the moment of epochal change, that is the Protestant Reformation as proverbial nail in the coffin of traditionalism, then in the gestation of everything European. Yet, the struggle for supremacy over Europe between the Germanic Empire and the Catholic Church ended with the Pope forcing Henry IV's long walk and his capitulation (Berman 1983), which in many ways drove the final wedge between the religious sphere's interests and jurisdiction and that of the polity's; something that had long been implied in Christ's famous dictum about God and Caesar. As we shall see in our discussion of law below, economic autonomy and Europe's rise had more to do with the church's decision to use *law as a weapon* instead of raising an army, withdrawing into monasteries, or merging with the polity to create a centralized theocracy that was the deciding factor (Unger 1976); a generation of legal entrepreneurs would spread throughout Europe looking for work and convincing the most important classes, including the urban merchant class, to adopt law instead of abject force (Berman 1983).

## A Brief Aside on Autonomous Economies

What separates the economy from other institutions is its ubiquity in terms of penetrating other institutions through the circulation of its generalized symbolic medium of exchange: *money* (Simmel 1907; Parsons 1963a;

Luhmann 1976). Markets are powerful forces because they do not require a physical location to operate (Collins 1990; Swedberg 1995); moreover, *money* becomes the key force making possible legal, educational, scientific, medical, sport, art, and other institutional domains autonomous (Turner 2004; Abrutyn and Turner 2011). That is, these other domains become possible because their entrepreneurs can monopolize certain goods and services desired by other strata, and in return, they are able to accumulate wealth; thus, these domains rarely reach a level of autonomy like polity, religion, or economy because their actors are always dependent on polity in patron-client relations (Eisenstadt and Roniger 1980) or they become economic entrepreneurs themselves, plying a service in exchange for *money*. Thus, law is technically about *justice* and *conflict resolution*, but can easily be corrupted and become about *money*; professors may be oriented towards *knowledge* and *learning*, or they may be looking for grants, consulting fees, or other sources of *money* that may or may not corrupt their pursuit of these other value-orientations. In Chapter 5, when we discuss the circulation of media of exchange, the idea of "colonization" in which "foreign" media of exchange penetrate, circulate, and outpace "indigenous" media will be discussed. As will the propensity for some institutional domains to be more resistant to corruption and colonization, such as kinship where *money* can be subverted to *love/loyalty* (Zelizer 1997) or in religious domains where religious entrepreneurs strive to *sacralize money* (Belk and Wallendorf 1990; Singer 2008; Smith, Emerson, and Snell 2008; Mundey, Davidson, and Herzog 2011).

## Law

There has been some debate as to whether law is indeed a universal institution or not, with many scholars following Weber's (1967) argument that custom and law are different. In a sense, he is correct—there were no full-time legal actors or organizations, yet mounds of ethnographic evidence indicate that preliterate people had laws in addition to and separate from kinship customs and religious norms (Malinowski 1959; Redfield 1967; Pospisil 1978). According to Hoebel (1973:26–8), law is comprised of three basic components: (1) norms backed by physical coercion, (2) an agent or body of agents authorized by society to adjudicate these norms and distribute these sanctions, and (3) the consistent enforcement of norms and sanctions. Law, as an institution, tends to address the universal human concern of justice (J. Stone 1965; Black 1998), which is increasingly believed to have a biological basis (Gospic et al. 2011; Proctor et al. 2013). Law also comes to be the central domain in which conflict resolution is achieved, even though resolution is not always attained and, even in modern societies, it is not the only domain where conflicts are resolved (Black 1976). Finally, where economy has achieved some degree of autonomy, law begins to replace religion as the mechanism most often used by political and economic elites for integrative, regulative, and legitimative purposes (Bredemeier 1962; Turner 1980). That is, it offers actors a unique impersonal mechanism that helps integrate actors by generalizing a set of norms and clear sanctions for their violation, while also becoming the weapon used to sustain inequalities (Turk 1976) and "immunize" against future conflicts (Luhmann 2004).

As noted above, the evolution of law has been a generally neglected aspect of the sociological historiography explaining the rise of the west. Weber (1927 [2002], 1967), of course, was aware of the importance of law in the story, but it has been less emphasized by contemporary sociologists than religion and economy have been. Yet, the west became distinct from the east, in part, because a cadre of legal entrepreneurs emerged from the contingent intersection of European primogeniture which produced a huge "unemployed" class of second-born sons during the population boom that occurred before and after the black plague, and the unpredictable decision on the part of the Catholic Church to draw its jurisdictional boundaries by systematically creating the first body of codified law known to humans (Berman 1983). The church's strategy was built on Gratian's (1582 [1993]) legal innovations surrounding the procedure for "glossing" legal texts and the church's "discovery" of 5th-century Roman emperor Justinian's legal digest (Kunkel 1966), which served as the foundation for Canon Law. Canon Law would become the first truly codified, general system of legal principles. The church began recruiting and training legal scholars who could learn Gratian's (and his colleagues) methods, travel to local parishes and help priests administer Canon Law.[2] Eventually, the training would be systematized and formalized in the burgeoning church-sponsored university system beginning in Salerno, Bologna, and Paris (Rashdall 1936). Eventually, a cadre of out-of-work legal entrepreneurs dispersed throughout the continent convincing political entrepreneurs (e.g., kings and princes) and economic entrepreneurs (e.g., manorial lords and urban merchants) that they needed law to compete against the church (Berman 1980; Unger 1976). The result: conflicts between and within classes became legal battles more often than not, which changed the trajectory of the west and made legal entrepreneurs the heirs to new parliamentary systems (Berman 2003), the architects of political philosophy (Montesquieu 1750 [2002]), and the writers and propagators of constitutions. Even today, nearly 44% of members of Congress were/are lawyers, with 60% of the Senate and 37% of the House composed of legal entrepreneurs. This story is beyond the scope of this discussion, although sociologists would be wise to begin examining the Gregorian Reformation more deeply and the impact legal autonomy had on the evolution of Western supremacy and the emergence of educational, medical, scientific, and even economic autonomy.

As law becomes autonomous, courts, judges, and the like become drenched in themes of *justice*, and it becomes the arena for conflicts to be legitimately and non-violently played out and resolved. It can carry powerful emotions, as violations of moral boundaries elicit strong social emotions

(Durkheim 1893). Though, the medium *justice/conflict resolution* becomes generalized and cooler in order to handle the diversity of conflicts in a systematic and relatively consistent manner; decisions are legal in principle and often conflict with the emotional orientations of non-legal entrepreneurs.

## Education

If there is an institutional domain that does not appear ubiquitous in time and space, it would be education. Education, like all other institutions, was deeply embedded in the very essence of the nuclear family, its physical organization of space and time, and its everyday activities (Bourdieu 1977; Nolan and Lenski 2009). Yet, the sphere of educational activities is a requisite component for group survival: everything must be passed from one generation to the next via some type of pedagogy otherwise the culture is lost and a group loses its claim to being a group. The birth, however, of formal education is slow going at first and does not really take root until the appearance of writing (Schmandt-Besserat 1992) and a real need for standardized training. Randall Collins (2000a) has created an historical typology of schools based on their form and function: the communal schools of Greece built for the purposes of socialization and community identity; patrimonial guilds that created closed systems of monopolized tradesmen; the monopolistic status group schools like those of the "great" professions in modern America; and the bureaucratic schools which are premised on standardized examinations, credentialism, and rationalization (cf. Collins 1979). At its root, education is about *learning*, though what is learned has varied tremendously across time and space.

Like all institutional domains, education can become autonomous, though it is by far the least autonomous of all the major institutional domains. It is precisely this paradoxical two-tiered universe within the educational sphere that makes it so fascinating. Mass education, at the primary and secondary levels, is far from being autonomous because educational entrepreneurs have little freedom to define their sphere of social action. Instead, education at this level becomes a serious arena of struggle between political, economic, kinship, and religious entrepreneurs who are aware that the basic problem of cultural reproduction is so important to the continuity of society as well as the interests of each entrepreneur. In the 1300s, however, the advent of the first universities (Rashdall 1936), coupled with the emergence of scientific scholars, began the slow march toward (higher) educational autonomy. Again, not complete because of the interests of various other entrepreneurs, research universities and institutes are sites in which educational entrepreneurs were able to secure some autonomy through the merger of scientific entrepreneurship. Universities, then, are not just physical, temporal, and social spaces of *learning*, but also the production and distribution of *truth* (Luhmann 1976) and *applied knowledge* (Parsons 1973; Abrutyn and Turner 2011). The mechanism and ideology of "academic freedom" has done a relatively good job of protecting these types of entrepreneurs from the corruption of the outside world. Yet, like every institutional domain, its integrity is always threatened. Private and public organizations provide money for research that can have real or perceived strings attached; administrators of public universities are provided monies from the government, and thus professors become governmental employees; many campuses have ROTC offices, chapels or churches, liaisons from the legal world (Title IX), and so on. Campuses and educational autonomy are constantly under the threat of external forces to succumb.

## Secondary Institutions

A secondary institutional domain is one which forms from within one or more of the six universal ones and becomes a discrete sphere of social action, exchange, and communication at a later period in human history. Four or five contemporary examples have been identified: science, medicine, sports, art, and media (Abrutyn 2009a, b; Abrutyn and Turner 2011). Like the previous six institutions, these newly autonomous domains have entrepreneurial classes with some degree of structural and cultural independence, deep generalized cultural systems—science is founded on *truth*, medicine on *health care*, sport on *competitiveness*, art on *aesthetics/beauty*, and media on *mass communication*—and they are differentiated physical, temporal, social, and symbolic space. What makes them different from the universal institutions is that they emerge rather late and come out of preexisting institutions.

Science, for instance, emerges out of the religious institutions where *truth* was once monopolized and still remains one of its central concerns (Gaukroger 2006; Lindberg 2007). As cosmological competitors (Abrutyn 2013a), scientific entrepreneurs struggle with their religious and metaphysical counterparts for monopolies over *knowledge*, *learning*, and *truth* (Ben-David 1965; Merton 1973). Remnants of their religious heritage remain: graduation continues to have religious overtones, as does the robe and the hood; the public refers to scientists as "they said this" as anecdotal evidence to support their understanding of the world; and science is an epistemology that classifies and seeks order to the world just like religion. The primary differences are in method and in science's ability to objectively demonstrate its success rate and track record, whereas religion requires leaps of faith.

Likewise, sport is a hybrid of economy and polity (Werron 2010): *money* and *power* (in the form of franchised authority) combine to form *competitiveness*, with *competitiveness* apparently having some biological roots (Gat 2006; Blute 2010). Indeed, this theme reflects both the struggle to succeed in a free market as well as the glory and valor of combat without the messiness of dying. Sport, however, is separate enough from its parents to have developed its own internal logic and system of evaluation. Sporting events "are ceremonial competitions, miniaturized confrontations, that oppose matched individuals or teams equally worthy of respect, competing in good faith, and in accordance with a shared set of rules" (Dayan and Katz 1988:168); "contests are *celebrations of these rules*" hence the fact that he two biggest sins in modern sports are "doping" and gambling because both call into question the integrity of the competition. Both Shoeless Joe Jackson and Pete Rose have been denied entry into the baseball Hall of Fame because of gambling—even though the latter of the two was betting on his own team to win; and the case against steroid using players is unfolding before our eyes with consequences yet unrealized. But these are not simply American traits: the Tour de France has very stringent performance enhancing drug policies and testing, as does the Olympics. And for all the money that goes into the business of sports, fans of teams continue to want their best players to stay, take "hometown discounts," and retire as an all-time great; players, often wanting to stay, are traded, whereas team and player loyalty is called into question during free agency. Thus, money penetrates and corrupts the "purity" of the competition, but the competition remains the defining qualities of the best of the best. Indeed, sports are often linked meta-ideologically with art as we consider the gracefulness of an athlete, or the simplistic beauty of the sport.

A more detailed analysis of these two secondary institutions, and the three others, requires more space and different forum. One of the biggest contributions a revamped historical institutionalism can provide to modern sociology is the exploration of these other domains. These spheres of social action, exchange, and communication have expanded the human life-world, enriched them in some ways, while creating more sites of domination that the average person must contend with (Weber 1946b). For now, it is enough to note they exist and that the theory is open to adding more institutions if they appear to meet the criteria above.

## CONCLUSION

In sum, autonomous institutions are real macro-level structural and cultural milieu in which myriad actors, resources, and authority systems are linked together through divisions of social and functional labor and the increasingly discrete cultural system that gives color and texture to these invisible, structural ties. The life-world of actors embedded within these domains are made real by the pursuit and acquisition of generalized symbolic media according to their relative position within the domain in question, and other domains that they inhabit or encounter. Importantly, institutions vary in their level of autonomy, which can grow or contract over time. Autonomy is a process by which entrepreneurs, or specialized corporate actors, come to monopolize knowledge, practices, solutions to existential, ubiquitous concerns, and the right to produce, distribute, and govern the circulation of institutionally-specific resources. As they are able to secure greater monopolies, they begin to carve out physical, temporal, social, and symbolic space to realize and protect their interests, to develop and disseminate their solutions and resources, and to meet some collective benefits; collective in the sense that a *significant* proportion of the population *believes* they have the legitimate right to these claims. These real niches they construct become the core or cores of increasingly autonomous institutions; the cores become the centers of institutional reality, both physically and cognitively. Around the cores form institutional environments, with individuals, collectives, and clusters of collectives unevenly distributed in relationship to a core. Their position determines the flow of resources, their position within the various divisions of labor, and their privilege; it also shapes how committed they are to one institution's core vis-à-vis all others; and, finally, it reflects the unique intra-institutional stratification system that generates distinct classes or categories of actors based on the generalized symbolic media and differential access to it.

In the next chapter, we will examine how institutions become autonomous by looking closer at institutional entrepreneurs and the process of entrepreneurship. This discussion will be followed by an elucidation of institutional ecology (Chapter 3), the structural linkages that tie actors together and act as conduits along which resources flow (Chapter 4), and the cultural system that forms around the circulation of one or more generalized symbolic media (Chapter 5). These discussions will set up an analysis of the stratification system of institutions (Chapter 6), and, in the final chapter, allow us to look closely at how the theory of institutions developed throughout informs other traditions in sociological theory.

# 2 Building Autonomous Institutions from The "Inside-Out"

> The test of any great charismatic leader lies not only in his ability to create a single event or great movement, but alsoin his ability to leave a continuous impact on an institutionalstructure—to transform any give institutional setting byinfusing into it some of his charismatic vision, orderly offices, or aspects of social organization, with some of his charismatic qualities and aura
>
> —S.N. Eisenstadt

## INTRODUCTION

Max Weber's (1946b) vision of the future was pessimistic as he saw the emergence of legal-rational authority in modernity as a harbinger of inertia and demystification that was not an improvement over traditional authority and, in fact, was likely to strip humanity of its humanness. But no matter how pessimistic Weber was, he offered humanity a singular force capable of radical change, of revitalizing a stale culture, and of re-mystifying the world—if only momentarily: *charisma*. We often teach charisma to undergraduates by pointing to specific leaders like Martin Luther King Jr. or Hitler, noting that it refers to authority predicated on a person's supposed personal quality(ies) and the subsequent feelings of moral duty or obligation on the part of the follower. But Weber's intent was far deeper than this, although it is essentially correct. Weber (1968), like Durkheim (1912), recognized the force emotions had in shaping how people oriented their actions and attitudes. In Eisenstadt's introductory remarks to an edited volume of Weber's work on charisma, he posits *charisma* is "rooted in the attempt to come into contact with the very essence of being, to go to the very roots of existence, of cosmic, social, and cultural order, to what is seen as sacred and fundamental" (1968:xix). Modern sociologists, whether Marxist materialists or post-structural cultural sociologists, often assume or imply that charismatic leaders or movements are not real: the former argues that religious leaders are not about salvation, but remuneration and material needs, whereas the cultural sociologists, like Bourdieu, see endless games of strategic manipulation.

Yet, Weber's argument remains sound and worth revisiting. For him, charismatic movements could only be transformative if the leader and his closest followers genuinely pursued ideal interests, in addition to the obvious needs to subsist. Moreover, movements of pure self-interest could not be successful in enlisting non-members, who would fail to derive any benefit from becoming entrapped in new moral obligations and duties. Hence, the charismatic leaders we remember in history were driven by ideas, by the desire to improve what they saw as problematic; their power rested on their ability to inspire through words and deeds, and to convince and influence enough people that what they offered should be desired and valued by everyone else. Charismatic leaders, then, are capable of compelling individuals and groups to blend emotions with substantively rational choices, thus elevating certain value-orientations, collective goals, material and ideal interests, while delegitimizing or obviating others (Weber 1946c; Eisenstadt 1989). And when the leader or innovator could draw a small group of people to him or her, this group could become a *charismatic carrier of culture*, able to potentially alter the fabric of society. They possessed charisma because they were "touched" by the leader, legitimated by his/her presence and blessing, and, upon his/her death, became the true successor to his vision of reality. The group member's actions are perceived as morally sanctioned, and the group comes to embody the substantive value or values espoused by the charismatic leader. It is for this very reason that charisma is unstable, and must be routinized into traditional or legal-rational forms of authority; having done so, charismatic individuals become enemies of the once-charismatic carrier group (Weber 1922).

When confronted with the question of institutional change and the process of autonomy, we look to the types of agents capable of reconfiguring the social landscape in a seemingly permanent way; after all, having the right to change the physical, temporal, social, and symbolic landscape in ways that effect a great proportion of a population requires having special "powers." Drawing from anthropologist Fredrik Barth (1963) and, of course, Weber, Eisenstadt (1963, 1964b, 1980, 1990) spent an entire career examining these historical agents, or specialized corporate actors he termed *institutional entrepreneurs*. For institutional change to be possible, the institutional analyst must determine "the presence or absence . . . of an active group of special 'entrepreneurs,' an elite, able to offer solutions to the new range of problems" (Eisenstadt 1965a:55); that is, "the creation of new institutional structures depends heavily on the 'push' given by various 'charismatic' groups" that constitute "the closest social analogy to 'mutation'". For Eisenstadt, entrepreneurs emerged in times of crisis, or perceived crisis and their efforts were devoted to resolving these crises through some type of innovation. That is, they could become an historical force, a 'switchman of history' to borrow Weber's (1946c:280–1) terminology, or a source of variation upon which selection mechanisms could work operate.

Thus, this chapter is about institutional entrepreneurs, their projects (Colomy 1985; Colomy and Kertzmann 1995), and their struggle for power-dependency/power-sharing relationships such that they can carve out autonomous institutional space for their activities and knowledge building, recruitment, and training (Abrutyn 2009a; Abrutyn and Van Ness unpublished).[1] That is, entrepreneurs are a principal force in the construction of autonomous institutions, often working from the inside-out and from the bottom-up (cf. Abrutyn 2013a, b). The old functionalists like Spencer, Parsons, and more recently even Turner have tended not to specify who does the building, choosing rather to see institutions as macro-structural adaptations to environmental pressures. In a way, institutional differentiation "unfolds" with little consideration of who does the unfolding. To be sure, Turner's (2010a; Turner and Maryanski 2008, 2009) recent work has begun to theorize about the evolutionary forces that pressure groups to act in ways that innovate, but the way meso-level actors actually change the macro-level of reality remains underdeveloped in his sociology.

## RECONCEPTUALIZING INSTITUTIONAL ENTREPRENEURS

### The Colloquial View of Entrepreneurship

Criticized for not having a theory of action or agency, new institutionalists began to search for some type of agent of change. Drawing from Eisenstadt, Paul DiMaggio (1988:14) settled on institutional entrepreneurs who he conceptualized as actors "with sufficient resources who see in them an opportunity to realize an interest that they value highly," and, consequently, are potentially able to create new organizational forms. In recent years, this concept has come to be used by all sorts of new institutionalists as a catchall for organizational actors able to innovate organizationally (DiMaggio 1991; Rao 1998; Endres and Woods 2006; Levy and Scully 2007; Hardy and Maguire 2008). The new institutionalists, however, diverged from Eisenstadt's (and Weber's) original intent in many ways. First, recent criticisms have asked how actors can be true agents of change when new institutionalists see all action as deeply embedded in routine, taken for granted structures (Leca and Naccache 2006)—or, what has been labeled the "abstract voluntarism of rational choice theory" (Emirbayer and Mische 1998). Moreover, a paradox emerges between the oft-assumed unintentional, script-following actors and the instrumental strategizers (Bourdieu 1990a, 1992)—that is, actors cannot be both (Fligstein and McAdam 2011, 2012). Third, new institutionalists ignore power and conflict, struggle and uneven change, while typically conceptualizing entrepreneurs as forces of linear, incremental change (Colomy 1998). Fourth, and closely related, the normative, moral side of action is omitted altogether, which retains the cynicism of contemporary sociological theories of action, at the expense of insights from Goffman (1959, 1967), Collins (2004), and others (Colomy and Rhoades 1994). Fifth, new institutionalist and Bourdieuian studies of entrepreneurs are ahistorical (Calhoun 1993; Abrutyn and Turner 2011) and, generally speaking, narrowly focused on publicly traded economic firms (Aldrich and Ruef 2006), which account for maybe 7% of all organizational units across the modern world.

These criticisms all converge on a highly limited and over-economized definition and conception of entrepreneurship that favors organizational innovation and subsequent efforts to legitimate these innovations, whereas Weber and Eisenstadt had in mind epochal, historically relevant, qualitatively transformative change, as well as reformist, modification. There is little hint of struggle or conflict, the pursuit of power or prestige, the normative or moral motives inherent in or undergirding many movements, and little acknowledgement of resistance, readjustment, re-strategizing, or failure; that is, new institutionalisms' entrepreneurs are as vague and convenient as the institutional environments that shape organizational dynamics. Thus, we must abandon this usage and return to the Weberian-Eisenstadtian conceptualization, which is centered on institutional change and evolution, or the processes by which

> the major institutional spheres of society become dissociated from one another, attached to specialized collectivities [or entrepreneurs] and roles, and organized into relatively specific and autonomous symbolic and organizational frameworks within the confines of the same [society, which in turn creates] . . . more difficult problems for [institutional entrepreneurs as] . . . the increased autonomy of each sphere creates more complex problems of integrating these specialized activities into one systematic framework. (Eisenstadt 1965a:51)

## Eisenstadt's Vision of Entrepreneurship

From a purely theoretical standpoint Eisenstadt (1964a, b, 1980, 1990) was committed to the structural-functionalism of Parsons, but was engaged in integrating historical agents and, thereby, a dynamism otherwise lacking in Parsons' work—even in his evolutionary models (Parsons 1964a). To do so, Eisenstadt drew heavily from Weber (1968), who Eisenstadt argued "came closest to recognizing" that specialized corporate actors were central to institution building and institutional change (1964b:384). It was the entrepreneur and their contingent efforts that led to a multi-linear theory of social change, in which broader sociocultural/ political/economic conditions, and unpredictable historical contingencies had to be accounted for. That is, "a given social sphere contains not one but several, often competing, possible orientations and potentialities for development," which Eisenstadt argues "Weber saw most clearly when he showed that religious institutions may take several forms" because of the historically bound social movements and their variation in success (1964b:384). Thus, Eisenstadt (1987) saw charismatic leaders and, in particular, charismatic groups he labeled *institutional entrepreneurs* as central forces of institutional change, capable of mobilizing human and material resources and innovating technologically, organizationally, and symbolically when dealing with both macro-exigencies like population pressures or resource scarcity as well as second-order problems predicated on the social division of labor and related to integration, regulation, and legitimation.

More concretely, institutional entrepreneurs are able to use their charisma to (1) shift the "global" worldview held by those around them, (2) supplement established group goals with new goals, (3) push collective goals above self-interested goals held by individual members, and/or (4) delegitimize certain extant individual and/or collective goals (Eisenstadt 1971:54–5); and, when truly successful, it is "the routinization of charisma [that becomes] critical for the *crystallization and continuation* of new institutional structure" (1965a:55). In essence, then, their new vision of reality (or worldview), organizational and technological innovations, and charisma makes them capable of reorienting other actors' goals, decision making, and allegiance in ways that can mobilize the resource necessary to exact real change. Drawing on emotional energy, a strong sense of normative, moral obligation, and a sense of injustice and unfairness in the way things currently are, entrepreneurs and their collectives can reconfigure the social landscape. If we return, for a second, to the hunter-gatherer example in the first chapter, we recall a society dominated by kinship. Five thousand years ago, political entrepreneurs in places like Mesopotamia, Egypt, and China began to distinguish their goals "from goals of *other spheres or groups in* society . . . [in that their] formation, pursuit and implementation became largely independent of other [spheres or] groups and were *governed* mostly be *political criteria and by consideration of political exigency*" (Eisenstadt 1963:19). It is in these moments, where the structure and culture is transformed that entrepreneurs are able to change the trajectory of a society.

Eisenstadt's career was spent studying two of these moments: the evolution of polity via entrepreneurship beginning some 5,000 years ago (1963, 1965b, 1977) and the Axial Age (Jaspers 1953; Eisenstadt 1986b) in which religious entrepreneurs began a concerted struggle for their independence vis-à-vis their political counterparts. From 900–100 BCE, some of the most dynamic moments of entreprenuership, recorded in texts, archaeology, and history, occurred in which control over the religious institution, which was gradually becoming autonomous, was the ultimate reward. There are other moments of entrepreneurship of note as well, even if Eisenstadt had little interest in them. Some are epochal, such as the legal revolution in the west during the middle ages (Berman 1983), others more reformist such as the struggles within and between political parties in antebellum America (Colomy 1990b). Thus, although we will need to modify and supplement Eisenstadt's theory, he provides us with a strong foundation for understanding why and how institutions evolve.

### *The Engine*

Entrepreneurship emerges in the context of real or perceived crises. There are generally two sets of crises: primary and secondary. Primary crises are often the initial engine driving selection pressures, or pressures for the creation of new structural and cultural artifices to reduce these pressures.

Macro-level dynamics like population pressures, resource scarcity, power differentials, and so on (Turner 1995) can intersect with each other in ways that threaten people's standard of living, often motivating them to act. Entrepreneurs emerge as innovators of solutions to these problems, and when they recognize their interests in monopolizing solutions, articulating the efficacy of their solutions vis-à-vis existing ones, and actively pursuing greater shares of resources, they can begin to mobilize as a real force of change. These selection pressures can open windows of structural opportunities, but as we shall see shortly, there are some basic conditions identified by Eisenstadt that could restrict their potential success.

The second type of pressure emerges from *within* existing institutional domains, and not from macro-level forces. As institutions grow autonomous and roles and organizations become distributed in horizontal and vertical space, new secondary exigencies related to creating trust (integration), distributing power (regulation), and imposing shared meanings (legitimation) become equally pressing problems for entrepreneurs. Some solutions to these problems involve minor adjustments or reforms, whereas other times entrepreneurs *create the conditions for ambitious intra-institutional social units to become entrepreneurs themselves*. Eisenstadt (1964b) called these actors "secondary" entrepreneurs as opposed to primary entrepreneurs who authorized their innovative projects. A limited number of outcomes can come from secondary exigencies: (1) new entrepreneurs can solve problems by adapting the institution to these exigencies and, thus, become mobile within the institution they operate within; (2) new entrepreneurs can struggle with the older, primary group to usurp their control over the institutional core; (3) old entrepreneurs can co-opt, destroy, or exile new entrepreneurs; and (4) in some cases, where the opportunities exist, new entrepreneurs can erect newly autonomous institutional space and gain their independence from the old entrepreneurs, creating tenuous power-sharing agreements.

Eisenstadt's (1964a, 1964b) identifies at least three structural/cultural changes that are necessary conditions for entrepreneurship. Although there may be others that become relevant on a case-by-case basis, these seem to be generic. First, a sufficient amount of resources, especially human and material, must be "freed" from whatever flows they are locked within. Second, besides alterting the flow of resources, entrepreneurs must construct special markets in which they coordinate the patterns of exchange, as well as the "price" or value of resources; considering the importance of generalized symbolic media as symbolic and material currency further deepens this argument. Third, existing power relations must be rearranged such that entrepreneurs can find alternative bases of resources that extricate them from being wholly dependent upon existing elites and, thereby, locked in a patron–client type relationship. To illustrate how these changes effect entrepreneurship, let's look at Eisenstadt's analysis of political entrepreneurs.

### *Political Evolution*

The initial engine of political evolution and entrepreneurship can be traced back to the "rapid" shift from hunter-gatherer life to horticultural subsistence about 12,000 years ago. As populations became sedentary, ecological niches filled, and pressure for segmentation and migration intensified (Cohen 1977; Fagan 2004). Within a few thousand years, most of the Earth's desirable land was occupied, leading to the appearance of ecological circumscription pressures (Carneiro 1970), especially around the great alluvial flood plains like the Yangtze or Euphrates rivers (Adams 1966; Yoffee 2005). Here, of all locations, populations could remain sedentary as the annual floods brought replenished the soil, and allowed for ever-greater populations; but these floods also created new conditions for conflicts over water rights, as well as amplified the danger of massive flooding, which perhaps accounts for the pervasiveness of flood myths in ancient Mesopotamia and its more famous descendent: Noah's ark (Kramer 1963). It is very likely that population pressures were driving resource production intensification, problems of distribution, and the emergence of early temple economies. In Uruk, the first recorded city, we find evidence of political entrepreneurship likely compelled to erect supra-kin institutional structure and culture (Liverani 2006) as several endogenous and exogenous crises—such as rapid migration, ballooning heterogeneity, and intensified inter-kin conflicts—rapidly shook the extant kinship institution's integrative efficacy and viability. Concomitantly, these pressures provided the opportunities for political entrepreneurs to seize the legitimate use of force and raise an army capable of protecting their newfound power (Abrutyn and Lawrence 2010); this maneuver, however, would have to be coupled with the search for new legitimating mechanisms.

Thus, as political entrepreneurs began to recognize their interests, they had to "free" resources from their anchorage in kinship, ascriptive, and territorial collectives (Abrutyn 2013b). Where local control over resources dominated the flow to an impersonal center, political entrepreneurs could not realize the types of goals they would set; they needed people and they needed surplus to build irrigation/canals, palaces, and temples; fight wars and subjugate foreign populations; and populate cities.[2] The emergence of corveé labor (Lipinski 1979), workshops, centralized grain storage facilities (Postgate 1977), mass production of pottery and other commodities exchanged for labor and loyalty (Potts 1997), and massive urban political centers that controlled agrarian hinterlands through a tenuous balance of coercive force, control over waterways as well as the mobilization of services like public projects that produce irrigation and canals, cultural integration through pantheonic religious systems, and military circumscription built on rival city-states looking to usurp land and water and uncivilized barbarians in the hills (Adams 1966; Flannery 1972; Stein and Rothman 1994; Yoffee 2005) began the slow, and still incomplete process, of tearing asunder the productive power and control over resources kinship and ascriptive collectives had always monopolized.

Furthermore, alongside the disembedding of resources came the growing importance of markets as political entrepreneurs needed a mechanism of economic exchange and distribution that was discrete from kinship patterns of exchange (Algaze 2005), and that they could control through standardized weights and measures (Scott 1998) while, incidentally, attempting to integrate disparate social units through economic mechanisms. The degree to which power is centralized and consolidated in the center made a huge difference in how freely resources flowed beyond the center into the environment, as well as became a key variable affecting the proliferation and success of other aspiring entrepreneurs as powerful political elites can interpret religious entrepreneurship as a threat and can marshal coercive and ideological force much easier when power is consolidated (Lenski 1966). In wresting resources from old patterns, political entrepreneurs were essentially reconfiguring the circuits along which material and human resources moved. Power, both in the form of force and in the generalized symbolic medium, became the cultural mechanism assuring the boundary maintenance of polity versus kinship. In these earliest states, of course, polity was far less autonomous then today, as it ceded much of its control to local kinship entrepreneurs who were far more capable of resolving blood conflicts, dealing with local trade and barter, and conducting ancestor-based religious ceremonies.

As resources are "freed," internal markets grow in size, diversity, and importance, and power differentials grow, entrepreneurs and their institutional cores become increasingly self-reflexive: as a group of actors, entrepreneurs come to share lifestyles, consumptive patterns, and experiences such that they are, in reality, different from other actors. Moreover, the size and diversity of these *specialized collectivities* grow such that the activities of entrepreneurs differentiates as some focus on external interactions—for example, long-distance trade—and others on the polity itself. And as the polity grows more autonomous, new social units are created by entrepreneurs and begin to form the outlines of the polity and its myriad divisions of labor (Rueschemeyer 1977). The emergence of a distinct internal life-world, with its own divisions of labor, and the gradual disembedding of kinship divisions of labor from political ones puts pressure on political entrepreneurs to find mechanisms of integration. These earliest societies are almost two distinct societies as peasant life could not be any further from the nobility, whose social world was nearly invisible from peasants concerned with the daily rounds and subsistence. Meanwhile, the disembedding of resources from ascriptive units, the increasing importance of markets, and increasingly specialized roles and organizations weaken the scope and efficacy of traditional authority (Weber 1927 [2002]), which consequently produces the second major problem entrepreneurs tend to deal with: *regulation* of diverse social units—a problem further exacerbated by the uneven distribution of resources, the potential for inter-kin conflicts over resources, and the weakened effectiveness of old modes of conflict resolution rooted in ascriptive communities (Yoffee 2000). Finally, as power differentials grow, traditional authority is weakened, and regulation becomes a salient pressure, the third problem entrepreneurs deal with emerges: *legitimation* of authority and a new social order rife with inequalities.

Ultimately, if it was population pressures and resource scarcity, and the inability of old solutions to conflict resolution to provide *justice* in the face of growing heterogeneity that "jump-started" political entrepreneurs, it was the emergence of secondary exigencies related to integrating two disparate institutional spaces, legitimating the claims political entrepreneurs made on kinship entrepreneurs, and regulating the activities of newly differentiated political units that solidifies entrepreneurial activities and makes them a near permanent feature in human societies. Where two or three exigencies appear in unison, however, there are strong probabilities that entrepreneurs will arise and, at the very least, attempt to innovate; symbolically articulate why their innovations are improvements over the current solutions and why the current solutions are unfair, unjust, or illegitimate; and, finally, struggle to mobilize resources for their projects. Where power is highly consolidated, their efforts will likely be mixed and, very often, they will have to adjust their goals or face potential annihilation. Where they do begin to succeed in reducing these problems, they generally parlay charismatic energy into institution-building efforts meant to "permanently" institutionalize their solutions, privilege and gains, and influence. Eisenstadt, to be sure, reminds us that their successes may be long-lasting or fleeting, as institutional differentiation is a process and not a state, and so is entrepreneurship. Figure 2.1 attempts to visually capture this political model, as a way of explaining the earliest political innovations, and as a way of alluding to contemporary political entrepreneurship that still is driven by some very similar, though more complex forces.[3]

In essence, what Figure 2.1 demonstrates is that as the initial variables get locked into a feedback loop, pressures arise for solutions to these macro-dynamics. But in the process of resolving them, the social divisions of labor are altered, and the previous solutions to problems of integration, regulation, and legitimation become tenuous. A second feedback loop emerges in which second-order exigencies, typically appearing at the meso-level of social reality between newly differentiated collectives struggling for their independence vis-à-vis existing elites and for power-dependent advantages with other strata, including potential competitors. It is in the midst of these two feedback loops that the structural opportunities for entrepreneurship are at their widest, as new organizational and normative frameworks that elevate collective goals over self-interested ones, carve out free space for

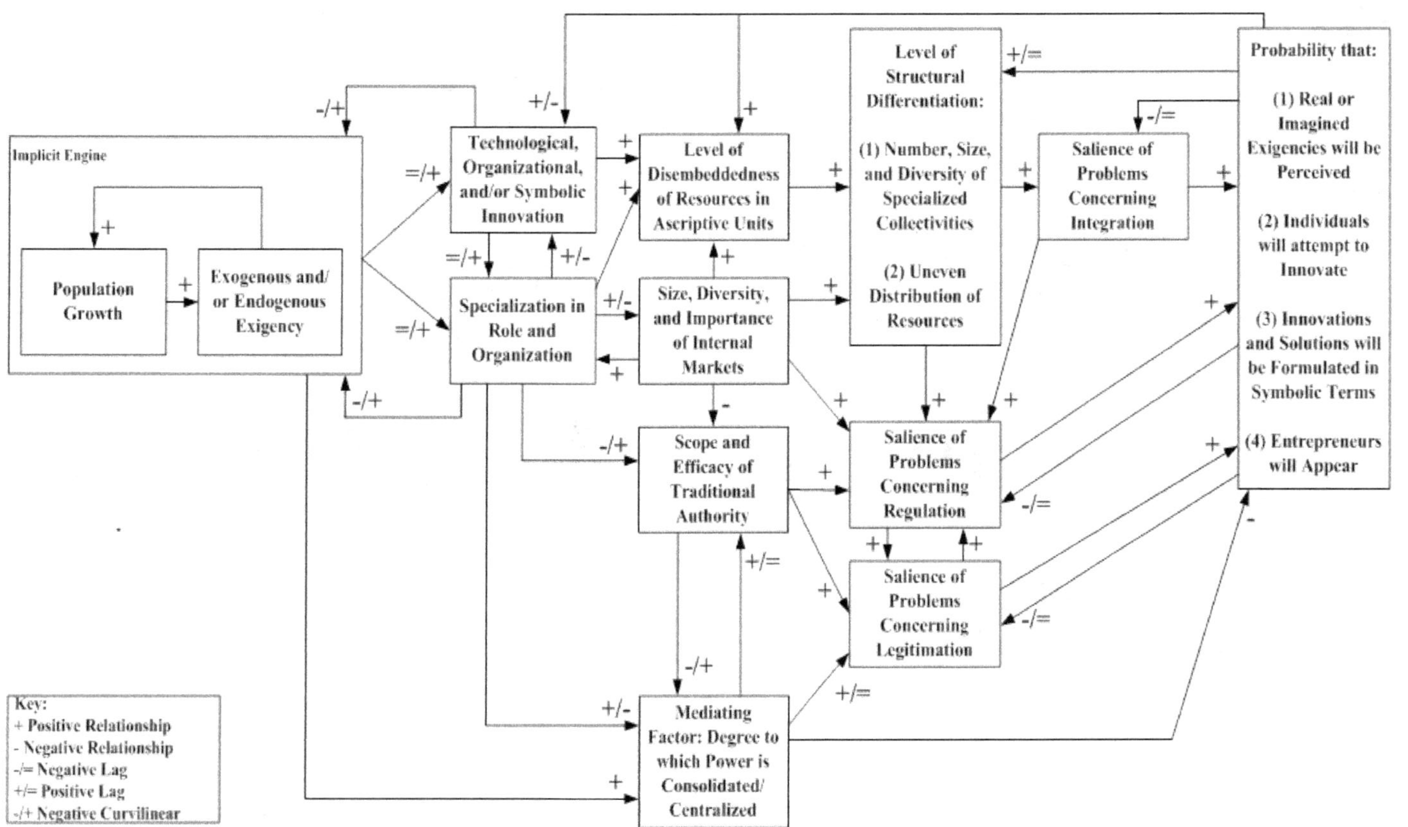


*Figure 2.1* Model of political entrepreneurship.

the aspiring entrepreneurs while compartmentalizing the new roles and organizations, and for (tenuous) power-sharing arrangements to reduce the amount of overt conflict found in society become possible.

Although this model is a more formalized way of looking at entrepreneurship, there are recent advances in institutional entrepreneurs we should consider, as Eisenstadt was far less systematic in his thinking. In particular, two separate but closely related threads of entrepreneurship have been built off of Eisenstadt's: Paul Colomy's neofunctionalist approach and my own evolutionary-institutionalist perspective. Colomy's (1990a, b, 1998; Colomy and Rhoades 1994; Colomy and Kertzmann 1995) work has looked to the overarching collective solutions to the most basic macrosociological problems of legitimation, regulation, and, especially, integration, while emphasizing the concrete problems, adjustments, and incomplete results of entrepreneurship due to the outcomes of struggles between collectives with power and without power (cf. Rueschemeyer 1977). My work has tended toward a neo-Weberian perspective that has emphasized monopolization of resource, power-dependency/power-sharing arrangements, and the tenuous balancing act entrepreneurs engage in between collective orientations and self-interest (Abrutyn 2009a, b, 2012, 2013a, b; Abrutyn and Turner 2011; Abrutyn and Van Ness unpublished). In many ways, I am interested in the struggles *between* autonomous institutions and their entrepreneurs for resources, attention, and influence over the "steering" of society, whereas Colomy is interested in the struggle over the institutional domain's power structure and the problems that entrepreneurs face as they attempt to disseminate new structural and cultural elements. Together, however, they provide a robust framework for explaining institutional change.

## A SYNTHETIC THEORY OF ENTREPENEURSHIP

### Entrepreneurs, Institutional Projects, and Institutional Autonomy

Paul Colomy (1985, 1998) began using the term *institutional project* to capture the entrepreneurial efforts directed toward "crystalliz[ing] broad symbolic orientations in new ways, articulat[ing] specific goals, and construct[ing] novel normative and organizational frameworks to pursue their institutional ends" (Colomy and Rhoades 1994:554). Colomy reasoned that projects could only be successfully pursued if entrepreneurs could tap into the charismatic dimension of social reality, that is, link their goals and decisions, strategies and intentions to something larger than themselves. By tapping into, or at least being perceived as having tapped into, this charismatic fount, entrepreneurs had the unique ability to "carve a free space between [their] actions and the macro environments in which they are pursued, imbuing [their] efforts with a degree of creativity and voluntarism" (Colomy and Kertzmann 1995:194). By elevating entrepreneurs to a potential creative force of qualitative transformation, Colomy has isolated the "revolutionary" dimension of Weber's charisma, while linking the instrumental-technical side of innovation to something deeper, and more normative. Put another way, the project became a balancing point between instrumental behavior that was self-interested, and the moral, voluntarism of the Durkheimian tradition (1912; also Parsons 1951; Goffman 1959, 1963; Alexander 1988a; Alexander and Smith 2003); charismatic, emotional energy was the key to "disembedding" rational action while giving it a moralistic coating.

The concept institutional entrepreneur, then, became multidimensional, nuanced, and indicative of a wider range of activities than just organizational adaptation or modification. To be sure, Colomy sees a continuum between reformist or *elaborative* projects, and those that are epochal, or *reconstructive* (Colomy and Kreutzmann 1995:196). In between, the types of projects emphasized by other theories of social change can easily be added: revitalizationist (Wallace 1956), otherworldly or retreatist (Hall 2003), fundamentalist (Almond, Appleby, and Sivan 2003). In all cases, entrepreneurs have to identify a problem, articulate why it is a problem, why the solutions they offered are superior than extant solutions—both technically and morally—, and seek out material and human resources to expand their efforts (Colomy 1998). I would add that [d]ifferent projects suggest a typology of entrepreneurs and, perhaps, a set of phases or sequences projects tend to go through. For instance, one might call those initial entrepreneurs innovators, as they are often the highest risk takers and the most charismatic (Stark 2007); the types of charismatic carriers Weber was interested in could be called primary entrepreneurs (Eisenstadt 1964, 1971, 1980), whereas reformist projects are carried out by secondary entrepreneurs or, perhaps, *elaboratists* (Abrutyn 2013a; Abrutyn and Van Ness unpublished).[4] The latter type are already embedded within the institutional domain, are elites or secondary elites/subsidiary organizations, and are oriented towards modifying, adapting, adjusting, or incrementally changing aspects of the environment in ways that sustain entrepreneurial influence and privilege, while also making changes that might not appear radical at the time—perhaps their innovations are couched in "returning" to some past golden age—but that have the effect over time of reconfiguring the institutional sphere.

### *Elaborating Projects*

Institutional projects initially "are rarely articulated in a systematic or detailed way . . . [until they] attempt to enlist support [and/or] fend off opposition" (Colomy and Kertzmann 1995:194n1). Eisenstadt's model anticipates this distinction, even if he did not explicitly make it himself: individuals and/or the groups they are mostly closely tied to perceive a problem and work to resolve it; they may be elevated by elites to find solutions, or they may do so on their own accord. It is the reaction of elites and other strata along with the emergence of self-reflexivity. That is, entrepreneurs are not yet entrepreneurs, and projects not yet projects, until they develop self-awareness of their innovations, the value of their innovations, the desire to sustain or even expand their access to resources, and the belief that what they can offer others is an improvement over what currently exists. It helps, of course, that they truly believe they can transform society or a segment of it for the better, as this further lends a sense of moral obligation and justification to group commitment and mobilization efforts, but it is not necessary for entrepreneurial success. Inescapably, projects are not simply techno-rational, but also involve a substantive-rational and, often times, affectual dimensions. Although these logics or motivations may be complimentary, they very often are sources of tension within and between entrepreneurs, and can only typically be balanced tenuously and for short periods of time before one dimension comes to dominate the underlying premises of a project and the entrepreneur's goals.

Projects range in terms of their content, but four generic goals tend to undergird entrepreneurial projects (Abrutyn 2009a)—although the importance of any one goal will vary across cases. (1) Entrepreneurial projects always look to monopolize resources that allow them to further realize the concrete project goals—resources being things like positions, material goods, knowledge and practices, symbolic elements, or even human resources. In addition, (2) entrepreneurial projects are always focused on the reactions of elites as well as securing as many alternative bases of resources as possible. If the first goal, then, is monopoly, then the second can be called legitimation as entrepreneurs take one of three approaches: (a) top-down in which they secure power-sharing agreements that confer credibility on their activities, reduce the efficacy of suddenly illegitimate competitors, and secure monopoly over goods and services—for example, the American Medical Association (Starr 1982); (b) bottom-up in which they build a grassroots movement in which significant proportions of strata become dependent upon entrepreneurial resources and, as such, they leverage power-dependency that may protect them from elite reprisals—for example, many of the Axial Age religio-cultural entrepreneurs (Eisenstadt 1982); or (c) a mixed approach that involves carefully calibrated strategies meant to secure power-sharing and power-dependent relationships—for example, the legal entrepreneurs in western Christendom during the 12th–15th centuries (Berman 1983).

Further, (3) entrepreneurs work to articulate and frame their projects (Colomy 1998). Regardless of the entrepreneurial units ulterior motives, they must develop culturally resonant frames that persuade people that existing problems are being poorly solved, their solutions are better, and what they are offering is difficult if not impossible to find elsewhere (Snow and Soule 2010). Projects rarely are solely self-interested, but instead seek to provide some collective benefits to some segment of the population, otherwise why would anyone ever waste their time or resources supporting the entrepreneur's aims (Eisenstadt 1971). The success of entrepreneurship often comes down to their communicative skills and their ability, as well as their ability to embed their frames in authentic performances and rituals (Alexander 2004). To be sure, the framing process often includes instrumental arguments about their innovation's improved efficacy and economy over existing solutions, as well as moral language that criticize existing solutions as unfair, immoral, unjust, elitist, and so on. Finally, (4) entrepreneurial projects have a self-reflexive goal that has two underlying components. First, as entrepreneurs recognize that their innovations or the resources these innovations procure for them are of significant value to their success, some members of the group begin to devote their time to further innovation to increase their value and position, others work to shape the resonant frames. Second, and closely related, the more success entrepreneurs have, and the more they are able to reconfigure the social world, the more secondary problems entrepreneurs face that require new problem solving. Whereas some entrepreneurs are focused on the outside, and some on the entrepreneurial class itself, other entrepreneurs must begin the arduous reformulation of the project to include dealing with intra-institutional regulation and integration.

To summarize thus far, projects generally involve the careful blending of instrumental rationality with substantive rationality, but this blend varies and, as we shall see shortly, can be the cause of project failure. Entrepreneurial ability to transform the social world rests on their project's efficacy, which is rooted in four interdependent, yet independent goals: (1) the pursuit of resource monopolization to justify their existence, realize their goals, and secure their position, if not expand it; (2) the search for legitimation from above or below, but ultimately through as great a number of alternative sources as possible to prevent dependency, while wrestling power-sharing and power-dependent relationships for themselves; (3) formulating and articulating culturally resonant frames that enlist new members, legitimate their claims, justify their existence to others, and delegitimize alternatives, whether those of extant elites or competitors; and (4) deal with second-order problems related to carving out autonomous space—primarily, new problems of intra-institutional regulation and integration. None of these goals is more important than the others, but all represent the concerns entrepreneurs have, especially when they are dealing with the material, self-interested side of projects versus the collectively oriented ideal side.

Before moving on, a few final remarks on the *dual logics* of projects—or what might be fittingly called the *orientational* axis—will help underscore the tenuousness of projects. Entrepreneurs are corporate groups, and corporate groups need resources to survive, but like any organization, survival and self-aggrandizement can become as important if not more so than other practical or ideological goals. Projects lend themselves to the pursuit, then, of self-interested concrete goals that shape the way the four underlying goals are expressed. Likewise, by their very nature, projects can also be prominently oriented toward the collective. Indeed, entrepreneurs perceive an existential crisis as destroying the vitality of the community, and rather than cynically assume their belief, commitment to the collective good, and push for change is self-interested, we must accept the fact that they may in fact be collectively oriented and acting with what they believe is the best intentions for the greatest proportion of a population. To be sure, no project can be one or the other *en toto*; groups must find resources to sustain their activities and their member's biological existence at the very least, whereas purely self-interested groups will fail to enlist interest from significant proportions of the population. That being said, entrepreneurs tend to be biased toward one orientation or the other, although these may vacillate according to the phase of the project and the broader environment in which they are acting. Too much of any one orientation, as noted, will likely destroy their chances, whereas it is nearly impossible to balance the concrete project goals perfectly. In fact, disputes between important entrepreneurial members may fracture the group, or weaken it against elite opposition. It may also produce rival entrepreneurs that lead to one succeeding, or all failing—or, in the rare case, dynamic heterodoxic institutional domains (Eisenstadt 1984). Either way, differences in orientation inevitably produce important variations across cases.

### *Project Variation and the Multi-Linearity of Institutional Change*

For Eisenstadt, entrepreneurs were the source of variation upon which sociocultural mechanisms of selection could work. But it was Colomy's emphasis on the institutional project that concretized the actual source of variation and, ultimately, provided a missing conceptual tool for explaining why institutional change was divergent and multi-linear. Entrepreneurs vary in their skill and ability, whereas their projects vary in terms of their content and outcome: "different entrepreneurial groups frequently fashion distinctive instrumental remedies and symbolic appeals, ranging from incommensurate projects to idiosyncratic but complementary versions of a roughly similar program" (Colomy and Kertzmann 1995:195). In addition, projects are greatly shaped by exogenous factors. The unpredictable reaction by elites and other important strata may be supportive, opportunistic, or resistant to the project's goals. Entrepreneurs must also compete against the "din," as they are not always the only voice articulating culturally resonant frames or looking to enlist members in the population (Colomy 1998:278–86; Colomy and Kertzmann 1995:194–6). As such, projects rarely follow linear paths, as they involve adjustments and accommodations that often lead to outcomes incommensurate with the initial goals. For instance, the *selective elevation* of one religious entrepreneurial unit over another by political elites could be random chance, one of strategy and instrumental rationality, or political expediency (Verkamp 1991); yet the act of elevation can have radical consequences for rival groups and for the society's institutional domains in that prestige biases could lead to easier diffusion of entrepreneurial innovations and the rapid ascension in power and privilege (Henrich and Gil-White 2001)—for example, the elevation of Buddhists during the Mauryan Empire (in India, *c.* 323—185 BCE) gave them an advantage vis-à-vis other Vedic and ascetic religious groups, whereas the fall and the later rise of Brahmanic power would lead to Buddhism becoming "extinct" in India (Keay 2000; Thapar 2004).

Even the decisions entrepreneurs make cannot be fully predicted. Strategies that emphasize conservative ideologies, like that of the Confucian literati, are just as likely as radical progressivist arguments. Either way, entrepreneurs are the historical forces capable of switching the tracks of history—for example, the earliest political kings faced with constant pressure for political innovation within an increasingly autonomous political domain vis-à-vis kinship (Frankfort 1948); religious entrepreneurs like the Axial Age Israelite prophets (Liverani 2005), Greek philosophers (Elkana 1986), or the myriad Indian ascetic sects (Thapar 1975); and the great legal entrepreneurs of the 11th century, like Gratian, who invented western rational law and the procedures for learning and arguing (Berman 1983). In some cases, variation is clear and so are many of its causes. The Axial Age was a time of convergent evolution, because it witnessed the birth of five religio-cultural revolutions and entrepreneurs in five independent regions with little evidence of much contact (Schwartz 1975). Yet, any observer would easily discern tremendous variation in ecological and demographic conditions, sociocultural factors, the initial projects, reactions from elites and the population, and the responses by entrepreneurs and, therefore, the content and outcome of their projects (Eisenstadt 1986b).

One further note is worth briefly addressing: Colomy (1998) has noted some entrepreneurial projects fail. However, their efforts may lead to transformative change via two unforeseen routes. First, elites may co-opt the entrepreneurs or, more importantly, their projects, throwing their privileged position and resource advantage behind the projects in ways that render the aspiring entrepreneur's redundant. In these cases, projects never result in the type of change entrepreneurs sought, but some of their goals become embedded in the collective fabric as a result of co-optation. Second, elites may choose to crush the entrepreneurs, but the goals and ideology may have already spread and inspired second-generation entrepreneurs. Indeed, the act of suppression may be cause for mobilization. Like the former case, the end is never exactly as the first-generation entrepreneurs wanted, but second-generation entrepreneurs often have the advantage of emerging within a sociocultural context in which the ideas and goals already of some acceptance and enlisting support is far less difficult or costly. Moreover, the elites may change their strategies upon considering the reaction to their oppressive strategy.

### *Phases of Projects*

Implicit in this discussion is the possibility that entrepeneurship has different sequences or phases in which different dynamics and problems shape the texture of each phase. Moreover, each stage presents new challenges that can lead to the collapse of entrepreneurship, the retrogression or readjustment of the project, or to other possible outcomes. To my knowledge, no one has tried to theorize what entrepreneurial phases might look like. Yet, it is possible to offer a tentative list of project sequences that are induced from the numerous entrepreneurial cases and the theoretical logic discussed above. The first phase is termed *nascence.* This phase is characterized less by entrepreneurship and more by perception, innovation, and recognition. As with the earliest years of children's lives, the earliest moments of entrepreneurs' "biographies" are central to their later success, mythology, and ambitions. Where did the collective form? On the margins of society or within an already autonomous institution, or were they "drafted" by existing entrepreneurs who were responding to a crisis and attempting to adapt? In the former case, we can point to the Israelite prophets as an example of peripheral groups resisting the center (Albertz 1992), whereas in the latter case the *elaborative* projects of theologians like Thomas Aquinas or Mencius, who reformed existing institutional structure in ways that may have initially led to small, gradual changes that eventually reached a threshold and became larger ones come to mind. Knowing where the entrepreneur comes from is important because it will also give the analyst a sense of what strata entrepreneurs have close affinity with, who their natural rivals will be, and whom they are dependent on and, thus, whom they will eventually have to confront and gain independence from. Ultimately, this stage involves perceiving a problem, innovating, and ends with the members of a loosely coupled corporate group of innovators or perpetuators of innovations recognizing their shared interests and becoming a bounded social group.

Once they have become a corporate group, entrepreneurs and their projects may transition to the second phase, *gestation.* Gestation is characterized by the clear formulation of the goals of the project, which involves a conscious and unconscious selection process that sees the group members begin to articulate ideological explanations (and somewhat coherent narrative) for their existence, what they aim to do and why they should be able to do so, and a clear conception of what problems their innovations may solve. This is a time of coalition building, the search for support in material or human resources, and the spontaneous effort to resist those in power. The third phase, *reaction*, is the period in which entrepreneurs must react to the responses of elites as well as their framing efforts. It is here where they may begin to pursue top-down or bottom-up strategies, and it is this phase that is most perilous for their continued existence. The swift, violent response by elites can lead to exile or death; a blasé or uninterested response by enough members of the population may drain energy and resources from the entrepreneurs, and, of course, entrepreneurs may stubbornly fail to change course. When they do react, projects enter a *readjustment* phase where goals, cultural frames, and other aspects are recalibrated in hopes of meeting the challenges proposed by elites and/or recruitment failures. The perils of this phase are found in the threat of internal factioning as rivals may emerge and struggle to lead the movement.

If their projects survive this phase and they are able to legitimate their claims, an *institution-building* phase begins, in which entrepreneurs have secured some independence and parlay this into the right to reconfigure the physical, temporal, social, and symbolic space. This phase may be slow or fast, and it may regress rapidly into the third phase as elites may not yet be finished reacting and forcing responses from entrepreneurs. The true complexity of entrepreneurship, however, comes on the heels of institution building as suddenly they are not only faced with inter-institutional interactions, but enter a *reorientation* phase in which their focus towards intra-institutional problems associated with legitimating their claims, integrating increasingly differentiated social units who are dependent upon the institution for existence, and regulating these disparate social units actions becomes equally as salient, if not more so, than their dealings with other entrepreneurs and strata. Thus, entrepreneurial projects do not end, but are a process that involves constant interplay between successes, response, readjustment, and so forth. One entrepreneur's reorientation phase may become the structural opportunity for an ambitious nascent entrepreneur's ascent to independence. Finally, failure during any moment in the process is always an option, and the contraction of autonomy, the usurpation of privilege from rivals within the institutional domain, or simply poor decision making for whatever reason may lead to rapidly deteriorating entrepreneurship. Indeed, autonomy is generally incomplete, differentiation uneven, and dedifferentiation, retrogression, and disintegration potential trajectories as well.

## Institutional Projects and Institutional Autonomy

Although each of these phases are important, of particular interest to this book is the institution-building and reorientation phases that culminate in some level of institutional autonomy. That is, entrepreneurs are responsible for differentiating institutions and making them autonomous. Although differentiation and autonomy are similar processes, autonomy, as noted in the previous chapter, is the process by which institutional structure and culture becomes discrete vis-à-vis other institutional domains. In part, entrepreneurial projects allow entrepreneurs to "carve a *free space* between [their] actions and the macro environments in which they are pursued" (Colomy and Kretzmann 1985:194, emphasis added); maintaining this free space implies institutionalizing a new organizational and normative framework that constitutes a new institutional domain's structure and culture. Moreover, it means literally differentiating physical, temporal, social, and symbolic space that, ironically, delimits much of the creativity and voluntarism the initial project gave to them.

In order to become a force of institutional autonomy, entrepreneurs must secure structural and symbolic independence vis-à-vis other entrepreneurs, competitors, and other strata (Abrutyn 2009a). *Structural independence* is a positive function of the degree to which entrepreneurs (1) monopolize the production, distribution, and consumption of some set of resources, goods, and/or services; (2) secure the legitimate right to monopolize these resources, goods, and services both from existing elites and/or a significant proportion of the population; and (3) leverage the monopoly and legitimate right into privileged positions and, ultimately, power-dependent advantages and (oft-tenuous) power-sharing agreements. In essence, structural independence is a result of becoming an indispensable source of something other groups of people want. It is not enough for these entrepreneurs to produce and distribute something only the elites want or can afford; they must also expand their base of resources by finding ways to make available and necessary their resources and services to other social strata.

Conversely, *symbolic independence* relates to the cultural and cognitive side of institutions—for example, the normative, symbolic, and cognitive elements. On the one hand, as entrepreneurs resolve human concerns, monopolize key resources, and secure legitimacy, they are also able to monopolize the production and distribution of one or more *generalized symbolic media of exchange* (see Chapter 5, this volume, for an in depth discussion on generalized media; for a recent discussion, see Abrutyn and Turner 2011; also Parsons 1963a, b; Luhmann 1976). In essence, generalized symbolic media of exchange are the *source of culture*, as they are bundles of symbols organizing talk, social exchange, cognition, and social action within an institutional domain, its smaller corporate units, and institutionalized encounters (cf. Turner 2010a, c); they are used to formulate worldviews and themes differentiating actors across domains (e.g., families versus universities, parents versus professors); and they are the symbolic ingredients of ideologies evolving within a particular domain. Media also manifest themselves in what I refer to as *valued external referents*—physical/social objects that are placeholders of value, dispositions, and attitudes that denote a person's position within the domain, and institutionalized rituals that imbue objects with value and internalize these dispositions, while also being key identity markers. Thus, media are real resources that can be accumulated, invested, and exchanged and, therefore, may be unequally distributed and hoarded by individuals and categories of individuals in ways that reflect dominant patterns of stratification and/or patterns specific to the institution. Part of the institution-building and reorientation phases involves creating these media, building the structural linkages along which they circulate, determining and standardizing their value, and imposing the symbolic-cognitive rules associated with their use.

Hence, *institutional* entrepreneurs pursue projects that result in newly autonomous institutional domains, expanded autonomy in the domain in which they are members, and/or the contraction of autonomy in rival institutional domains. They do this by literally reconfiguring the physical, temporal, social, and symbolic dimensions of a society and demarcating the real and cognitive boundaries of the domain. Entrepreneurs "colonize" buildings (e.g., churches or courthouses) and geographic zones like "residential" or "financial" districts, entire cities (e.g., Washington, DC or Jerusalem), and, in some cases, entire regions (e.g., "western Christendom" or Islamic civilization). They also demarcate the appropriate times in which these physical spaces are to be entered, the goods/services entrepreneurs offer are available, or actions and goals unique to the institutional domain may be activated. Additionally, entrepreneurs are responsible for creating generalized roles like "consumer," "patient," or "client" that have very simple membership criteria and somewhat generalizable expectations and obligations across situations and institutional domains (cf. Eisenstadt 1965a:30–1). Finally, entrepreneurs seek to install their vision of reality by "drenching" the aforementioned spaces in the symbolic elements found in the circulating generalized symbolic medium: the architecture of buildings becomes synonymous with its institutional entrepreneur's activities and act as cues for cognitive orientation; monuments represent symbols of heroes, ideas, or iconic things; uniforms and emblems differentiate actors and organizations from each other as well as orient action and attitudes; and roles become symbolically meaningful things. On the micro-level, discrete lines of action, goals, and decision-making processes are institutionalized and permeate greater numbers of the broader population as generalized roles like consumer or patient, as well as institutionally specific "generalized others," become available to more people and their meanings diffuse and taken for granted.

In essence, the variation in the level of a given institution's autonomy is really a function of entrepreneurial independence, which again depends on its skills, historical/sociocultural contingencies, the responses and efforts of other types of entrepreneurs, and other factors. Projects are not "about" autonomy, but generally have some focus on gaining, sustaining, and sometimes expanding structural and symbolic independence. In the process, entrepreneurs look to "crystallize broad symbolic orientations in new ways, articulate specific goals, and construct novel normative and organizational frameworks to pursue their institutional ends" (Colomy and Rhodes 1994:554) that have the end result of carving out autonomous space and institutionalizing their domains distinct structural and cultural space. It also means, as we shall discuss in detail in Chapter 6, building a stratification system unique to the institutional domain. Thus, institutional entrepreneurs are the *architects* of autonomous institutions and thus a force of true qualitative transformative change. They may build from the inside, or from the outside, but when they succeed, they reconfigure the social world by altering the physical landscape, the temporal reality, the social relationships, and the symbolic essence of human societies.

Ultimately, the last components we can add to a synthetic model of entrepreneurship comes out of the growing independence of entrepreneurs and the generic emergent problems rooted in the process of institutional autonomy. In particular, building a new sub-system or sphere of social action, exchange, and communication means new exigencies that require solutions or the level of autonomy becomes threatened. That is, they must deal with the same basic problems related to their claims to monopolies over the production and distribution of institutional resources (legitimation), the linkages between disparate corporate and individual actors dispersed within the institutional domain's newly autonomous environment (integration), and control and coordination of these divisions of labor (regulation) (Abrutyn 2012). That is, entrepreneurs must find ways to link individual and collective actors, as well as niches, such that the flow of resources can be controlled, conflicts reduced, competition regulated, and stability enhanced; in part, this involves connecting the core of the institutional domain and its mundane, techno-rational functions to some broader normative/moral dimension (Shils 1975). Using various types of mechanisms of integration that include institutionalizing patterns of domination and/or exchange (Turner 2011) as well as monopolizing the production and distribution of a distinct generalized symbolic medium of action, exchange, and communication, entrepreneurs attempt to stabilize the internal milieu; stabilization implies even greater institutional autonomy. Indeed, the reconfiguration of structural and cultural relationships within an institution goes beyond the boundaries of the domain as non-institutional actors "enter" the discrete physical, temporal, social, and symbolic space of the autonomous sphere in pursuit of goods or services being offered. Furthermore, the circulating of some generalized symbolic media across institutional boundaries also forces other domains to reconstitute their internal environment—for example, *money* entering polity, law, or science forces all three to adapt and change to accommodate the medium while also protecting against colonization from foreign media (more on this in Chapter 5, this volume).

Their efforts have consequences for other entrepreneurs across time and space. First, they offer future or aspiring entrepreneurs a script or blueprint for success. It is not shocking that the earliest efforts at state craft included building bureaucracies meant to manage large territories and disparate populations as efficiently as possible (Eisenstadt 1963, 1965b). These efforts were repeated over and over, with adjustments and adaptations being common but radical change was not. Second, entrepreneurs may offer cautionary tales to future entrepreneurs. Failures are just as important to future entrepreneurs as successes. For example, kings throughout the ancient near east kept libraries filled with their predecessors successes and failures (van de Mieroop 2004). Political innovation could be accomplished by learning from failed policies, like the Babylonian's propensity to deport elites, which was not replicated by the Persians.

Finally, entrepreneurs are also engines of new entrepreneurs. Existing entrepreneurs authorize potentially ambitious actors (e.g., kings giving power to scribes or bureaucrats) to deal with problems that they do not have the time or energy to handle. Unintentionally, they pry open the structural holes through which nascent entrepreneurs can emerge. In creating the space for ambitious actors to become entrepreneurs, they sow the seeds of their own possible demise or reduction in privilege. In other cases, they paradoxically try to control resources but at the same time expand their influence to the point with which mechanisms of integration become inefficacious. It is on the margins, where groups have some free space due to costs of monitoring and sanctioning so far from the center that resistance-focused entrepreneurs form. And the freeing of resources from ascriptive groups makes it far easier for these marginalized entrepreneurs to mobilize resources, even under the auspices of traditional structure and culture.

## FINAL THOUGHTS

We are finally in a position to define what entrepreneurs are and offer a synthetic model that accounts for Eisenstadt's insights and adds the discussion above. In essence, then, *institutional entrepreneurs are defined* as *bounded corporate units who (1) perceive real or imagined crises, (2) pursue institutional projects that include (a) symbolic, organizational, and technological innovation meant to resolve the crisis, (b) efforts to articulate and frame their solutions vis-à-vis existing solutions, (c) the pursuit of monopolies over innovations and goods/services that make them unique and, possibly, indispensable, and (d) leveraging power-dependent and power-sharing relationships with various strata, which (3) results in some degree of structural and symbolic independence and, thereby, some ability to build autonomous institutional domains by reconfiguring the physical, temporal, social, and symbolic space around themselves.*

Like biological mutations, entrepreneurs and their projects are the sources of sociocultural variation that selection, when the conditions are ripe, can work on. Because the content and success of projects, and the entrepreneur's skill, vary, projects do not follow linear, predictable paths. Rather, they are subject to interference from without, competition from other aspiring entrepreneurs, or an unmotivated population. It was suggested six phases or sequences capture the generic direction projects follow under the perfect conditions: *nascence*, *gestation*, *reaction*, *readjustment*, *institution building*, *reorientation*. At each phase, regression, factioning, and failure are possible outcomes. It would seem, then, that entrepreneurship is a challenging enterprise, although the rewards are mobility, greater shares of desired resources, and, in some cases, a stake in the "steering" of society. Tenuously balanced between self-interested goal pursuit and collective-oriented innovation, projects offer dynamic cultural and organizational frameworks that can replace, adjust, destroy, or revolutionize existing frameworks. The success of these frameworks is not guaranteed, but clearly entrepreneurs are evolutionarily advantageous as human societies are still going strong, and they have been able to handle greater population sizes distributed over large tracts of geographic territory. In the next chapter, we turn to the question of what happens when entrepreneurs are successful.

# 3 The Ecological Dynamics of Institutions

> To be a society, a social system must have its "center of gravity"within itself, i.e., it must have its own system of authority within its own boundaries. It must also have its own culture. Part of its culture it will necessarily share with other societies from which it derives and with which it has intercourse—but part of this culture will be particular to itself. Some of this particular culture will be about itself. It will consist of beliefs about the history and nature of the society, its relationship to certain ideal or transcendent entities or values, its origin and destiny. It will include beliefs about the rightfulness of its existence as a society and about what qualifies its members to belong to society.
>
> —Edward Shils

## INTRODUCTION

The remarkable moments of creativity and freedom from structure that occur during certain phases of entrepreneurship are thrown in sharp relief to the highly constraining, embedded agency of routine, institutional life. As entrepreneurs carve out their autonomous institutional space, they begin to erect the scaffolding that will, over time, become the framework through which their goals, decisions, actions, and strategies are eventually channeled. In Weberian terms, charisma must eventually be routinized; where entrepreneurs are successful, charisma or, more succinctly, the link between the mundane and the effervescent transmundane—whether sacred in a religious sense or a secular, civic sense (Durkheim 1912)—is institutionalized in a physical and cognitive institutional core (Shils 1975; Eisenstadt, Abitol, and Chazan 1987). That is, institutions are real things in terms of their demarcation in physical, temporal, social, and symbolic space. As such, as they grow more autonomous, entrepreneurs increasingly become associated with one or more physical loci in which their activities, practices, and recruitment/training occur, as well as a cognitive-symbolic locus toward which people can orient their actions and attitudes even when not in the physical presence of the core or its constituent entrepreneurs. The core, in a sense, is like a factory, warehouse, and distribution center for institutional resources—material and symbolic (Abrutyn 2012); it is the "sacred" center in which the human concern or concerns entrepreneurs are believed to deal with is institutionalized and dealt with (Eisenstadt 1977:72ff.); it is a space in which generalized symbolic media of exchange are produced standardized, distributed, exchanged/transferred (Abrutyn 2009a); in short, it is the material and symbolic center of the institution.

The core is the lynchpin for understanding the way institutional autonomy works, the variability and divergent trends within the institutional domain, the structure of intra-institutional stratification. The functionalists had it right: institutions channel the way people act, exchange, and communicate. But where they went wrong was in assuming some sort of blanket consensus filtering down throughout the entire institution (Parsons 1971; Luhmann 1995). Rather, actors are distributed in uneven positions throughout an institution's divisions of labor, nearer or farther from the institution's core, or one of its cores. Proximity to the core dictates the level of conformity and congruence an actor or set of actors display in terms of action, exchange, and communication. This proposition holds true regardless of whether conformity is predicated on deep acting, habit, or callous calculation. But not everyone or every group or every cluster of groups finds itself near the core. Some are quite far from the core, whereas others sit in the boundary overlaps between institutions, and still others find themselves closer to the core of another institution. As identity control theory suggests (Burke 1999; Stets 2006), each actor is a composite of myriad role-identities and their general prominence and salience to their self-concept. Each role-identity and its relative value reflects the nearness or farness from one institutional core or another, culminating in a role-identity matrix. We can predict quite a bit about an actor or group's decision-making, strategies, and goals based on their institutional role matrix because the matrix is shaped by the ecological-institutional dynamics. Ecological dynamics also point to the way stratification emerges naturally within an institutional domain and, importantly, presupposes a theory of social change as it implies a set of locations where resistance and social movements are more likely to form—for example, the margins, the interstices between institutions, and so forth.

As such, this chapter sets up the next three chapters by positing a theory of institutional ecology. The theory rests on a simple proposition called the rule of proximity. In essence, the rule states that the closer are individual, collective, or clusters of collective actors to an institution's core, the greater are the constraints on interaction, exchange, and communication and, thereby, the more predictable are their goals, lines of action, and decisions. Being a probabilistic statement, we assume that there is variability even in actors close to the core. A professor may be fully devoted to the educational core and the values and ideologies of its generalized symbolic media learning, yet is entitled to have an off day in his or her role performance, or may like the research side of education and thus shirk committees and teaching responsibilities. The point, however, is that the more a class of actors orient their attitudes and actions towards an institution's core, the more stable and predictable the institution becomes, and the more stereotyped their actions are.

## ECOLOGICAL DYNAMICS

As entrepreneurs carve out autonomy, institutional domains become discrete in physical, temporal, social, and symbolic space. What this means is that entrepreneurs first begin by demarcating a physical location or set of locations that become the *institutional core*; around the core are zones filled with various individuals, collectives, and clusters of collectives, or what will be termed the *institutional environment*. For heuristic purposes, Figure 3.1 visualizes what an institutional domain might look like.[1]

Inside the core, entrepreneurs produce and distribute resources associated with whatever the institution does, recruit and train new entrepreneurs, develop and disseminate knowledge and practices, and, generally, reproduce the institutional world, protect the boundaries of the core, and often engage in their own disputes and discourse. The greater the degree of institutional autonomy, the greater the degree to which the core becomes the central locus of resource production and distribution, the symbolic link between the sacred and mundane, and the base of institutional authority.[2] The core, very often, is a real physical place, especially when an institution has reached a certain threshold of autonomy. It could be a single building, a complex of buildings, a diffuse geographic zone,

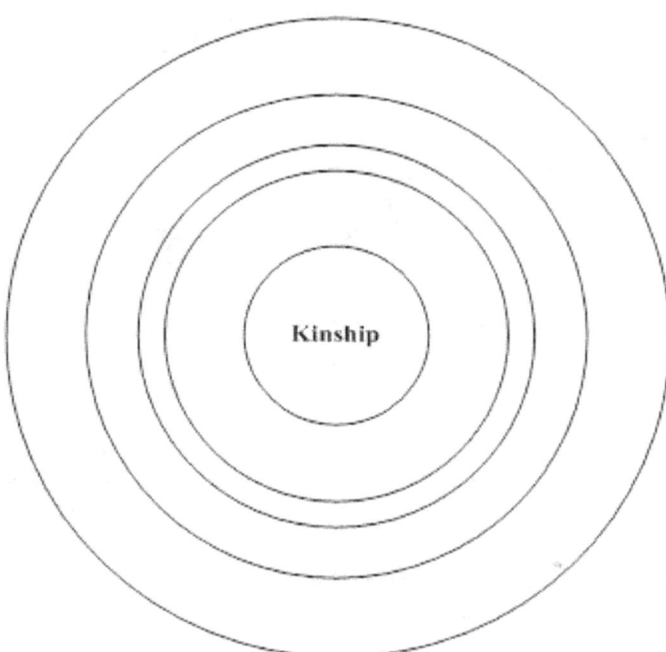


*Figure 3.1* Generic model of institutional ecology.

or even an entire city, state, region, or vague civilizational space. The most ideal cores also become the cognitive cores we call up in our mind when thinking about our role performance within an institution. Education is often synonymous with brick buildings and ivy; religion with a cathedral; polity with a palace or the White House or some other iconic physical site.

The institutional environment is much more fluid than the core, as it involves numerous types of actors. In one sense, the environment is composed of physical "blocks" of actors surrounding the core—for example, the law offices, bail bondsmen, restaurants, and other corporate and individual actors that exist around a downtown legal core. But the environment is far more complex than this. It consists of open spaces in which actors orient themselves by the symbolic markers or "signposts" indicating what type of action occurs here and what the actor's expectations are. An American visiting a city will know where he is almost immediately by the "landmarks"; if he was taking a stroll downtown, for instance, and the number of bail bondsman and law offices rapidly multiplied, it would be clear that he had entered a legal zone. Thus, around the core, we find support or subsidiary actors and what we call liaisons, or a class of actors who are most readily able to traverse the real and imaginary boundaries between institutions in order to act as "translators" between institutions, providing access to a foreign institutions core to people desiring the resources of that core and delivering and ensuring a steady flow of "consumers" to entrepreneurs. Support actors, then, are oriented toward the core and its entrepreneurs, and help maintain institutional autonomy; liaison actors are more complicated and have allegiances to two or more institutions, even if their principle function is towards one—for example, lawyers translate law into other institutional "languages," and although we would expect them to be legal actors, they are sometimes closer to the core of another domain.

Besides these two types of actors, there are others. There are "consumers" and "tourists" who enter the space of the institutional domain with very different motives and goals. There are "extra"-institutional entrepreneurs, or entrepreneurs from other domains who travel along special networks of elites and can move from one core to the next to exchange and communicate with their counterparts; there are competitors or rival entrepreneurs that faction and construct their own discrete rival cores, which underscore contradictions, pluralism, and heterodoxy.. At the same time, the physical and temporal space is also cut according to the rule of proximity. A lawyer who walks into a deli during a lunch break is suddenly free to orient to "law" or can re-key the frame she is using in exchange and communication (Goffman 1974); even a brief aside can build a temporally defined interaction within the larger interaction and cognitively shift away from the physical core. Or, consider the bail bondsmen physically distant from the courts and legal zone, located perhaps in a seedy neighborhood. His interactions are going to be far less monitored and sanctioned, and thus the gravitational pull of the center will be less felt by him and his clients than by the bail bondsmen located down the street from the court. And, eventually, as one travels far enough from the core, the lines between one institutional domain and another begin to blur, and eventually they grow clearer and the signifiers point to a different orientation.

## Intra- and Inter-Institutional Penetration

The core is not just a site of production and distribution, but also contains the mechanisms through which entrepreneurs try to penetrate the environment; impose a vision of reality and erect a generalized system of action, exchange, and communication that regulates behavior; and, very often, expand their influence in order to increase their access to greater shares of human and material resources. It is through certain structural and cultural linkages that entrepreneurs are able to integrate disparate social actors dispersed throughout the environment and arranged within a series of divisions of labor. These divisions of labor act as structural

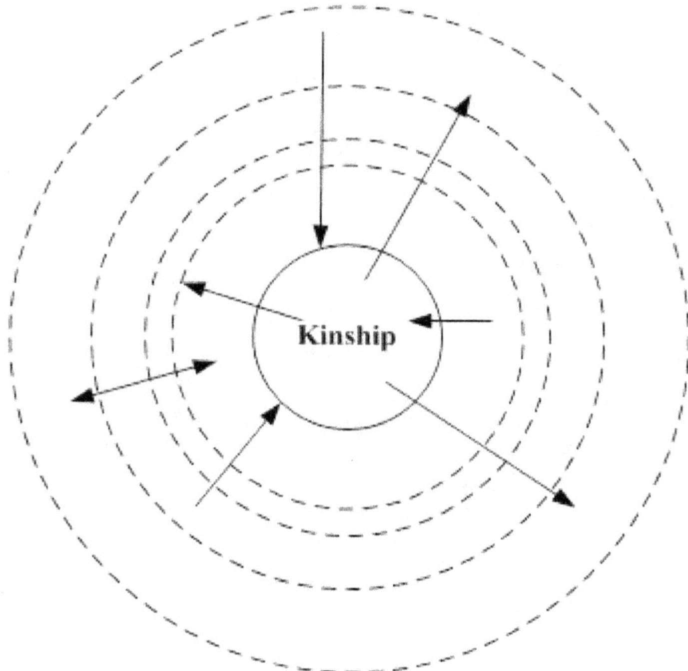


*Figure 3.2* Resource flow from institutional core.

mechanisms controlling experiences, mobility, and the flow of resources; the flow of resources, which travel along these linkages like generalized symbolic media, "coat" or "drench" the linkages, the actors distributed across these linkages, and the physical spaces (see Figure 3.2 for visualization of resource flows) giving meaning to the social order, unevenly distributing some of this meaning and interpretation/evaluation of events, and making the divisions of labor normative.

No matter the level of institutional autonomy, however, institutional domains are never free from the penetration of other domains because they are not closed systems. That being said, entrepreneurs and their support actors do try to maintain the integrity of the core vis-à-vis would-be colonizers or polluters. But even their best efforts are not always successful. Structural and cultural linkages, like highways, connect myriad cores together, as elite networks form along which entrepreneurs from one institution can become mobile in others, generalized media from one domain, depending on certain conditions, can circulate uneasily alongside the "indigenous" medium of another domain, and of course, resources are constantly flowing across environments from one collective to the next, one individual to the next, and from clusters of collectives to other locations. Figure 3.3 illustrates several examples of ecological arrangements and the flow of resources from one space to the next. It is meant to underscore the complexity of institutional complexes and resource flows, the interpenetration of institutional space, the lack of full autonomy, and the highly variable social landscapes human societies reveal. Only through empirical and historical research can one ascertain a case's configuration. For instance, Figure 3.4 provides an example of what hunter-gatherer societies looked like: kinship was relatively autonomous with the institutional cores of polity, economy, religion, and so on embedded within.

As an aside, embedding is tricky. On the one hand, embedding one institution into another provides the dominant institution with greater control and coordination of resources. Entrepreneurs often pursue *abolitionist* projects meant to absorb or subordinate institutions for greater power and prestige. On the other hand, embedding, as in the case of Figure 3.4, reduces autonomy to some degree because it creates severe antagonisms between, say, kinship decisions and political goals. That is, actors do not have a clear temporally/physically defined way of dealing with the two different spheres of social reality, and thereby, must balance the "demands" of two different institutional logics.

## A Note on the Physical-Cognitive Distinction

What does it mean to say institutional cores manifest in physical and cognitive space? As institutions grow more autonomous, they tend to

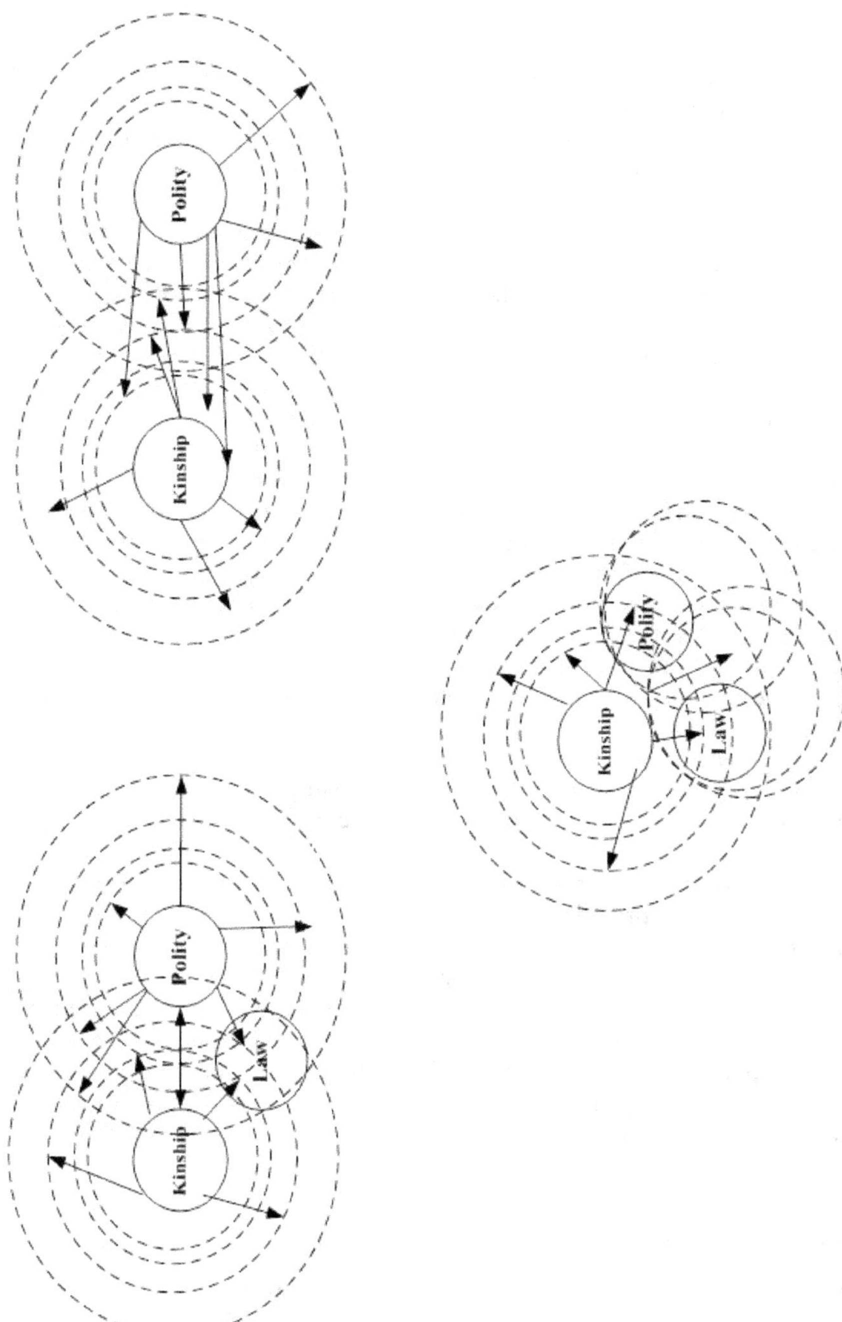


*Figure 3.3* Variation in resource flows within and across institutional domains.

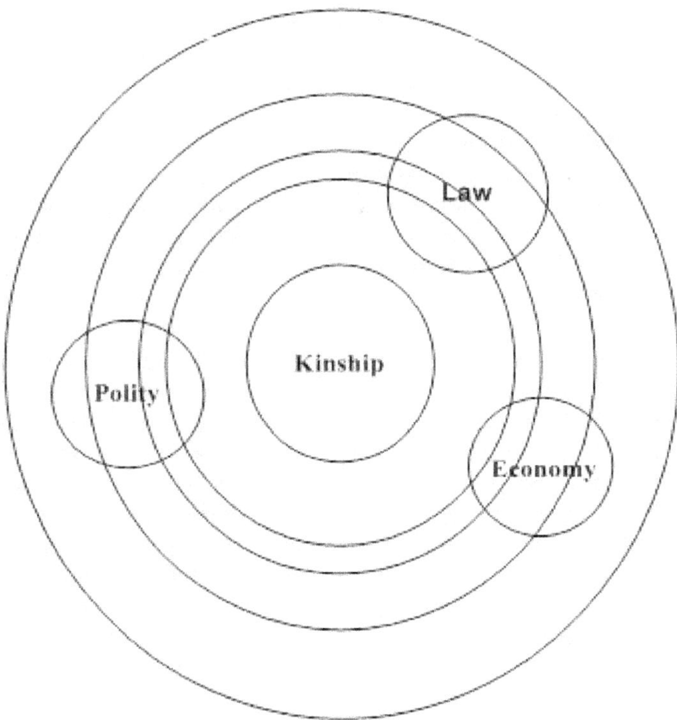


*Figure 3.4* Institutional ecology of generic hunter-gatherer society.

become more cognitively discrete, or compartmentalized in a significant proportion of the population's minds, while also become increasingly visible geographically. Consider three anecdotal examples. First, an abandoned church. Physically, it is likely differentiated from other types of buildings like apartments and houses in terms of its size and scale, and symbolically in terms of its architecture. Seeing one, even a dilapidated one, acts as a symbolic cue to call up one's own religious experience; both the real biographical religious history and the one that has been constructed through networks, media, and so on. Its physical and cognitive dimensions are inextricably linked. Second, economic cores tend to have less physical tangibility, and are more often cognitively real. To be sure, a mall or an industrial zone are economic cores in the physical sense, but online shopping and financial markets are far less tangible, especially when the commodity being exchanged are futures or securities (Collins 1990). Third, a college classroom may be a physical site for education and science, but the attitude of the student may be cognitively oriented elsewhere—for example, the degree and the specific class may be means to a better job, more money, and the American Dream, hence the student is economically oriented while physically present in the educational sphere.

Regardless of the degree to which physical and cognitive cores are coupled, institutional cores are real and, thus, have real consequences. Where polity has achieved autonomy, entrepreneurs erect massive public buildings with large, cognitively imposing expanses of space—for example, the National Mall in Washington. Humans often take for granted the way the physical space shapes our understanding and orientation, but consider Rosemary Joyce's remarks on Mesoamerican political organization of space:

> By creating different kinds of space within sites, the continuing monumental architecture served to create spatial areas with restricted access, a constantly visible form of exclusivity . . . [whose grandeur and immensity altered] the patterns of habitual movement of all inhabitants of the site, stratifying space, and hence the people who were allowed access to different space, [while] creating and marking centers and peripheries . . . [Moreover,] monumental art *permanently inscribed a small number of figures as actors linking the natural and the supernatural world* . . . [which] provided a history . . . that gave members of new polities a *ready-made store of understanding about the meaning of such architecture*. (2000:71–2; emphasis added)

Thus, the reconfiguration of physical space has significant effects on how people understand their place in the social universe. It effects how people walk around, the obstacles and awe-inspiring things in their path—as well as stratifies space around who is authorized to use it and when; it "inscribes" historical events, myths, persons into the geographic space; and it legitimates the claims entrepreneurs make about their authority, the institution's history, and the expectations all actors have when physically or cognitively near (cf. Postgate 1977; Chang 1986; Scott 1998). It is the physical demarcation of the core through grandeur and massive architecture that *links* the mundane and transmundane, and gives living, breathing proof of which actors have special access to this link—or, in some cases, as within the religious sphere, not just access but also a duty to care for and maintain the link. For instance, the very act of inventing a (new) political capital is a supra-human deed and a political innovation as old as the first known empire (Akkad) and the world's first known conqueror, Sargon the Great (*c.* 2334–2279 BCE) (Liverani 1993; Michalowski 1993).

The link between the sacred and profane is central to understanding the duality of the core, and to understanding the depth of entrepreneurship when it manages to qualitatively reconfigure the social landscape. Every autonomous institutional domain has a "center of gravity" in which entrepreneurs will enshrine institutional culture "about itself . . . beliefs about the history and nature of [the institution,] its relationship to certain *ideal or transcendent entities or values, its origin and destiny* . . . [and,] the rightfulness of its existence [or] . . . what qualifies its members to belong to [the greater] society" (Shils 1975:36–7). The institution, entrepreneur, or core need not be religious, as the process of demarcating physical space is the same for all institutions: the process of autonomy implies "consecrate[ing], that is, to sanction and sanctify" the world as is (Bourdieu 1991:118); civil attachment may be weaker than sacred, but it still draws people into a constellation of normative frameworks shaping the color and texture of action, exchange, and communication—especially when one is close to the center of an institutional domain and the institutionalized/routinized charismatic objects. The core, then, is that link between the transcendent, suprahuman, routinized charisma its entrepreneurs claim to have access to and the mundane goods and services it provides to those who desire access to the core, and/or its resources. It is this supranatural aspect that makes it cognitively distinguished. Washington, DC is not just a physical site with big buildings and political actors doing political things; it is an idea, a beacon to citizens and other political actors, and an object people can orient towards even in Alaska or Hawaii. To be sure, it has subjective meaning for actors—for example, libertarians may see it as the bane of their existence, whereas some civic-minded folk see it as a source of human rights and rational discourse. Yet, it acts as a "center of gravity" for polity, and legitimates political autonomy through the attention it garners (Abrutyn 2013b).

Ultimately, the core's integrity is a positive function of the level of institutional autonomy. Elementary schools are physical cores of education, but education is far less autonomous than polity or economy. A school is *differentiated* from other buildings, but it is heavily penetrated by entrepreneurs in other institutional domains and, therefore, educational autonomy is severely delimited. Hence, educational culture competes with political, economic, kin, religious, and legal cultures for attention and space, even though superficially it is a physical site of education. In the former Soviet Union, courts were physical sites of law. However, law was often about *power* and *political loyalty* first, and *justice* second, which meant that it was superficially legal, but actually actors generally oriented themselves politically (Berman 1955). In a later section below, we will explore some of the dynamics of hierarchical cores—for example, when a state-level polity is embedded within a national-level polity; diffuse cores—for example, markets horizontally spread throughout cities and states; and pluralism—for example, a single religious domain has competing churches, denominations, and sects, or myriad legitimate cores. First, however, we should explore the basic principles and dynamics of institutional ecology.

## THE RULE OF PROXIMITY

If we accept as true the argument above that institutions are indeed real things, occupying physical space and existing within the minds of various actors, then it goes without saying that institutions have ecological dynamics that are founded on the relative distance between individuals, collectives, and clusters of collectives and the core/entrepreneurs. It is proposed, then, a *rule of proximity* which states that *the closer are individual, collective, or clusters of collective actors to an institution's core, the greater are the constraints on interaction, exchange, and communication, and, thereby, the more predictable are their goals, lines of action, and decisions.*[3] Put another way, the effects of institutions on actors is most pronounced the closer they are to the institutional core. Resources are more visible, and thus their pursuit is more desired, the rules of pursuing them more clear, and the consequences for obtaining them more known (Abrutyn 2012); the agents of authority can more easily monitor and sanction those close to the core, whereas encounters are formalized and rules more often taken for granted; closeness also puts actors within reach of whatever charisma has been routinized, and, thereby, orientations are often duty-bound, or perceived to be (Shils 1975).

The physical location, then, of a person, or where they perform a certain role on a regular basis may be close to the core, or even in the core. It is predicted that this closeness will have consequences for the individual actor's goals, preferences, access to means to achieve goals, strategies (and diversity of strategies available to him/her), ideologies, and so forth. It is also expected that their behavior will be more stereotyped and routinized than the actor who finds himself further from the core. In terms of groups or clusters of groups, we can expect that the closer they are, (1) the more often they are responsible for supporting the core or entrepreneurial activities, (2) the more "positively" privileged (and thereby so are their members) they are than other groups further from the core, and (3) the more they come to be identified as representative of the institution, its concern, its underlying symbolic essence and meaning, and perhaps even the source of charisma.

Physical distance is often correlated with cognitive distance, although not necessarily—for example, some people can be physically close and not cognitively, and vice versa. The closer actors are, cognitively, the more normatively committed they are to the institutional domain and the more predictable their actions will be. We can expect their performances to be authentic, genuine, and substantively driven (Alexander 2004; Reed 2011). Conversely, those cognitively far from the domain have more freedom to act in novel or disruptive ways (Goffman 1971)—that is, they may be purely instrumental, strategizing, interested actors who employ strategies of misrecognition and condescension (Bourdieu 1977:81–2, 1989:16). To be sure, organizations and, especially, clusters of organizations are not sentient beings and therefore it is not that they are cognitively oriented in the same way as people. Yet, collectives (and clusters of collectives) that are very close to the core are often under intensive external pressure to "behave" in predictable ways. Moreover, they may be the producers of valuable institutional resources like generalized media, or they may be privy to greater shares of these resources, which means they will come to look, act, and appear much more stereotypical than those further away. As such, some of their members are very likely aware of what it means to be in that collective, what the collective itself stands for, and what its ultimate goals are.

The question, then, is why does the *rule of proximity* work? Three central dynamics will be explored below. First, the level of role or organizational commitment generated by the properties of an individual, collective, or cluster of collective's social ties. Second, the way proximity shapes actors' (or clusters of actors') nearness to the system(s) of authority and the mechanisms of social control. Third, and finally, the degree to which the central symbolic system and vision of reality imposed by entrepreneurs is visible, internalized, and successful vis-à-vis other institutions and their symbolic systems. These three dynamics are independent of each other, but are clearly interrelated. An actor or group may "act" authentically because of the fear of sanctions or external mechanisms of regulation, whereas his or her counterpart may be normatively committed because they are not just afraid of the system, but because the constitution of the social ties are configured differently than the former actor. What matters most is that the *rule of proximity* predicts (1) the degree to which individuals or collectives set institutionally sanctioned goals, use (and have available) institutionally sanctioned means to achieving these goals, and understand their choices through the logic of the institutional domain and not other institutional logics; (2) the diversity of an individual's or collective's strategies; (3) the degree to which the actor pursue, accumulates, exchanges, and invests an institution's generalized symbolic medium of exchange/communication; and (4) the degree to which the actor or cluster of actors has a vested interest in supporting the core and shaping the institutional domain.

## Role Commitment

Sheldon Stryker (1980) proposed that identities, or the individualized meaning structures attached to each role a person plays (cf. Stets 2006), were identifiable in terms of their prominence (self-perceived importance), salience (likelihood of being activated in any given situation), and commitment (size, density, and significance of networks a given identity is embedded within).[4] Prominence is deeply psychological, although powerfully shaped by the salience of and commitment to a particular identity (Burke 1991; Burke and Stets 1999); commitment, for Stryker, is purely structural—that is, it is shaped by the properties of the social ties related to a given identity, which, in turn, affects how often and to what degree an identity is salient. As such, salience is sort of the mediating mechanism between one's own personal feelings about their list of identities and the way their social ties shape and constrain their personal choice. The greater the salience of an identity, the more committed the actor or collective will be to performing authentically and normatively (Stryker 1980), predictable/ stereotyped performances (Goffman 1959), and feeling negative emotions when performing poorly (Burke and Reitzes 1981).

Stryker proposed that we all have an identity salience hierarchy that governs our total self-conception, or who we see ourselves as and who others see us as. An actor's "professor" identity might be most prominent to them, but the configuration of social ties may lead to her "mother/wife" identity's activation more often and more deeply. As such, her identity hierarchy, which is fluid and often situational, will be defined by two contradictory identities and, thus, her behavior and attitudes will be tenuously balanced between the two. By looking closely at Stryker's commitment dimension, we can discern what institutional domain(s) a person is physically and cognitively near. On the one hand, *intensive commitment*—or, the depth, significance, and shared history the social ties of a given identity possess—is also shaped by the *rule of proximity*: *the closer an individual or collective actor is to an autonomous institutional core, the greater is the probability that specific institutional actors will be considered significant others, and hence the greater is the likelihood that the institutional identity/role will be considered prominent vis-à-vis other identities*. On the other hand, *extensive commitment*—or, the sheer number of social ties a given identity is linked to—is shaped by the *rule of proximity*: *the closer an individual or collective actor is to an autonomous institutional core, the greater are the number of actors who identify and activate his/her or its institutional identity, expect generalized behaviors, and act/exchange/communicate via a specific generalized symbolic medium*. Thus, the frequency of identity activation will be high. Again, there are no guarantees that intensive and extensive commitments will overlap, and in fact they often do not: some institutional domains and their roles are anchored in socioemotional moorings, which generate intensive commitments, while other institutional domains foster cooler, universalistic, impersonal relationships, and thereby, provide greater numbers of actors that one might interact with. Let's look a little closer at each type of commitment.

### *Intensive Ties*

Intensive commitment is rooted in the types of relationships actors have with the people that they consider to be more important or who have the longest, most durable and intimate relations with; hence the term intensive. The logic is simple. Identity/roles associated and activated frequently by significant others like spouses or parents are highly valued because the rewards are multiplex, trust and commitment are high, and sanctions are often face-to-face as is monitoring (R. Turner 1978). Failure to play a role activated by intimate others produces powerful negative sanctions like disappointment, disapproval, gossip, and, in the worst case, being thrown from a relationship that offers strong social and emotional support. The rewards are "multiplex" because relationships are rarely one-dimensional: one gets love, affection, gratitude, other emotions, monetary support, and so on. It is true that what comes to be defined as "intensive" may change as the actor's definition of reality changes, but it does not change the effects intimates have on us. This discussion should not be taken as reductionism. Our intensive ties are far more complicated than they seem at face value. A husband may derive status from his wife's profession and income, whereas she may derive status from his education and occupational prestige/title (Stets and Harrod 2004). These bonuses are transferable across institutional boundaries, but they also intensify the possibility of conflict. In order to make the money that he derives extra status from, she must prioritize work; yet, prioritizing work also reduces the salience of her wife role/identity and could cause dissatisfaction. When we have two or more identities that are prominent in our salience hierarchy, we try hard to manage both of them and tend to be highly committed to both institutional domains, which, in turn, creates the distinct possibility of role conflict. Intimate ties also shape our cognitive closeness or farness to an institutional domain. Obviously, family draws us into the kinship world; we put pictures of kids and spouses on our work desks, carry them in our wallet, and shape much of our non-work hours and days around activities with them. But these ties can also shape our religious identities by either drawing us deeper into a religious organization or pushing us further away; likewise, our parent's political affiliation often shapes our adult affiliation, while our father's and perhaps mother's educational attainment and occupational prestige shapes our future pursuits and aspirations—and successes to some degree (Blau and Duncan 1967; Bourdieu 1984), and our parents and kids and spouses can even shape our degree of cognitive nearness to sports, art, and so on.

### *Extensive Ties*

On the opposite side of the spectrum, we all have social ties that are not as intimate, typically one-dimensional in exchange and situation, and, because of this, dynamically different. Here, performance has more to do with dynamics related to the number and density of social ties a given identity is linked to. The more people we know that activate a given identity, the more salient that identity is. First, it is just more likely to be salient because the probability of it being activated is higher when we know more people who think of us as a mother, a professor, or a doctor. When we are in "unfocused" encounters, like the supermarket, and someone sees us and begins the ritual of interaction that draws us cognitively into a specific role, it makes this role salient regardless of who we think we are outside of the physical environment. For instance, a new professor in a new city and university is likely to have extensive ties primarily to people who know her as a professor. The vast majority of people she interacts with are students; if she runs into one at the supermarket or restaurant, they will only react to her as if she still is their professor. Her colleagues and friends are likely all professors or their spouses. Besides her spouse, she may have few face-to-face interactions with anyone beyond her university role. Prominence predicated on extensive commitment, in this case, is a function of practice, frequency of activation, and atrophy of other role/identities. It may also speak to a concerted effort on her part to embrace this role and put herself in situations where it is activated because she understands it as good for her career.

Extensive ties are both products of physical and cognitive proximity to an institution's core. On the one hand, the closer one is to the core of an institution, the more it is likely that the vast majority of actors we encounter are also oriented toward the institution and, thus, more likely to activate the institutional identity we carry. When I go to work at the university, I am likely to only run into colleagues and students; this is also true of conferences and other academic events. On the other hand, extensive ties mean having a greater number of specific counter-role players one can visualize interacting with. A student sends me an email, I run into a colleague at the grocery store, or I get an acceptance or rejection from a journal; all of these encounters activate my professor identity and the more often this happens the closer I move towards the core. Extensivity also makes the identity seem important or prominent because one may have high regards for their performance based on external responses, as well as the number of people they know as a professor. Thus, again, we are pulled closer to the core and will act increasingly stereotypically.

### *The Merger*

When a role/identity is activated by both forms of commitment, we should expect it to be very high in a person's salience hierarchy. Let's stick with the young professor as an example. Fast forward 30 years and picture a woman at the peak of her career in her discipline of choice, married through the whole process and successful as wife, mother, and professor. It is very possible her success in academia is predicated on her prioritizing scholarship first and family second; to do so, her husband may have had to reprioritize. It is very likely that the older she gets and the more accolades she receives, the more her husband's own status is derived from being connected to her. He begins to think of her more as a professor and then as a spouse. Her kids probably even think of her as that because she has consistently remained in role throughout the course of their lives! What you get is a merger between person identity and role, and very strong levels of predictability. In some ways the person becomes the ideal type, the caricature, the perfect representative of a particular role; they are the model that neophytes point to. In reality, though, the merger is rarely complete or perfect, as merger requires subordination of other role commitments and, therefore, living in near-constant role tension. Institutional domains, in part, compartmentalize our role/identities in ways that should simplify things by defining when we should act in expected ways. However, we all know from personal experience that institutional domains, their entrepreneurs, and the agents as found in our intensive and extensive ties pull and push us in contradictory and competing ways. Yet, I believe if we sought to measure one's extensive and intensive ties, we would get one dimension of his or her self that could give us some idea as to why he or she chose to act in a given situation. These ties tell us a lot about which roles are salient and likely to be salient, as well as, which lines of action and goals are likely to be predictable.

## The Moral and Social Order

Institutions also contain systems of authority that compel compliance; the force of these authority systems is predicated on the relative distance actors' stand from the core. Besides the relative force, the type of mechanisms of control also change based on proximity. For instance, nearness implies some degree of commitment to the appropriate role performance because it is expected from those around us and to not do so would elicit powerful feelings of shame or embarrassment. Further from the core, agents rely on instrumental and external mechanisms like material incentives and agents authorized to monitor and sanction inappropriate behavior. Finally, institutional cores are centers of resource production and, thereby, also distribute resources which act as sanctions (rewards and punishments) to role-players (and groups).

### *Visibility and Presence*

The closer one is to a core, the more visible are desired resources as well as agents of social control (Abrutyn 2012). As people get nearer to entrepreneurs in the core, the successes and rewards these actors have secured become understandable or, at the very least, clear enough that actors may perceive them as within reach even if they under- or overestimate the situation. Moreover, nearness to the core means being closer to the seat(s) of authority, which makes the thought of mobility and privileged position a reality. It is for this reason that we often find those middle managers or lieutenants most committed to the norms and values of the group, because they are so close to securing privilege (even if it never happens), and are so close to those who have it, that much of their self-worth is derived from their near-privileged position (Michels 1911 [1962]). What's more, these second-in-commands are close enough to power to feel it and are often empowered enough that they may even believe they are in control. In every profession, for instance, there are two types of "close actors."

There are those who shape the reality through their relationships with actors beyond the realm of the institution and, thus, derive their power and privilege through elite networks. Then there are those "careerists" who are devoted to the ideals of the group, its values and norms, and the legitimate path to success even if it never gets them there, but because it is "right." These actors obtain nominal power and prestige, and may even make a difference in the social reality of others. Yet, their predictability in action and attitudes is shaped more by the core and its entrepreneurs being within reach.

The other side of closeness is related to the physical presence of external agents of social control. Being near the core means interacting with elites, or at least being ordered around by elites. It also means interacting with those actors whose function is to protect the elites, whether in the physical sense of police or security or in the figurative sense as in gatekeepers. Either way, being near the centers of power often humbles actors, pushes them toward deferential positions, and also heightens the threat of punishment for inappropriate action. As actors find themselves farther away, this threat lessens and, eventually, become nominal and unevenly manifested. It becomes increasingly costly on the margins of an institution to station external agents and, in many cases, the interstices of multiple institutional environments raise jurisdictional questions better left unasked.

Briefly, consider a professor at the top of her game. First, she will likely serve on various committees and boards which put her into contact with others like herself. The norms and values will be espoused both in formal statements of purpose as well as in how veteran members carry themselves. Second, she will be privy to information others do not have, whether truly important or not. This position makes her a gatekeeper and also acts as a reward. Third, she may begin to have an easier time publishing as she meets editors of journals, becomes considered a go-to expert, and is asked to speak at conferences or invited to colloquia at universities. At this point, the rewards are quite visible even if she is never going to become the best in her field or an international presence; the point is she has reached a level where she is on the cusp of the core and in possible line to be an entrepreneur. Finally, she will be travelling in networks that overlap with the best, and these people and their closest allies will become agents of control, whether purposively or unconsciously. It becomes increasingly obvious that her behavior conforms to the expectations of the group and education science in general and thus is more predictable.

### *Normative and Regulatory Control*

Sociologists have long acknowledged social systems employ normative—or controls anchored in socioemotional, moral meanings; taken-for-granted—or controls rooted in the implicit assumptions about reality and habitual behavior; and regulatory—or controls founded on the existence of external agents and the threat of force or some punishment. There are few social systems that do not utilize all three types of forces, but the former two are cheaper in terms of time, energy, and other resources than the latter type. This is for two reasons. First, actors prefer not to feel coerced or bossed around (Boehm 1999). Second, the use of, say, material-incentives to regulate behavior does not produce high levels of normative commitment and thus does not lead to moral behavior all of the time outside of the physical presence of an agent (Hechter 1987). Institutional entrepreneurs work very hard to internalize their vision of reality in institutional actors and produce cognitive closeness. When actors are cognitively close, they are subject to normative controls, or that is they act not because they feel forced to but because it is a moral imperative or duty to act correctly. Parsons referred to this as "voluntary" action, or the feeling that one is choosing their actions when in fact they are being guided by external, sociocultural values and norms (Alexander 1988a); Goffman was perhaps more accurate when he remarked, "As performers we are merchants of morality" (1959:251). For Goffman, all role performances touched on the normative because the activation of a role implied some commitment and awareness of the most basic underlying expectations and rules no matter the reasons for performing—for example, whether for personal reasons (e.g., self-esteem, self-gain) or for unconscious collective reasons. Because most interaction is ritualized (Goffman 1967; Collins 2004), most of us are somewhat close to the institutional core at least cognitively whenever playing a role. Yet, as Goffman also noted some people are "distant" from their role and the performance and thus can be cognitively distant as well. Some reasons include commitment to other prominent roles, lack of reward, and poor self-evaluation.

That most people have some cognitive commitment should not detract from the importance of regulatory mechanisms. Humans are emotional creatures and are often unpredictable under the right pressure. In a courtroom, for instance, most of the performers in the legal drama "know" what is expected of them and will act accordingly based on cognitive nearness. That does not prevent the existence of a bailiff or two to ensure that all actors observe the norms and rules if only to keep the performance going. Physical nearness almost always leads to some compliance and conformity because of fear of punishments because people's actions are more visible and, therefore, more sanctionable.

### *Formalization*

Weber (1978) may have been the first to explicitly recognize that the degree to which a situation is formal—for example, standardized, ritualized, routinized—varies positively with the degree to which actors will comply unthinkingly (see also, Goffman 1974; Collins 2004; Turner 2010b). For

Weber, what was most important about enduring social orders were their ability to make things routine to the point that we took for granted those things as having always existed. It was not that they were morally right or that punishments could follow; the point was we followed many rules or acted in certain ways because it was traditional and typical, and thus action was "automatic" (and easy). The closer one gets to the core of an institution the more typified situations become. In part because many of the buildings where institutional exchange occur do the same tasks day-in and day-out, and their personnel are highly constrained by formal rules internalized through training and explicit in handbooks, posters, and other real manifestations. Furthermore, entrepreneurs or, what I prefer to call "support" actors (more on this below), tend to inhabit the core and closest zones near the core and thus "demand" deference through their clothing, titles, and other status markers which, again, condition people to act in stereotypically subordinate ways.

## Translating Underlying Meanings

One of the unique dynamics of institutional autonomy is the emergence of a distinct intra-institutional culture, or system of symbols that provide the basic tools for individuals and groups to communicate, act, and orient themselves (Abrutyn 2009b, 2012; Turner 2010b; Abrutyn and Turner 2011; Luhmann 2012). This culture grows out of the generalized symbolic medium that institutional entrepreneurs monopolize and employ in institutional exchanges and communication. In Chapter 5, this concept will be elaborated in far more detail, but for now we can say a few words that highlight the way media shape reality. Simmel (1907) was perhaps the first elaborate a theory of generalized media in his Philosophy of Money. Money, once generalized in "meaning" and exchange-value, intensifies economic exchanges by making them more frequent, more complex, faster, and more ramified. An "empty" placeholder of value is durable and portable, which changes the way homo economicus orients him- or herself to the economic sphere of action because it promotes future-orientation, the ability to save for a future purchase, the improved ability to rationally calculate debts and credits, etc. (Weber 1927 [2002]). Money is also responsible for "fetishizing" commodities or hiding their true value by converting labor-value into pure monetary terms (Marx 1867 [1990]). Parsons (1963b) would take this a step further and argue that money is not just a token used as a placeholder, but in fact was a symbolic medium of exchange (La Valle 1994), or a specialized language that was, in a way, a symbolic bundle comprised of norms, values, ideologies, strategies, expectations, and goals. That is, the possession of *money* means, for the actor, an understanding of the things it can be exchanged for, the strategies surrounding its use, and a normative framework for "*doing*" economy. Luhmann (1976, 1982) extended Parsons by arguing that *money* is not just a symbolic referent of the entire economic system, actions and attitudes, but also a mode of communication. In later work, Luhmann (1995, 2012) would emphasize the tendency for media, as a *mode of communication*, to impose themes of discourse and text on the social system. *Themetization*, in his terms, captured the way polities or religion were identifiable by the different vocabularies used in everyday exchange.

*Money* becomes the central focus for all things economic where the economy has secured some degree of autonomy. That is, *money* becomes the symbolic "cornerstone" of economic goals, actions, and decisions (Abrutyn 2009a). Each institutional domain has its own medium of exchange as a way for entrepreneurs to regulate and integrate disparate units, legitimate stratification and their vision of reality, while linking the domain to other institutions—for example, polity's is power (Parsons 1963b; Abrutyn 2013b) and religion's is sacredness/piety (Luhmann 2012; Abrutyn 2013a).

Understanding that generalized media are not just physical resources (e.g., how many dollars are in your wallet), but also symbolic resources, makes a major difference for understanding intra-institutional culture and the predictability of actors in relation to the distance from the core. The experience of acquiring specific material goods transmits shareded meanings: getting a new car has various types of meanings for the purchaser such as positive feelings about a more dependable or better looking vehicle, a statement of their position in the status hierarchy of society, and more diffuse associations of freedom. But generalized media are not just material objects as they are symbolic bundles internalized and activated in oral/written communication (Luhmann 2012), and non-verbal communication as conveyed through our embodied dispositions. Hence, having lots of money has exchange-value in the tangible sense that it can get a high-status car, while it also implies a wider range of strategies for using *money* wisely and maximizing its exchange-value. And, despite the fact that one cannot consume *money* like other commodities, themes surrounding money include accumulating it, saving and hoarding it, investing it for bigger returns, and converting it into other media as a strategy of getting more at a later date. Having more of money means having access toa greater number of themes of economic discourse which links them to more economic actors and gives them a greater chance of improving their economic position. *Money*, then, is something larger than the currency; it is a cultural toolkit for the economic sphere of social action, just as any medium becomes the toolkit for the autonomous institutional domain it circulates within. Thus, as individuals or groups get closer to the core, they either acquire more of the medium of exchange, gain access to the productive/distributive centers of the medium, or the medium becomes increasingly visible and thus becomes a goal motivating actors to follow institutionalized paths to attainment.

## THE ENVIRONMENT AND ECOLOGICAL DYNAMICS

### The Institutional Environment

Up till now, the institutional environment has been at the periphery of our discussion. Yet, the environment is the milieu of the vast majority of actors in any given society. The environment is a strange place, because it varies tremendously in composition and, unlike the core, is not necessarily clearly demarcated from other institutional domains' environments. There are, for instance, resource niches within the environment that are clearly distinguishable from other domains, and yet the environment is more often than not pock-marked with organizational units and individual actors from various domains. In a neighborhood that rests on the edge of a busy road in a medium-sized city, there are rows of houses that are truly reflective of kinship, churches or other houses of worship on the corners of smaller and major roads, strip malls or other economic good/service providers, and schools. When one enters these physical spaces, his or her orientation is drawn into the dominant sphere (religion, economy, or education), yet the building and organization remains rooted in a kinship space that constrains and shapes the "foreign" entity. It is for this reason that communities that can, resist industrialization near neighborhoods or the placement of prisons or nuclear waste facilities. The desire is to deepen the core's boundaries and build buffer zones around the core to protect the integrity of the actors. It is possible, then, to create a typology of environmental actors based on proximity to the core and their general function.

#### *Core Support*

As the core develops, entrepreneurs try hard to develop buffer zones between the core and the rest of society. There are no closed cores, but there are protected cores. "Buffer zones," where extant, are inhabited by actors best labeled *support actors*. Their primary function is analogous to middle managers. They have authority and some degree of access to the core, but they are not producers or innovators; they are enforcers, regulators, and executors. They ensure the core's ethos permeates through the environment. They may be assistants to executives: for example, middle managers in a corporation, sports fans, or civil servants in the government. Indeed, the line between entrepreneurs and the support actors blurs oftentimes as career bureaucrats certainly derive certain privileges from polity, but do not have the real power to reconfigure the institutional space. Or, consider nurses who are important support actors in the production and distribution of the generalized symbolic medium of the autonomous medical institution: health care. Indeed, they have a high degree of access to these and other medical resources and their relative prestige and power reflect that. However, nurses are generally not entrepreneurs in the truest sense of the word:

they rarely have the ability to reconfigure space in meaningful ways. Their primary role is to act as the go-between for doctors and patients.

### *Liaisons*

Some support actors find themselves located in the interstices of multiple institutional environments and are no longer "support" in the truest sense of the word. Instead, these actors are better labeled *liaisons*, as their primary function is not so much a buffer between core and environment, but actually communications and relations between one institution and another. Lawyers, for instance, are legal actors, and through their efforts to "test" law they are entrepreneurs to a certain degree. However, one of their most important functions is translating the problems of individuals or groups in one domain into legal language so that the legal core can provide resolution and/or justice; they are then responsible for re-translating the legal language into the language of the institution the actor comes from (Luhmann 2004).[5] Thus, entrepreneurial classes can become sub-divided as some entrepreneurs continue to worry about the core, while others bring the core into other domains through liaison activities—for instance, big economic firms often have a legal department whose sole purpose is to help the organization adapt to the law and use the law when necessary (Sutton and Dobbin 1996).

The unique position of these types of actors leads to some of the most fascinating institutional dynamics, dynamics often taken for granted by organizational actors who overemphasize the role of closed clusters of actors like fields (DiMaggio and Powell 1983) or sectors (Scott and Meyer 1983). On the one hand, they supposedly represent the interests of the entrepreneurs and institutional core to which they most prominently belong to. Lawyers are trained at accredited law schools and must take the bar exam and can be disbarred by the American Bar Association for betraying legal ethics and principles. Yet, lawyers are also economic actors exchanging their access to *learning* (legal education) and *justice* (personal and professional relationships with judges; skill and legal ability) for *money* (fees); their loyalty, of course, is to their client(s) and thus may or may not be in the best interest of the legal institution. People are more likely to trust judges, whose interests, motives, and actions are presumably embedded within law and law only, while negative narratives of lawyers abound. The problem, then, is that groups that find themselves in the overlapping environments of institutions are not simply tempted, but truly oriented toward myriad cores and the pressures for compliance and conformity across domains. And where *money* is the generalized medium between two other media (e.g., lawyers exchanging *learning* so that an economic entrepreneur can gain *power-authority* over his/her employees is facilitated by *money* or fees rendered for legal services), the values and norms of the economy are always present and can intercede in instrumental, amoral ways.

### *Consumers*

Non-institutional or institutional actors pursuing the goods and services of the core are deemed consumers, even though this term may over-economize the actions and motivations of non-economic actors. Congregants of a church, or potential converts, are consumers seeking access to *piety/sacredness*, communication with the supranatural, the networks found within the specific church, and whatever other goals may be of interest. In this case, obviously, these people are not consuming these things as one would consume bread or milk, but they are consuming institutional goods and services through adherence to behavioral patterns, exchanging tangible and intangible resources for other desired resources, and communicating through symbolic media with other actors. They have to choose among a set of alternatives, figure out the terms of exchange that secure what they most want, and then acquire the good and/or service. The case of religious consumers is no different from the person going to the grocery store for bread: it is rarely a one-time only exchange, but actually a gradually developing relationship between consumer and support/entrepreneurial actors. This also means that emotions become a part of the exchange, as norms of reciprocity and obligation form (Blau 1964), and the exchanges deepen to include more goods and services being exchanged (Lawler 2001). Consumers, unfortunately, vary tremendously in motive, motivation, distance from the core, resources desired, and means to acquire these resources. Some students in my classes are in it for the degree, some for the job promised after the degree, some to achieve something after having a family, and so on. Some, of course, see the degree as a path to *learning* and *truth*, and thus begin the slow process of conversion to entrepreneur-hood.

### *Extra-Institutional Entrepreneurs*

Like liaisons, extra-institutional entrepreneurs have the potential to be beneficial to an institution's entrepreneurs or a serious threat. Above we noted the fact that some entrepreneurs are embedded both in their institutional domain as well as networks of other entrepreneurs. They share similar lifestyle patterns, life experiences, consumptive habits, and often material and/or ideal interests. Furthermore, through social exchange, entrepreneurs are able to exchange high-level access to institutionally specific resources, as well as prestige goods rooted in social and cultural capital. But what links these types of actors together most powerfully is their dependence on each other for legitimacy. Political entrepreneurs in the U.S. need the independence of legal entrepreneurs for their own claims to legitimate authority, whereas legal entrepreneurs rely on political entrepreneurs for the enforcement of their decisions (Weber 1967). The importance of religion in the U.S. has led to the deepening of network ties between certain religious entrepreneurs and their political counterparts (Brint and Abrutyn 2009).

The dynamics of extra-entrepreneurial action is predicated on the fact that in spite of overlapping interests and cultural habits, a society's total entrepreneurial class does not compose a homogeneous class of actors (Weber 1946b). Quite the contrary, expansion of one institutional domain often has to come at the expense of other domains and their autonomy. Sometimes, this encroachment is out of necessity in terms of the goals an entrepreneur sets. For example, nearly every political entrepreneur *needs* the population to reproduce biologically for continued material and human resources. Without new members fewer surpluses will be produced, and there will be fewer eligible soldiers. Although biological reproduction has been the primary role that kinship institutions play, and still play, the polity intercedes more often than not. In the U.S., for instance, the polity offers material incentives (via tax breaks) for having children. In this case, political entrepreneurs are not pursuing malicious or nefarious plans to weaken the independence of kinship entrepreneurs. However, there are plenty of times where entrepreneurs do pursue strategies of "contraction." Using the same example, consider the various laws against child and spousal abuse; although these are humane and necessary, they are direct usurpation of kinship autonomy. The Catholic Church's efforts during and after the Gregorian Reformation (*c.* 1050–75 CE) also reflect a conscious attempt to reduce the autonomy of the kinship domain in return for the expansion of the religious institution's reach and, thereby, autonomy (Gies and Gies 1986).

In the most extreme cases, entrepreneurs can subordinate entire autonomous institutional domains and subvert their logic. In the former Soviet Union, through a revolution that installed a powerful political entrepreneurial unit, nearly every institution was re-embedded into polity (Armstrong 1961). Unlike the arrangements we find in autonomous legal institutions, law was about *power* and political *loyalty* first and *justice* and *conflict* resolution second (Berman 1955); additionally, Paul Froese (2009) lays bare the concerted effort under Stalin and his successors to pervert the Russian religious institution, eradicate the *supranatural*, and intertwine *piety/sacredness* with *power* and political *loyalty*. As history has shown, these efforts were for naught as the Soviet Union is no more. Yet, autonomy is tenuous and entrepreneurs have plenty of incentives to embark on institutional projects aimed at expanding their influence vis-à-vis other entrepreneurs influence. In one sense, it is adaptive for entrepreneurs to do so; in another sense, it is a maladaptive strategy as the ubiquity of some institutions, like law or religion, likely points to their importance to human societies and to addressing problems humans continue to find troubling—for example, justice, conflict resolution, and communicating with the supranatural. This point should not be taken, however, as a celebration of societies with highly autonomous institutional domains like, say, the United States or Britain. The payoff for greater adaptive flexibility is (1) the growing magnitude of macro-level exigencies like population pressures and (2) a greater number and more diverse set of centers of domination.

Societies, and their institutional domains, are "survivor machines" as Jonathan Turner (2010a) is fond of calling them, but survival is relative and collapse seems fairly common.

### *Marginal Actors*

There are two types of marginal actors: Those who are intensely oriented toward the core of one or two institutional domains at the expense of other domains and those who are neither physically nor cognitively oriented toward any particular institutional domain. The former type is an interesting case because they continue to be affected by the domains they willingly or unconsciously withdraw from. Humans do desire certain things; prestige and respect are absolutely universal needs for humans (Lenski 1966). In the event that some institutional domains become "removed" from everyday reality, grow cold and impersonal, and alienate actors more than find ways to draw them in, some actors seek out groups within domains that provide the social support and resources they desire and need. There is a fairly large segment of the American population that considers the instrumental rationality of the autonomous American economy and the political expediency of the American polity to be repulsive and amoral. On the one hand, these actors may be turning away from these dominant institutions because they actually gain little in the way of *money* or *power*. That is, the core is so distant that there is little reason to commit to the economic or political roles. On the other hand, it is also probable that their families and church offer powerful incentives to commit strongly to the kinship and religious cores. Given that humans have limited amounts of time, attention, and energy to devote to anything, why not devote it to the domains that offer them the most prestige, reciprocal goods and services, and socioemotional anchorages? These domains have created power resistance meta-ideologies crafted through the fusion of *love*, *loyalty*, and *piety/sacredness*; these meta-ideologies refract the interpretation of economic and political values, norms, and ideologies and provide a buffer for these cold, impersonal spheres of social action. To be sure, few people can truly escape the penetration of the universal, dominant institutional domains because *power* shapes the vast majority of non-religio-kin relationships these actors exchange within, as does *money*. Yet, that does not mean these marginal actors have to believe in the legitimacy of these domains and their entrepreneurs. And, as many scholars have shown, these resistance meta-ideologies, when wielded effectively by their respective entrepreneurs can change the meaning of the media of exchange—for example, as Belk and Wilkerson (1990) label it, churches can *sacralize money*.[6]

## The Multiplicity of the Core

A key aspect of institutional ecology we must address is the fact that societies do get larger and as a result, second-order problems related to regulating and integrating geographically dispersed groups within a common institutional domain become pressing. Empires collapse when they overextend (Collins 1981a), suggesting the limitations of autonomy and the need on the part of entrepreneurs to innovate if they are to extend their geographic influence. Two solutions have been used most typically: *proxy* cores and *multiple jurisdictions* that hierarchicalize institutional cores.

### *Proxy Cores*

As one Mesopotamian polity grew from the failures of the next, each cast of political entrepreneurs had to either use what they felt worked from their predecessors or invent something new. In the earliest dynasties, such as the Akkadian and Ur III, the transportation/ communication technology available led to the creation of *proxy cores*, or physical sites that were to be reflective of the central core found in the empire's capital, and were supposedly a physical extension of the emperor's *power* (Nissen 1988; Liverani 1993; van de Mieroop 2004). The "governors" of each city-state or colony answered to the king, whereas temples built within the city were directed toward the religious center, or the city of Kish (Frankfort 1948; Kramer 1963), with each local deity being introduced to the regional pantheon and thus independent, yet subject to the king of the gods, either Enlil or later Marduk and Assur (Jacobsen 1963).

It is not enough, then, for entrepreneurs to create a real core or for the specialized language of the core to be internalized through socialization; instead, proxy cores must be developed to overcome the problems associated with real distance. Polities, historically, have had numerous political innovations in trying to intensify their autonomy and to increase the flow of resources—all of which were constrained by available transportation and communication technologies (Hawley 1986). Proxy cores are noticeably smaller than their originator and are weaker at generating solidarity and control because they are stripped down versions of the real core and the entrepreneurs or support actors physically present are not always authorized to lead collective, public rituals of solidarity. They basically serve as a visual reminder of the institution, while also having functional qualities for entrepreneurs—for example, local federal buildings collect taxes or protect local environments. Recall, then, our previous discussion about the U.S. polity and entrepreneur's desire to penetrate the further reaches of American society for regulation, integration, and legitimation. Washington, DC cannot physically be moved everywhere, and the threat of coercive force is always expensive and, eventually, unstable. One solution is to literally build federal buildings in every state and big city to serve as symbolic reminders of the political core's control, as well as to have real representative actors present to interact, if need be, with citizens; some services easily lend themselves to localization. In addition, the state has military and national reserve bases located throughout. Again, these serve as reminders of the core's supremacy over power, and from a functional sense, represent political entrepreneur's unique ability to mobilize an army at moment's notice to protect against threats and, importantly, quell rebellions.

### *The Jurisdictional Dimension*

A second solution to this problem has been to create multiple jurisdictions that reflect a loose coupling of numerous levels of social reality. The inclusion and embedding of each level weakly links one core to the next, while the cultural equivalencies generated by the circulation, and somewhat independent production and distribution rights of each core's entrepreneurs, of the same generalized symbolic medium of exchange and communication. The physical core of the polity in the U.S., for example, rests in Washington, DC, where the most powerful entrepreneurs facilitate and constrain political action, exchange, and communication. Yet, state- and local-level cores exist that have some degree of relative autonomy from the higher-order levels. Governors have the legitimate right to produce and distribution power, while respecting federally imposed limits; the same is true, of course, of local cores where city councils and mayors shape the daily lives. In one sense, this is incredibly adaptive as local problems can be dealt with quickly and with political entrepreneurs more familiar with the specific contours of the problem. But this also sets up multiple layers of domination for non-political entrepreneurs who must wade through a labyrinth of "red tape" and some uncertainty about whose power is most valuable. The larger a society becomes, however, the more difficult it is for a single core and the more efficacious multi-jurisdictional solutions can be. It is at once adaptive as it produce numerous centers of creativity and problem solving, while also increasing the level of domination and the potential for elite conflicts as lower-order cores can and often do challenge higher-order cores for greater autonomy—for example, the eternal battle between federal interests and state's rights. In the effort to deal with distance, regional cores must also embed local, previously autonomous cores into the institutional domain.

### *Intersecting Core Dynamics*

The dynamics become fascinating when multiple jurisdictions emerge side-by-side with proxies. Consider, for instance, a small town in the U.S. of, say, 10,000 citizens. In nearly every one of these towns, the geographic layout is the same: a downtown area with a "main" street upon which one finds the Mayor's office, town hall, numerous businesses, the courthouse, and probably a once-dominant church. Around that general main street complex one will likely find the chamber of commerce, an Elks club or multiple (formerly) men's voluntary associations, the county jail, law offices, and other key goods and services. Finally, it is very likely that within a stone's throw of this downtown one will find neighborhoods filled with older houses that were once occupied—if they are not still—by the most prominent families in the city. For citizens of this city, this configuration shapes their everyday interactions with local institutional entrepreneurs and domains. The clear lines indicating autonomy are not there: for example, in many towns like this, powerful families sit on powerful boards, are linked with city councils, own lots of property, attend the most important church for social networking, and thus, play a series of entrepreneurial roles across domains. The decisions they make are important because they do indeed affect others in less privileged positions. Yet, the local macro-level of social reality cannot be divorced from the regional or national levels. For one thing, local governments are affected by state and federal law; local churches typically belong to a national association, although the level of centralization of power in the association varies tremendously; courts are shaped by lawyers and legal entrepreneurs who are beholden to a centralized association that professionalizes and sanctions their behavior; local law is different from national law because the plaintiffs and defendants and their legal counsel and judges may have personal relationships beyond the court—nevertheless the principles, in theory, are not any different. Moreover, through the penetration of more diffuse institutional domains like the arena of public schools, mass media, political campaigns, markets both real and internet-based, and so on, the larger regional and national domains penetrate the lives and cognitions of everyday people. In sum, local people's interests and orientations may be shaped daily at the local institutional level, and dealing with property zoning may seem most salient for instance, but they are also embedded in a larger institutional complex. The blurriness of the local institutional level and the compartmentalized national level creates confusion in role performance and cognitive meanings. It may very well be that groups like the Tea Party or the unfortunate label "bumpkins" for "country folk" has more to do with the level of distinction made between one institution and the next; when dealing with regional or national forces that draw clear lines between morality and *justice*, morality and *power*, loyalty and *money* it likely tears these actors from their cognitive anchorages in unsettling ways.

Now, consider the difference in everyday and long-term experience of a city dweller in the U.S. A federal district sits beside a legal district, which both likely sit beside both state and city courts and governmental offices. The clear lines are less between these buildings and their location than between these institutional spaces and other institutions. Places of worship have their own location, more often dictated by population density than political links; the economy, diffuse as always, exists to provide goods and services wherever people are. Yet, the "financial" district comprised of banks and other types of finance as well as an "industrial" district are severely demarcated from other types of institutions. The sheer population size and density make people compartmentalize their roles and the meanings behind these roles because of the level of complexity and need for greater certainty and simplicity across interactions. Lest one think the needs of the local are sacrificed to those of the national, this is just not the case. New York City's mayor plays a role akin to a governor of a mid-sized state, which is why his or her visibility on the national scene is so much brighter. Moreover, New Yorkers do not exhibit bizarre characteristics by favoring national issues of *power* over local issues like trash collecting, zoning, construction, and so on. Instead, what I am suggesting—and what would require further empirical examination—urban folk are already oriented towards the compartmentalization of institutional domains and because local, regional, and national niches overlap physically—for example, a state courthouse sitting beside a federal courthouse—they experience less anxiety, cognitive uncertainty, and stress when shifting from one level of jurisdiction to the next.

There is one final point worth making, but which will not be able to be developed as fully as it perhaps deserves. That there are multiple levels of jurisdiction also implies the potential for conflict across levels. Those entrepreneurs in the core at the apex of an institutional domain's resource flow *always* are in more privileged position because they have more control over the flow of resources across the domain. Yet, local entrepreneurs can and do often struggle for some autonomy and thus may pursue interests contrary to the central core. These struggles for freedom may be ignored is deemed non-threatening, may be met with new restrictions or intervention, or, in extreme cases, crushed; these struggles may also amount to rebellions and revolutions, schisms or sects, as local entrepreneurs self-determine and create new boundaries.

## CONCLUSION

If institutional domains are spheres of social action that organize people and resources according to some system or systems of authority, then there must be some variation both in terms of how these spheres are constructed and in how actors orient themselves to the various spheres they must contend with. It was argued above that although there are a finite number of institutions across time and space, the degree to which any given one is autonomous relative to the others varies tremendously and it is this variation in autonomy that accounts for the variation in societies both in the temporal sense, as well as cross-culturally. As institutions grow in autonomy—thanks to the efforts by institutional entrepreneurs pursuing their own independence in knowledge and practices, as well as monopolies over certain goods and services that make them an indispensable social group for other groups—they become increasingly discrete spheres of social action in physical, temporal, social, and symbolic space. Buildings, hours of operation, roles and counter-roles, and totems, emblems, and uniforms emerge to make distinguishable the political sphere from the economic sphere from the kinship sphere. *There is never a time when an institution can be fully autonomous.* Full autonomy implies the creation of a new society with its own institutional complex—or set of institutions and their relationships with each other.

In addition, institutional domains that are autonomous lead to the formation of resource niches labeled *institutional cores* and surrounding areas called *institutional environments.* The cores become the physical and cognitive "centers" of institutional life: entrepreneurs reproduce the domain, develop and disseminate a vision of reality, produce and distribute resources associated with the institutional domain, and create and enforce rules regarding the use of resources. The greater the level of autonomy, the more bounded the core becomes. Around the core are various layers of institutional life characterized by different types of role players, organizational units, and resource niches. Generally speaking, the closer a person, group, or field of groups is to the core of an autonomous institution, the more predictable are their actions, goals, decisions, attitudes, and strategies. This is so because (1) resources and rewards are far more visible to actors the closer they are, (2) mechanisms of social control are more present and efficacious, and (3) the symbolic system is more visible and penetrates the actors/groups more as they get closer. Ultimately, variation in the way people and groups feel about an institution, how committed they are to the collective goals and norms, and how much they identify as part of one institution as opposed to any other depends greatly on their relative distance to the core.

By considering institutional domains as real spheres of social action that can become more *or less* autonomous it is possible to refocus the lens on the ways actors adjust to institutional environments as well as provide explanations for why they act the way they do. The ecology of institutions pushes the idea that (1) actors in one autonomous institution are "governed" by different sets of principles than actors in other institutions, hence the variation in subjectivity; (2) reducing all action to economic or political motives ignores the very real possibility that a given actor, organization, or set of organizations is operating on very different values and thus is motivated very differently; and (3) the macro-level of social reality has a tremendous impact on defining the rules of engagement, what is being struggled over, explanations and justifications for the struggle itself and the strategies used, and the meanings actors impose on their reality. It also provides us with another lens for comparing societies across time and space, and thinking through some of the larger issues related to social change, human sociocultural evolution, and the macro–micro link.

# 4 The Invisible Framework

## Intra-Institutional Structure

> Without social institutions of some sort, without the organizationof social attitudes and activities by which social institutions are constituted, there could be no fully mature individual selves or personalities at all . . . in so far as each [person] reflects or prehends in his individual these organization social attitudes and activities which social institutions embody and represent.
>
> —George Herbert Mead

Institutions have both structural and cultural dimensions that shape the life-world of the individuals, collectives, and clusters of collectives that reside within their space. A structural analysis is essential to understanding institutions because it is the structural linkages that facilitate and constrain interaction, exchange, and communication—that is, they give shape and texture to, and sustain, institutional culture (the subject of which will occupy the next chapter).[1] Like roads leading into a city, structural arrangements allow actors to "enter" and "exit" institutions. Functionalists were well aware of this fact, and regardless of the criticisms leveled against them, a structural and material account of institutions is requisite for a robust theory of institutions; in most contemporary accounts of institutions, it completely ignores or simply takes for granted the structural side of institutions (Powell and DiMaggio 1991; Thornton, Ocasio, and Lounsbury 2012). Even a staunch critic of Parsons, C. Wright Mills wrote (in an unfortunately little-read text), "The concept of role . . . is . . . the major link of character and social structure . . . [and] institution *is the unit with which we build the conception of social structure*" (Gerth and Mills 1953:23; emphasis added). Later, he and Gerth would say that institutions "form" individuals as impulses "and sensitivity are channeled and transformed into *standard motives joined to standard goals and gratifications*" (ibid. 173; emphasis added).

To be sure, structure may be fluid, or ephemeral in the case of encounters (Goffman 1963a; Luhmann 1995), but the combination of structural elements undeniably constrain *and* facilitate how actors, collectives, and clusters of collectives relate to each other—and how they relate to themselves. In Chapter 5, we will examine how culture gives color and texture to structure, but for now it is the framework we are interested in. Although structures are erected within institutional domains for various reasons, they generally deal with three basic problems: the creation of trust and commitment among heterogeneous, impersonal, and often socially/geographically distant actors; the distribution of power, as well as the means to controlling and coordinating these disparate social units; and, finally, supporting the cultural systems ability to impose a baseline for shared meaning, and thus making interaction, exchange, and communication possible. In addition to the fluidity of structure, the efficacy with which they do what their architects intend them to do varies across time and space, as well as across the institution's environment as well, but the underlying impetus to erect structures remains rooted in these three problems.

## A DESCRIPTIVE LOOK INSIDE OF AN INSTITUTION

Consistent with previous discussions, institutions are both physically structured, as in they occupy and organize real space, and cognitively structured—for example, through ritualized encounters, acquisition of a generalized role-status, and membership in various corporate actors—such that people come to orient themselves in patterned ways. At the most micro-level of social reality, institutions consist of stereotyped, formalized encounters between generalized role-status positions. Roles are the vehicles of structure (and culture), as their performance is powerfully shaped by situation, setting, and a more diffuse (often imperceptible) moral obligation (Goffman 1959; also Gerth and Mills 1953; Turner 2010b). Institutional generalized roles are the most basic mechanism of integration, regulation, and legitimation. They integrate actors by offering an easily accessible set of behaviors and expectations—many of which apply across institutional boundaries—and generating structural equivalencies that reduce uncertainty across a range of encounters while encouraging trust between actors (Luhmann 2008); generalized roles regulate actors as they are often activated in formalized, monitored settings that restrict the degrees of freedom any given incumbent might have (R. Turner 1976); and, finally, shared position, generalized experiences, repertoires, and the like facilitate consensus or at least a belief that others in the same role and position will think, act, and react the same way (Berger and Luckmann 1966).

It goes without saying that there are two caveats to this discussion. First, the degree to which any role is generalized depends entirely on the level of institutional autonomy. Second, the degree to which a generalized role is salient to any given (potential) incumbent continues to depend on the *rule of proximity*. As actors get closer to the core, the more pressure there will be to act stereotypically. One actor may be cognitively distant, yet physically near and, hence, we would expect him or her to continue to behave as expected—within reason of course.[2]

Generalized roles, of course, are not the only micro-level institutional units. Encounters are also structured social units (Goffman 1963a; Turner 2010b). More formal and directed than unfocused encounters, institutional encounters activate institutional roles, make use of institutional resources, and are manifestly directed toward reproducing the institutional domain in some capacity. Again, as the encounters occur closer to the core, certain dimensions, such as the rigidity from role entrance to role exit, increase in their salience because they are more deeply embedded within a series of structural levels that are more easily monitored and sanctioned. Of course, an encounter can happen physically near the core, such as two university professors encountering each other as one leaves a classroom and the other enters, yet this encounter is nominally educational. One will have just exited her formal generalized role and a ritualized educational encounter (a class) while he might be "going over" in his head how he anticipates the impending encounter will go. They are likely to act more formally, or professorial, toward each other because there is an audience, they are in a professional setting, and both are in educational mindsets, yet their guards will also be down and expectations will be lowered as they are cognitively far from the educational core.

## Levels of Embedding

Encounters are embedded into meso-level social units like groups, formal organizations, communities, and categoric units (Granovetter 1985; Turner 2011). As organizational theorists have noted, informal groups allow actors to "escape" the rigidity and formality imposed by formal organizations pursuing corporate goals. Nevertheless, an informal group of professors (gathering near the educational core, e.g., a university department) will certainly act, talk and orient themselves differently than an informal group of doctors (whose gathering occurs nearby the medical core). The "traces" of institutional culture will continue to color their interactions and communication—that is, their "ecological huddles" will remain thematized by their dress and dispositions; they may use the informal gathering to "blow off steam" and exchange stories of students or patients, respectively, that bond them on a more personal level. The gatherings change as they get further from the core and the composition of any given gathering changes: in a coffee shop or at a dinner party, non-professors or doctors will likely mingle with the professors and doctors, and interactions will be more nimble and novel. Despite this, being around persons one knows from more institutionalized settings increases the "magnetic" pull the cognitive core has on entrepreneurs especially—for example, three professors at a dinner party may wind up in a more ritualized encounter, often to the dismay of their spouses and/or friends.

The more formalized a collective and the closer it is to the core, the more isomorphic pressures will shape the culture and structure of the collective. That is, the manifest goals it sets, the way it makes decisions, the strategies it uses or has available to use, and the means employed to achieving these goals will be more readily understandable and predictable. In part, this is because the chances of the organization being run by entrepreneurs or influenced by them increases, along with the pressure to act in legitimate ways that reproduce the institution and protect their individual privilege, and the patterns built through training all contribute to structural and cultural equivalencies. Moreover, collectives are nearly always embedded in larger clusters of collectives.[3]

Within institutions are a series of resource niches composed of various similar organizations (Hannan and Freeman 1977; McPherson 1988). They are similar in the sense that (1) their position relative to the core, and therefore the niches level of resource access, is the equivalent; (2) their "biographies" are often very similar; and (3) their structural relationship to other niches is equivalent. Niches provide collectives with real actors to reference their own behavior, set strategies, and mimic in times of uncertainty. They capture the uneven distribution of resources across institutional domains, as some niches have more privileged resources and are composed of a greater number of entrepreneurs, whereas others have fewer and are shaped by the more dominant niches. Despite this subordination, niches also capture the "locality" and variation found throughout institutions. An Ivy League niche will produce very different organizational cultures then an on-line university or small liberal arts college niche. Cultural variation, then, not only reflects differential access to resources, but also survival and resistance strategies to domination from more powerful collectives or clusters of collectives—for example, the Ivy League may shape much of the higher educational field by propagating and reproducing certain value-orientations like *knowledge production*, whereas an online niche may emphasize its instrumentally-rational goals. In both cases, the niches will look culturally similar because they both are embedded within the educational institution, yet they are not equivalent in many important and meaningful ways because of the structuration of an institutional domain. Some niches, of course, can be located in similar positions and hence share structural equivalence that makes the organizations look and act more similarly, while also facilitating greater interaction, exchange, and communication between them. In one sense, they are competing for similar resources—for example, a mid-level teaching university and a small liberal arts college struggling to draw human resources from the same population—yet, when they set goals and make decisions, their references are drawn from their niche.

Like the institution's core, which is an elite niche, all institutional niches have physical and cognitive dimensions. It would be too convenient, for instance, to lump all of the universities in the University of California system together, as this is just not the empirical case. It is true that they are drawing from similar pools of human resources, and a common pool of material resources, which does put them into a niche. Yet, UCLA and Berkeley look to other more prestigious universities as references, hence their membership in other niches. A strange pecking order develops within the UC niche, then, because some of their organizational units belong elsewhere despite being regionally linked: San Diego looks to UCLA and Berkeley with national ambitions, whereas Davis, San Francisco, Santa Barbara, Irvine, and Riverside have specialized in ways that define their unique missions; Santa Cruz is physically isolated, and thus opts out of the UC culture in many ways, whereas Modesto is too new to have defined its place. Thus, they are tied by resources, but there is tremendous diversity as to where their orientation lies.

Niches are embedded in larger configurations of collectives which we will call *fields*. Fields are more diverse because they encompass a larger swath of niches filled with segmented and differentiated collectives. The higher education field, for instance, encompasses Ivy League niches along with public and private research one universities, state schools, and so forth. Fields, furthermore, can cross institutional boundaries and be constituted by collectives from very different institutions. Higher education, for instance, does not just include universities arranged in niches, but it also includes political organizations interested in the research output of universities, curricula, the recruitment of potential soldiers, and the enforcement of broader laws; religious collectives nearly always are found on or very close to campuses, as they provide students with pastoral and social services; legal collectives, of course, exist on campuses in the form of Title IX; and, of course, economic collectives have vested interest in universities, often forming partnership programs with business, engineering, and other colleges that have technical-instrumental degrees. All of these organizations interact, exchange, and communicate in ways that determine the shape of

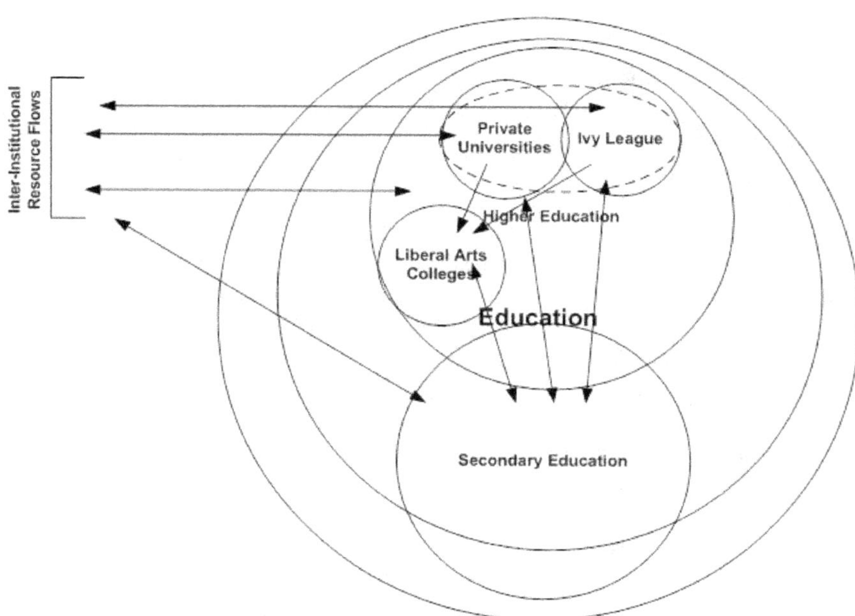


*Figure 4.1* Example of structural embeddedness of educational institution.

the field. Thus, fields can be *intra-* or *inter-*institutional amalgamations of collectives. Although, even the former type are easily penetrated by the collectives from outside the institutional domain, as generalized symbolic media circulate across institutional domains more often than not (see Chapter 5). Figure 4.1 provides a visual representation of the structural inside of an institution. In many ways, the diagram should be three-dimensional to reflect the way structure intersects with core-environment ecology.

Real briefly, Figure 4.1 illustrates how a single institution might look. Higher education, as a field, is hierarchically arranged above the secondary education field to denote its greater power in controlling the production and distribution of *learning* and *knowledge*. The arrows connecting both fields denote the reciprocal flow of resources, such as high school graduates going to college and then returning as teachers, administrators, and so forth. Within the higher education field, hierarchically arranged niches like private universities (e.g., Stanford and Ivy Leagues) again underline the power and privilege differentials found in a field. A dotted ellipse captures the existence of an elite network coordinating resource flows, especially human resources. The arrows are not reciprocal as these niches generate powerful isomorphic pressures on small liberal arts colleges. The education field, at all levels, is punctured by the flow of resources from outside, as well as the flow of resources from the educational domain to other institutions.

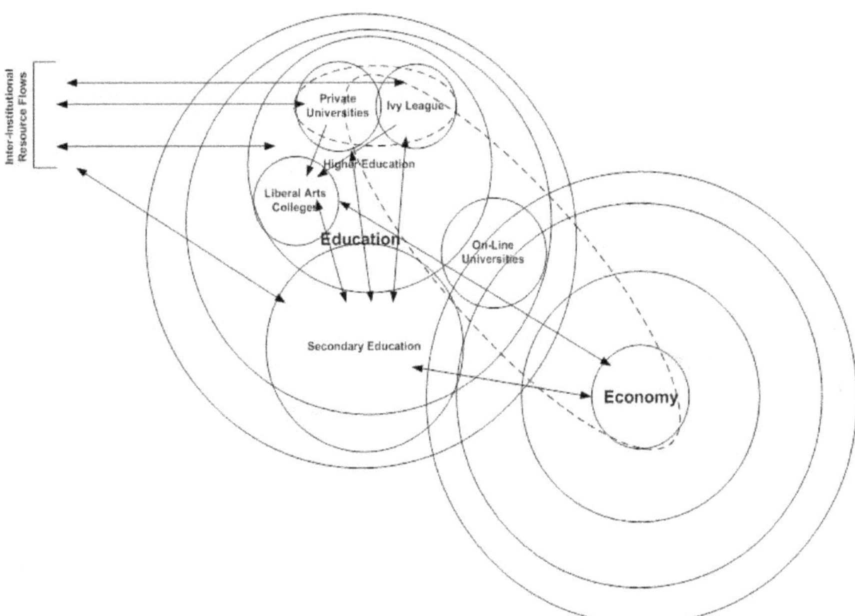


*Figure 4.2* Example of inter-institutional penetration.

## Inter-Institutional Structural Links

Figure 4.2 elaborates on Figure 4.1, adding a second institution to highlight some inter-institutional structural features. In particular, a dotted ellipse links the "cores" of the educational domain with the core of the economic sphere. This feature underscores the institutionalized paths of mobility, the flow of *money* in exchange for *learning*, and the right of each core to manipulate the foreign mediums value and meaning within their respective domains.

Additionally, reciprocal arrows link the economic core to the liberal arts and secondary education levels, as human and material resources clearly move from one space to the next. Finally, notice the penetration of economy into the secondary education field, as the diagram clearly shows overlaps between the economy's environment and the boundary of high schools. This illustrates the lack of autonomy in this area of education, whereas the integrity of higher education remains intact, although the economy's boundaries are quite close, and actually are bridged by the "online university" niche which co-exists within both institutions, drawing complementary and contradictory structural and cultural elements. Secondary education, then, is a contested arena. If other institutions like polity and kinship were modeled alongside education and economy, we would find secondary education being penetrated by all institutions as entrepreneurs from every domain have a vested interest in how culture is reproduced. On the other hand, even though universities depend on economic actors for grants and donations, academic freedom reduces the chances of corruption. However, online universities, like the University of Phoenix, do not hide their organizational goals, which is matriculation and job placement. They are for-profit collectives, and thus cannot be detached from the economic sphere, even if *learning* is the principle medium through which many ritualized exchanges and communications are governed.

## A Word on Macro Space

Too often, in conflating organizations and institutions, the structuration of space is blurred. Organizations, for instance, physically constrain and shape action by embedding it within a building, a particular floor that serves a specific department, a cubicle or office, and so forth. Institutions shape action by reconfiguring the social landscape: entire zones become residential in physical and cognitive reality; malls serve as economic zones that attract restaurants, subsidiary strip malls, and service industries; downtowns become seats of government and law, with courthouses, town hall, jails and police, law offices, and bail bondsmen. Recall, anthropologist Rosemary Joyce (2000:72) noted that political entrepreneurs stratified space so as to alter the "patterns of habitual movement of all inhabitants of the site," limiting access to some areas, while making public others—in essence, "creating and marking centers and peripheries." Entrepreneurs do not just bind member action in a building, but are architects of geographic space. Political entrepreneurs place palaces on hills symbolizing their position relative to other actors (Kramer 1963), build thoroughfares that coordinate traffic and allow for quick movement of security forces (Scott 1998), and they extend waterways, enhance transportation, and pacify hinterlands in ways that expand the physical and cognitive space with which ordinary people must contend; religious entrepreneurs erect massive temples and churches, make sites as small as a cave and as a large as an entire city (Jerusalem) sacred (Abrutyn 2013a), and contend that the sacred resides in the soul (Eliade 1978). They structure the physical world while also structuring the temporal world: when one has legitimate access to a site, when and how long a generalized role should be played, when and how long one's focus and attention should be directed towards which "direction," and so on. Finally, they "coat" and sometimes "drench" the physical and temporal spaces with symbolic elements unique to their existence and the institution's *ethos*. Churches and religious sites are filled with symbolic objects meaningful to adherents, but clearly solemn to those who have no initiation; the role performances themselves involve the use of identity equipment that further connotes the deeper significance of the physical and temporal reality; political sites employ paraphernalia like flags, seals, podiums, paintings/statues of past politico-military heroes and so forth; stadia are adorned with team colors, murals of past glories, whether by team or individual player, slogans of *competition*, fans rapid with anticipation and desirous of victory, "living legends" walking around or participating in the organization's many annual rituals, on and on. The more autonomous an institution becomes, the more entrepreneurs paint their spaces with coat after coat of vivid symbolic paint. The ritual performances serve to make the space and its denizens symbolically attached to the institution (Alexander 2004; Reed 2013), while the physical arrangement of that space serves as a reminder of this symbolic attachment even in times of dormancy.

Any academic from the U.S. that has taught as a visiting scholar at a university in Germany knows just what I am talking about. In the U.S., campuses are sprawling, filled with brick buildings, and brimming with activity; in Germany, they look far more like research or business parks in the U.S.: non-descript high rises, steel and concrete, normal business hours. Entrepreneurs try to construct physical space in ways that make sense to their projects, and it is very often the space and not the psychological character or cultural assemblage of a society or group that generates habitual patterns of action, exchange, and communication. American campuses are designed to facilitate social interaction in open, inviting expanses whereas German campuses are rational-instrumental in their design, and thus impose a very different milieu for socializing new students.

## Generalized Roles

Before we look more closely at the specific meso-level linkages of institutions, I would like to return to the micro-level briefly, and elaborate the importance of generalized roles as structural conduits. Institutional domains can only be as autonomous as the number of people who can access the core to some degree. Autonomy, and entrepreneurship, requires material, symbolic, and human resources to be sustained and expanded. Hence, entrepreneurs try to legitimate their vision of reality, regulate the flow of resources from other institutions and from their own environment toward the core, and integrate as many actors as possible into their institutional web. Entrepreneurs, like doctors or professors, need counter-roles that are as generalized and diffuse—for example, patients or students. As noted above, roles are the vehicles of structure as they are structures themselves that deal with all three exigencies: they integrate actors into a role set and provide expectations that can easily be transposed across a series of settings; they regulate actors by delimiting the actions and attitudes appropriate across said settings; and they legitimate the social order, as role performances are tacit acknowledgements of, at the very least, a basic acceptance of a normative order and shared sense of reality. Accessible generalized roles means greater proportions of the population are primed for potential institutional exchanges or communication, and thus, explicitly or implicitly believing in the institution's realness. To be sure, many people come to see the economy or polity as an object and an actor, reifying it in ways that a social scientist would be apprehensive to do; yet, the very fact that people reify institutions alerts us to an awareness that an institution is distinct vis-à-vis other institutions.

Generalized roles, of course, compete with each other for attention and scarce resources. Like other structural elements, they are subject to the *rule of proximity*, and it is not uncommon to meet people or entire collectives who are distant from one generalized role or another. Role distance produces a possible axis along which conflicts can simmer and explode. Many Americans, for example, feel alienated and detached from the impersonal and amoral polity and economy, choosing instead to embed themselves in the local kinship and religious roles that are moored in emotional, personal, level relationships. For many liberal scholars, this is a sign of their ignorance or lack of education, but the global growth in conservative religious movements predicated on a fusion of traditional kin elements with religious orthodoxy (Almond, Appleby, and Sivan 2003) reveals sites of resistance against the powerful institutions of the modern global world. This reorientation of action and attitudes is not without contradictions: the objective structure of society still demands their adherence to the basic expectations and obligations of generalized roles, while it is their subjective (or more accurately inter-subjective) understanding of the situation may allow them to perceive they are, in fact, not participating at all.

## INTRA-INSTITUTIONAL STRUCTURATION

There are five basic structural linkages that entrepreneurs can combine as they construct their institutional space: *segmentation*, *differentiation*, *exchange-networks*, *domination-hierarchicalization*, and *inclusion/embedding* (Abrutyn and Turner 2011; Turner 2011). In essence, "the particular configuration of an integrative [and regulative] mechanism will exert large effects on how, and to what degree, the structure and culture of an institutional domain and other domains influence the operation of a specific organizational unit [or set of organizations such as those found in particular niche]" (Abrutyn and Turner 2011:291).

### Segmentation and Differentiation

At the meso-level, two processes are at the core of structuring the action, exchange, and communication within institutional environments, and between the core and institutional environment: *segmentation* and *differentiation*. Analogous to mitosis, segmentation is the process by which a social unit, be it an actor, collective, or cluster of collectives, is reproduced nearly symmetrically. Entrepreneurs often have a hand in segmentation, as they can either formulate the "official" form or the rules constraining organizational construction, or they may present, in their own organization, the idealized organizational form to be copied. In its symmetry, structural and cultural equivalencies create powerful forces of trust and meaning, as solidarity and the moral order is *mechanical*. Segmentation, as a source of structural linkage, can be found in all institutional domains in the generalized roles that actors inhabit, the form of many basic organizational units (families, corporations, schools), and in the replication of resource niches. Indeed, it is the propensity for collectives to often adopt the forms most visible to them and create structural equivalencies out of the "belief" that those forms must work and must be legitimate, that led DiMaggio and Powell (1983) to focus on isomorphic pressures, especially the mimetic type. Although considerably primitive and often hidden from plain sight, structural equivalencies should not be underestimated as a capable mode of integration and regulation, because their powers lie in the taken-for-grantedness of perceived similarity (Berger and Luckmann 1966; Goffman 1967, 1971).

Where segmentation exists, there is undoubtedly differentiation structuring social reality as well. In hunter-gatherer societies, families segment, whereas individual roles differentiate according to sex and age (Turner and Maryanski 2009). Differentiation reduces competition through specialization and mutual interdependence. It also allows for greater social complexity, as differentiating physical and temporal space allow different activities to occur in different places and at different times without disrupting the flow of social life. Over time, and as institutional domains become increasingly complex—for example, more actors, greater size and scope, and so forth—differentiation becomes inevitable across the domain. Implicitly, the process of institutional autonomy already leads to differentiation between entrepreneurs and non-entrepreneurs, but differentiation accelerates as the domain grows in autonomy. The diversity in behavioral repertoires for generalized roles increase, as does the expectations that some repertoires fit some situations, whereas others are reserved for different tasks or encounters; specialization and organizational density lead to the fragmentation of niches both in horizontal and vertical space; collectives themselves differentiate as hierarchies form to pursue collective goals and regulate member behavior; categories diversify—for example, the entrepreneurial class splits into entrepreneurs who are focused on inter-institutional, intra-institutional, and intra-entrepreneurial matters. As Durkheim predicted, some differentiation is healthy as it replaces structural equivalencies with mutual interdependence as the mechanism of integration in the face of heterogeneity. To be sure, niches and generalized roles continue to create structural equivalencies, yet the institutional domain grows so complex as to render segmentation inefficacious across a larger level of reality, such as the field level or inter-field level. Yet, differentiation also contributes to the expansion of a social division of labor and, thereby, heterogeneity and greater chances of conflict between disparate actors thus rendering older modes of regulation and integration useless (Black 1976).

Vertical differentiation, or the emergence of leadership and authority, does not emerge until groups have grown large and dense[4], and problems associated with subsistence pressure groups to create redistributional systems founded on a centralize politico-kin member coordinating labor, spreading risk by collecting the surplus of all produce, and redistributing it to ensure everyone survives (Johnson and Earle 2000; Earle 2002). And although research on small groups has shown that the differentiation of leadership plays important roles in the group's ability to meet certain collective goals (Bales and Slater 1955), humans are not "wired" to happily subordinate themselves (Boehm 1999), give up resources without reciprocation (Blau 1964), or give up autonomy and independence in movement and decision-making (Maryanski and Turner 1992). Differentiation creates jealousies while also creating heterogeneity that can easily sever the efficacy of the kin-based *conscience collective* and the moral order. It exacerbates underlying grievances about resource distribution and self-worth, while *demanding* supra-kin modes of integration, regulation, and legitimation—that is, socio-structural linkages layered on top of segmentation and differentiation.

Not surprisingly, the three most common solutions build on these more natural machinations. *Exchange* is a horizontal linkage that combines principles of segmented reciprocity with the specialization of goods and services, and the generalization of exchange patterns found in increasingly heterogeneous societies (Mauss 1967; Levi-Strauss 1969; Ekeh 1974; Gillmore 1987). *Domination* is a vertical linkage that relies on differentiated status, privilege, and power (Lenski 1966; Rueschemeyer 1986) and exchange principles predicated on redistribution (Polanyi 1957). Finally, *inclusion/embedding* is the synthesis of exchange and domination, as a "distinct" network of collectives is embedded within a series of jurisdictional levels that have varying degrees of power over lower levels—for example, the American Medical Association or the American Sociological Association, as well as the American judicial system. The three socio-structural mechanisms, then, are analytically distinct, and institutions vary structurally based on which one tends to be the primary or overarching form of structural integration and regulation. To be sure, all three tend to appear in all institutions, yet one tends to become the force that shapes the variation in institutional logic.

## Exchange

Autonomous institutional domains integrate meso-level social units through the exchange of valued resources, and the subsequent construction of powerful norms of reciprocity and obligation (Blau 1964), as well as external regulatory agencies that offer formal paths to conflict resolution. When one adds generalized symbolic media to the exchange equation, the sociocultural foundations of institutional exchange become clearer. It was Simmel (1907) who explicated the consequences that *money*, as a generalized symbolic medium, had on economic interaction: its durability and portability allowed for future-oriented attitudes and even longer-distance action; its generalized and (relatively) standardized value accelerated, intensified, and made more frequent economic exchanges; it began to circulate across other institutional domains in ways that encouraged aspiring entrepreneurs, like legal or eventually medical entrepreneurs, to struggle for their own independence and carve out new autonomous spaces (cf. Collins 1990; Turner 2004). All institutional domains, as they become autonomous, have a generalized symbolic medium that produces cultural equivalencies across the environment that integrate structurally disparate actors; regulates action by coordinating and controlling the pursuit and acquisition of the medium, as well as the explicit and implicit rules regarding its exchange; and, finally, imposes a basic normative system of exchange that implies a tacit shared sense of "what is happening" and "why the medium if worth pursuing." Blau (1964:24–5) notes that it is the elaboration of the most basic dyadic exchange relation into macro-institutional structure that preserves the "basic values" underpinning social relationships, as well as constrains the patterns of exchange and creating social solidarity.

As such, it is accurate to consider institutions generalized systems of exchange (Mauss 1967) and, as Luhmann (1976; Goffman 1963a) insists, *communication* because media are not just tokens that act as placeholders of value—for example, the dollar bill—but symbolic bundles replete with the codes and rules shaping specialized institutional language (for more detail, see Chapter 5; also, Parsons 1968; T. Turner 1968). Generalized exchange is "indirect and impersonal [wherein everybody] presumably receives and everybody presumably gives . . . [which] fosters high levels of *interdependence* among the actors" (Lawler 2006:257), even though coordination is often the central problem as free riders and motivating actors becomes an issue (Coleman 1988). Generalized symbolic media assuage this problem within reason: the pursuit and acquisition of media require the tacit belief in its exchange and use-value, the adherence to a normative and coercive system of rules governing exchange and communication, and the legitimation, within varying degrees, of the entrepreneur's vision of reality. In Luhmann's (1976) terminology, generalized media help resolve the double-contingency problem in communicative action, thus making communication more likely to be successful in any given interaction as trust becomes an institutionalized feature of exchange and communication (Goffman 1967)

Thus, the integrative effects of exchange are clear. First, where generalized symbolic media are being exchanged between groups, cultural equivalencies—that is, homogenization of values, ideologies, and other symbolic elements—are created and reinforced across these circuits. When a person engages in the exchange of *money* or *competitiveness*, there is a tacit agreement that she has bought into, at the very least, the most basic normative rules of exchange as given by the institutional domain's system of authority because she understands that a dollar has an objective value. Second, when media cross institutional boundaries (*money* in exchange for *learning*, and reciprocally, *learning* in exchange for *money*), the two are more easily mixed and the ideological foundations behind, say, credentialism are born. Generalized exchange also generates positive emotional affect directed not toward a person or relationship, but to the group and structure itself (Lawler et al. 2009). Thus a scholar's self-worth and positive esteem is less tied to a personal relationship, then to the diffuse academy, even if he or she would not consciously talk about it this way. This was, in essence, Durkheim's (1912) big point regarding ritual and collective effervescence: feeling positive emotions during a collective ritual forces actors to search for the cause; in a large enough impersonal group, say, a political rally, the person may misattribute where the source is, but it nevertheless pushes the actor to want to return to political rallies more often. If exchanges produce enough actors who attribute their success, survival, and emotional effervescence to something transcendent, then they are duty bound to exchange ethically and normatively with others who they assume must attribute these things to the same source.

The final integrative advantage of generalized exchange comes from the legitimacy it provides those in positions of privilege and power, or entrepreneurs. That is, generalized exchange can reduce the social distance caused by power differentials because, in all reality, entrepreneurs *must* provide something to those who are subordinate to themselves or risk destabilizing the entire institutional domain. Consider, for instance, the tenuous exchange relation between Mesopotamian kings and their people—which, not coincidentally is a blueprint for all political entrepreneurs and their counterparts. Where power was usurped either through conquest or coup, the kings almost always had to win the loyalty of both the local priests and elites, as well as enough of the masses. This meant expanding the political institution as an exchange system to include these different strata (Abrutyn 2013b). Now, kings do not have booths or stores where people come buy wares from them. Rather, complex generalized exchange rituals generate "contracts" that reveal the real exchange relationship. Thus, it was typical of a king's first public works project to be a new temple to the local deity (Kramer 1963; Postgate 1977). The reason was quite obvious. First, it was a tacit agreement with the priests that he would protect, support, and sustain them in return for an exchange of *sacredness* that legitimated the king's claims to authority. Second, it was a tacit agreement with the people that the king would ensure material prosperity for the people and the city by pleasing the gods; that is, he was their *representative* in the exchange with the supranatural. Third, as a sign of good faith, the king would provide food and drink for the people for a weeklong festival that freed the people from work. This was the most tangible gift the king could give in exchange for *loyalty*, *money* (in the form of tribute, corveé labor, or taxes), and other intangible resources. The king did not directly, besides laying the cornerstone to the temple in person, exchange with each person. Rather, he became the central node in a massive political exchange system that saw *power* flow upward and then redistributed to the priests and compliant local elites through *loyalty*, *money*, and *sacredness*. In return, the king distributed *power* in the form of authority; redistributed *money* in the form of slaves, land, surplus grains, and other resources to the elites and the army; and acted on the behalf of the people to the supranatural, which, in a sense, redistributed *money* in the form of fertile land as well as *power* through defense against external threats and internal conflict resolution. If this sounds bizarre, it is likely so because it is very rare to think of ourselves as partners in an exchange with President Obama. We do not know him. Yet, like a Mesopotamian king he is the central node in a political exchange system that distributes *power* via rights and duties, *money* in the form of entitlements (e.g., Medicare) and collective goods (e.g., infrastructure), *justice* in the form of an independent judiciary and the promise to execute its decisions, and so forth. He reaps the rewards of the exchange system, while we are further integrated because we partake in it.

### *Domination*

Exchange links individuals and groups horizontally, whereas *domination* integrates them vertically (Collins 1975, 2004). Coercive force alone eventually destabilizes social order, but when legitimated by those being dominated, authority actually stabilizes social relationships and integrates them into a vertical exchange relation (Summers-Effler 2004). In some cases, people are motivated to act appropriately out of a feeling of duty, other times because it easiest or taken for granted, and still other times because it is in their best, instrumental interests to act accordingly; or, more accurately, power differentials may be predicated on symbolic-ideological power, administrative/political power, or material-incentive/economic power (Mann 1986). Each of these bases of power is not without its advantages and disadvantages. Coercive force is the most primordial, terrifying, and effective in the immediate moment, but, as noted, it is unstable in that over long periods of time it proves expensive and provocative (in that resistance can intensify into a feedback loop with increasing measures of suppression). Theorists of power routinely recognize the necessity in building up other bases of power for effective, long-lasting domination (Weber 1978; Mann 1986).

There may be no base of power more compelling than symbolic power because it gives its possessor "the power to make groups, to manipulate the objective structure of society . . . [and] to impose and inculcate a vision of divisions" that are otherwise implicit (Bourdieu 1989:23, also 1991). Sociologists have conceptualized symbolic/ideological power as deriving from control over psychic violence, the means of mental production, or the right to determine the legitimate vision of reality. All of these capture the possessor's unique ability to shape culture and ideas, while manipulating important symbols to shape opinion and motivate action—and, perhaps most importantly, mobilize emotions (Collins 2004; Lawler 2006). Symbolic power relies, in part, on the power holder's charisma, which is only effective when he or she continues to appear as special and unique to the audience (Weber 1968). A second weakness derives from what we could call *heterodoxies*, or the emergence of multiple, competing visions of reality (Eisenstadt 1982). In a single institutional domain, the entrepreneurial class may or may not be unified and there could become a fracture in the perception of reality. In modern two-party polities, where political entrepreneurs still share the same interest because they all belong to the ruling elite, fractures along the progressive/conservative binary still generate as well as speak to distinct cultural milieu throughout the polity.

Administrative power comes from being in a position to, in essence, legislate the minutiae of everyday life. Bureaucracy produces what has been called "callous" violence (Collins 1981b) as it banally imposes order on the environment and makes resistance difficult by creating a maze of authority characterized most by limited spheres of influence, authority, and tasks. Indeed, it is administrative power that leads to a taken-for-grantedness about certain things in our world. The biggest weaknesses administrative power faces comes from (1) detachment or alienation from duties; (2) bounded rationality, or the tendency for those with severely limited spheres of authority and tasks not knowing much else and thus rigidifying a system in the face of environmental change; and (3) the possibility of corruption that paralyzes an organization or system's ability to do what it explicitly sets out to do. The last base of power, material-incentive/economic based, derives from control over the distribution of key material resources or some type of reward. Every employer, for example, has this type of power as they provide wages or salaries to their employees. Control is most effective when (1) the good, service, or resource is scarce; (2) access to it is exclusive and guarded; and (3) the group is small enough to make monitoring and sanctioning cost-effective (Hechter 1987). That being said, material-incentives are probably the weakest form of control because it plays to people's self-interest more than the collective good. Free riders are common where groups are very big and access to the good is not entirely exclusive.

Power dependencies are exchange relations (Eisenstadt and Roniger 1980) and thus are likely to produce norms of reciprocity and obligation (Dahrendorf 1959), even if they are also likely to create tension, underlying conflicts, anger and jealousies, and, ultimately, conscious and unconscious strategies of resistance or pathological defensiveness (Summers-Effler 2004). Nevertheless, the person(s) in power *depend* on those willingly subordinating themselves for all sorts of important things, whereas those subordinating themselves do so only if they feel like they are benefiting somehow from the relationship. Benefits may not be real in the objective sense, nor might they be tangible returns (Rueschemeyer 1977); all that matters is the exchange relation is providing something for both parties. For this reason, power can be used to "crystallize broad symbolic orientations in new ways, articulate specific goals, and construct novel normative and organizational frameworks to pursue their institutional ends" and impose these common realities on entire resource niches and organizational fields (Colomy and Rhoades 1994:554). More specifically, institutions (and more specifically their entrepreneurs) "devise collective goals, and make it possible for their members to pursue these goals in a systematic manner," while still pursuing individual goals (Eisenstadt 1971:10). The desire to "serve" or the compulsion to act brought on by a belief in the moral order and the rightness of the system is a powerful force that obfuscates inequalities. Domination, then, becomes most efficacious when vertical power-dependent exchanges form around the generalized symbolic medium of *power*, or its more typical non-political form, *franchised authority*. However, all autonomous institutional domains facilitate domination vis-à-vis institutionalized rituals and paths revolving around the use, transfer, and acquisition of a particular generalized symbolic media, and thus these institutionalized rituals reinforce the vertical system of exchange. These rituals stabilize social relationships in spite of the power differential and tensions produced by subordination (Collins 2004). The specific "shape" of domination, or the base or bases upon which entrepreneurial authority rests, further distinguishes one institutional domain from another, or one resource niche within a domain from another. Institutional domains use domination as a mechanism meant to control the flow of resources in vertical circuits; this flow of resources, especially generalized media, integrates actors by making them interdependent on each other for the continued uneven distribution of resources—even if that seems bizarre!

### *Embedding/Inclusion*

The third mechanism of integration is built on the foundations of *exchange* and *domination*: *embedding/inclusion*. Embedding involves either the construction of a resource niche and the selection of some members and the exclusion of others, or the construction of a field that contains a number of niches. Both are entrepreneurial projects, and both are directed at reducing complexity, integrating differentiated social units, and regulating their actions as well as the flow of resources. In particular, this strategy has been effective for controlling and coordinating actors who are geographically separated, and thus frequent interaction is costly or difficult. It is also a weapon or tool useful for keeping competitors at bay, as they are either co-opted and integrated into the niche/field, or are simply delegitimized by being excluded.

For example, in carving out autonomous institutional space, legal and medical entrepreneurs must "franchise" their claims to authority from the autonomous political domain and, as such, must search for other mechanisms of entrepreneurial control. The solution was to create centralized associations (e.g., American Bar and American Medical Association respectively), whose primary function is to regulate the application, development, and transmission of legal or medical knowledge. Unlike religious entrepreneurs who can claim transcendental supra-political authority, these actors are dependent to some degree on the polity's "certification" of their claims., the latter of which backs these claims with the threat of force. These associations, however, developed different solutions to the problem of order because they are predicated on a sense of professional ethics, even if a doctor or lawyer can have their rights revoked: to control geographically dispersed, and decentralized fields and niches, law and medicine employ an embedding strategy that integrates through segmentation, exchange, and domination. At the local level, law schools or hospitals develop unique cultural aspects based on specific sociocultural factors and the type of personnel available to fill roles. Yet, in each case the larger association has the distinct authority to determine the legitimacy of the smaller units, hence their tendency to resemble each other in ways more important than they diverge. Law schools, then, act as individual organizations, but belong to a regional association that can, at least, monitor the behavior of the individual members; the regional associations also create certain cultural equivalencies that lead to regional similarities that, again, encourage integration. Regional associations, of course, are embedded into the national associations (American Bar Association), which impose structural and cultural constraints that tightly integrate their lower-level members. These sanctions are only as effective as the monopoly the elites have over knowledge and activities, and the potential rewards for acting in appropriate fashion. The ABA, for instance, can in the last resort disbar a member or, theoretically, an entire law firm; it can also decertify a law university. This power on top of the fact that one cannot practice law without an ABA certified license makes their vision of reality *the* vision of legal reality. However, legal actors do not often think of the sanction side of the equation, because the potential rewards for being a successful jurist far outweigh the costs of conformity—for example, wealth, prestige, or potential power.

Consider a very different case: the American Sociological Association (ASA). Again, the dynamics flow from the degree to which a governing body can sanction its members and the rewards for compliance. What we see in the ASA is very different from the ABA because there really is no centralized governing body. Departments must apply for a doctoral program, for example, but there is little oversight of what they are teaching; what constitutes sociological knowledge is nearly always contested. In essence, the association is a loose conglomeration of scholars who study anything and everything they personally deem sociological (Abrutyn 2013c).. Thus, training is highly dependent upon one's mentor and success on the department's prestige; these two factors likely contribute to one's ability to publish in the top journals and to move up in the sociological world. Each university, then, is loosely embedded in a regional and national association that really does little to control its members. That being said, the elite sociologists travel in similar networks, whereas journal editorships travel along these circuits and create informal standards that do in fact control sociologists. However, new journals are started and alternative paths to success emerge because the rewards are far more muted in sociology than, say, law or medicine. Thus, embeddedness has the double effect of integrating lower-level social units while also regulating their behavior. To be sure, in the case of the ABA vis-à-vis that of the ASA, the amount of integration and regulation is variable. Nevertheless, both remain bounded microcosms of their respective institutional domains.

Embedding builds both horizontal and vertical structural ties, and circumscribes the texture of relationships. The imposition of culture is far more effective, as less-advantaged social units are engaged in exchange relationships with privileged entrepreneurs and can see what is most appropriate. A law school professor at a lower-tier law school certainly has flexibility in her pedagogical choices, yet her training and embeddedness in a broader niche and field of better law schools makes some texts, cases, and methods requisite for successful training. Moreover, the law professor herself likely was trained at a better school than the one she ended up teaching at. Indeed, if one niche or a set of niches is the center of entrepreneurial training, and it is generally entrepreneurs trained in these niches that move to lower-level niches, they will impose the culture they internalized in their training into other domains. Thus, a recent study found that the top 11 departments in the U.S. had their students placed in 50% of the research-intensive job openings for assistant professors, leaving the other 100 Ph.D. programs and their graduating students fighting for the other 50% (Oprisko 2012; see also Grafton and Townsend 2008). In this case, as in many others like it, entrepreneurs are able to reproduce elite culture through mobility and imposed isomorphism. The result is greater cultural equivalency across a wider swath of collectives and clusters of collectives, while structural constraints are erected through admissions criteria and the conscious and unconscious desire on the part of hiring and admissions committees to protect or enhance privilege and prestige.

## *Mobility Within and Across Domains*

This last point leads right into our discussion of *mobility*, or a key structural linkage that ties collectives to each other, clusters of collectives within a domain together, and, importantly, collectives and clusters of collectives across institutional boundaries together through structural networks. Mobility refers to the "systematic and regularized movement" of actors "across corporate unit boundaries within and between institutional domains" (Abrutyn and Turner 2011:293). There is not a more efficient way of integrating differentiated social units than formally standardizing paths from one institutional domain to the next, because the paths become taken-for-granted forces of cultural reproduction and obfuscate the inequitable structural constraints on other forms of mobility. Ubiquitous paths also make anomalies, such as the classic "rags to riches" narrative, "evidence" that stratification and inequality are myths, hence further mitigating class tensions. The most obvious example is the educational domain, and it is also the underlying reason for the relative lack of educational autonomy in nearly all cases. In most contemporary societies, actors cross the boundaries of the kinship domain into the educational domain to participate in a more impersonal and generalized process of socialization and cultural reproduction. Although this process is stratified in terms of what socialization and cultural reproduction means for different categories of actors (e.g., children from rich backgrounds are obviously learning different things than those from middle, working, or poorer classes), it is a standardized process and therefore has similar structural effects as children gain a new, achieved status and role: student. Each year, the child moves from one collective to the next, eventually jumping from one niche (elementary schooling) to another (secondary schooling), and in many cases, a final jump from one field (schools) to another (universities). Again, the subjective experiences vary and the cultural consequences vary across categoric units, yet the standardized pattern of mobility has structural consequences that integrates children and comes to coordinate and control their behavior, while also legitimating numerous societal values inculcated through explicit teaching as well as the implicit and latent socialization process. Some values and ideologies are shared by all students and are really a function of the standardized process, whereas others are unique to the experiences of each grade, region, category of student, and so forth. As we shall see in the next chapter, the process itself becomes a source of pursuing and acquiring the *institutionalized* form of the *generalized symbolic medium* of *education*—a source of cultural isomorphism and reproduction.

At the end of the educational process, however, students traverse institutional boundaries and travel along structural links between education and the economy, law, medicine, polity, or science. The process itself is also somewhat standardized, as there are legitimate paths to obtaining meaningful employment—even if, again, access to these paths are unevenly available to all students, the fact remains that they are visible paths and as long as a significant proportion of the population continues to believe they are available, mobility will remain a viable source of integration, regulation, and legitimation. Thus, mobility creates and reinforces meta-ideologies built up from actors following stereotyped paths, these stereotyped paths becoming normative, and new narratives being constructed to explain changes in social structure. Learning leads to money; the empirical or objective validity of this path is beside the point because people buy into the "Horatio Alger" myth that one can pull themselves up from their bootstraps and make it if they just go to school and get the necessary skills. The process, in most industrialized nations, is systematized in the sense that the number of years typical of college attendance, the age of entry, and the process of applying for jobs remains relatively the same across societies. Moreover, the degree itself as both an objectified and institutionalized form of learning has a somewhat standardized value in the exchange for money or power. The empirical or objective link between these two media matters little, because the paths has become well-worn through repeated, systematic mobility and, like most humans, when presented with a well-worn path and an indiscernible shorter route through high grasses, most choose the former over the latter. Mobility is often closely tied to another structural mechanism: boundary overlaps.

### *Boundary Overlaps*

There are numerous boundary overlaps that help deal with exigencies concerning trust, power, and meaning. Some of these overlaps are consciously created by entrepreneurs, whereas others are more natural to the ecology of institutions. Niches, for example, are not always closed. In the American higher education field, the Ivy League niche is somewhat bounded, but it is not closed from other niches that contain prestigious and important research universities like Stanford, Berkeley, Michigan, and so on. In fact, they belong to a set of niches that overlap and create the structural linkages along which key human resources travel, reproduce the higher education culture among the elite, and impose their culture on lower-level niches and organizations. It is the overlaps among the elite, however, that facilitate the construction and maintenance of an elite network and culture across geographic boundaries without embedding, hierarchically, the individual collectives (see, again, Figure 4.2).

Boundary overlaps also facilitate the emergence of *liaison* actors whose function is to translate the language of one institutional domain into another, and vice versa. Lawyers, for example, exist within the interstices of multiple institutional domains, drawing their clients from religious or political collectives, translating their conflicts into legal language, and translating the legal decisions into more understandable language for their clients (Luhmann 2004). Liaisons are power brokers, who can use these structural positions to leverage greater independence or resources for themselves (Burt 1992), but who also facilitate the integration of differentiated institutional domains. On the one hand, most economic, political, or kinship actors will seek out a lawyer when they have a conflict needing resolution, or at the very least, they share an understanding that the legal system is the *legitimate* way of airing grievances (Black 1998). This suggests a degree of cultural integration that is expressed in the regularized use of lawyers for most conflicts.[5] The process further standardizes the exchange of legal media (*justice*) as well as other types of media (e.g., *money*), as it does not just involve the circulation of individuals and their mobility, but it involves entire corporate actors spreading generalized media through liaison activities; liaisons become experts in the eyes of the laity, and their word is taken as truth because the layperson(s) does not have the time or resources to discern the truth. Overlaps, thus, help spread narrow cultural elements from one domain to the next rather than subject non-institutional actors to the entire gamut of cultural elements. It is as if lawyers provide a stereotyped version of law and legal symbols, and thus it engenders a more ubiquitous generalized legal role for the laity: client.[6]

As would be expected, boundary overlaps do not only or always generate integration as they tend to structure and reinforce inequalities (see Chapter 6), boundary overlaps may restrict mobility and the flow of resources in ways that stimulate tensions. Recall the example above: if certain academic disciplines, like political science (Oprisko 2012) or history (Grafton and Townsend 2008), create closed boundary overlaps among the elite graduate programs and, consequently, the hiring of assistant professors is highly restrictive, then a large proportion of graduate programs will be in intense competition with a small set of elite departments. Thus, whereas cultural equivalencies are produced that integrate collectives and other niches through the mobility of these elite graduates, upward mobility is constrained and a large number of non-elite actors fight for a small percentage of positions. This could lead to massive irregularities, strains, and, in some cases, outward conflicts. The power, however, of institutional structure and culture is quite apparent in that papers might be written, talks given, and informal complaints lodged by many non-elite political scientists, yet the system remains intact and operating unfairly nevertheless. On a larger scale, C. Wright Mill's (1959) *The Power Elite* captured this same dynamic: he found relatively closed structural overlaps between certain kinship and educational niches and mobility into specific political/military and economic niches. The result, in other words, was standardized, restrictive circuits of mobility. These circuits facilitated the creation of certain media of exchange and communication that trickled down into other parts of polity, economy, kinship, and education, shaping the culture of all of these domains and their niches; hence the terms "dominant culture" or "dominant values." Much of American society was defined by so-called White Anglo-Saxon Protestant values and culture; over the last 50 years, their monopoly has been reduced through increased mobility among minorities due to outward conflicts as well as demographic changes. In the earlier era, a small segment of the population controlled the fusion of generalized symbolic media and its distribution across all institutional domains; the criteria for elevation to entrepreneurial positions were restricted to WASP men, which functioned to protect the dominant meta-ideology. Over half a century later, it is quite obvious that political party leaders continue to mingle with the titans of industry, but the networks and overlaps have changed in ways Mills may never have anticipated. For one thing, contrary to many cynics, it is clear that women and minorities are far better off today than previously. Is there more work to be done? Absolutely. Are these groups equal in opportunities? Absolutely not. But positions in the government and economy have changed dramatically and, over the last 20 years, rapidly.

Other changes have happened too that have changed the way boundary overlaps and circuits of mobility work. The GOP, or Republican Party, has become a religio-political body whose membership is still somewhat restricted to white males and evangelicals (Brint and Abrutyn 2009). The Democratic Party has white males as well, but it's become the path to mobility for a wider swath of the population. Leadership and positions of power, however, have become less about race and ethnicity, and more about one's access to learning. We elect Ivy League and elite private university graduates for the most important positions, no matter how much a challenger or incumbent pretends to be an average American. A new elite has formed around education, with religion being a key sorter of party affiliation.

## CONCLUSION

Structure still matters, even if sociology has moved toward a greater emphasis on cultural analyses. Institutional domains do occupy real space, and the reconfiguration of physical and temporal reality has just as much impact on humans as that of social and symbolic space. Indeed, as is clearly the case, culture is not always reproduced perfectly or evenly across settings within the same domain. Kids from lower-class families will be socialized differently than kids in upper-class families, meaning value orientations, ideologies, and even norms will vary across categoric units. Yet, despite this cultural stratification, societies continue to function to some degree most of the time. That is, going to the doctor may mean something different for a woman than for a man, a black person or a white person, or a rich man or a poor woman, but the patterns remain somewhat regularized enough that a significant proportion of the population *knows* what is expected of them as a patient when with a doctor, and they know what they can expect from a doctor.

In part, this is because institutional domains create structurally equivalent collectives and role through segmentary forces, while fostering mutual interdependence via differentiation. Thus, patients are patients in most cases, and television shows, magazines, and the like reinforce this in ways that are isomorphic; meanwhile, doctors are doctors, and the doctor–patient relationship is standardized and formalized, and in some ways, it is the mutual interdependence that creates trust, the acceptance of power differentials, and meanings that are shared enough to fulfill the most basic roles in most settings. Beyond these two basic forces, we find exchange, domination, and the creation of a micro-system of exchange–domination relationships called *embedding* as entrepreneurial efforts to integrate disparate social units, maintain the right to control and coordinate their actions and the flow of resources, and legitimate their claims. Finally, mobility and boundary overlaps is what spreads elite culture throughout a given institutional domain and across institutional boundaries, as actors from the elite spaces move from one place to another and impose entrepreneurial visions of reality wherever they go. In the following chapter, we will explore in depth how these structural linkages facilitate the flow of intra- and inter-institutional culture by creating circuit along which generalized media circulate. Like structural mechanisms, this cultural mechanism integrates and regulates action and attitudes; like structural mechanisms, it has dual consequences: it stabilizes social reality by imposing cultural equivalencies, while also creating and reinforcing patterns of stratification in ways that always threaten whatever ephemeral stability they create.

# 5 The Roots of Intra-Institutional Culture

## The Circulation of Generalized Symbolic Media

> Religion and art spring from the same root and are close kin. Economics and art are strangers.
>
> —Nathaniel Hawthorne

### WHY CULTURE MATTERS

If structural dimensions of institutions provide the frame of the institutional "house," then culture is what gives it texture, character, idiosyncracy, and life. Though autonomy does not mean total independence, when institutions reach certain thresholds of autonomy it is because their entrepreneurs have successfully created distinct cultural sphere in which action, exchange, and communication becomes discernible to significant portions of the population. At the core of our discussion are generalized symbolic media, an old functionalist concept (Parsons 1963a, b; T. Turner 1968; Luhmann 1976, 1982; La Valle 1994) that never really took purchase in sociology.[1] However, it is ripe with utility for bringing together a disparate body of sociology that emphasizes the underpinnings of integration and regulation/domination. It also opens the door to talking about institutions and their relationship to emotions (Turner 2010c), communication and language (Luhmann 2012), interaction rituals (Collins 2004), a link between the macro and micro realities (Vandenberghe 2007), and public performative rituals (Alexander 2004; Reed 2013). Drawing from Simmel's (1907) discussion of money as a generalized medium of economic exchange, media have generally been described as a mechanism facilitating and constraining generalized (and therefore impersonal/indirect) systems of economic exchange found in capitalist societies. As a durable and portable physical object, currency is imbued with a standardized and depersonalized value that can be exchanged for a good or service of which the provider can turn around, immediately or at a later date, and purchase a good or service he desires or reinvest the value into his business. The consequence of this innovation was the collapse of cultural and physical distances, as well as the intensification and acceleration of economic exchanges; and, more importantly, the creation of trust and commitment between strangers because the economic exchange and/or communication was coordinated by the medium and its underlying normative meanings and not by the actors.

Being that media remain undertheorized, it is a concept pregnant with potential. Different scholars have conceptualized it in complementary ways that could be synthesized in fruitful ways: as a language (Luhmann 2012), a normative system of exchange (Parsons 1963a), the source of institutional culture (Abrutyn and Turner 2011; Abrutyn 2013a, b), and as a resource to be monopolized (Turner 2010c). Furthermore, it shares many of the same qualities as Bourdieu's (1986) capital, but it differs in important ways. Most importantly, we do not see *money* and economy as the ultimate arbiter of exchanges and communication as Bourdieu sees economic capital. Rather, economic exchanges are *one type of* social exchange, and not vice versa. Indeed, *money* is a cultural mechanism of exchange and thus what appears as instrumental or self-interested action or exchange is merely the mode promoted by autonomous economies. Polities and religious domains operate on different cultural logics because different media circulate. And, by differentiating these media from their economic cousin, a more satisfying theory of institutional culture can be posited that does unnecessarily bias economy over spheres of social life like kinship or religion that *mean* something very different to their constituent actors. Thus, one of the most essential shifts in this chapter is to move further away from *money* as the primary example and emphasize the diversity of media and thus uncover some of the taken for granted aspects of *money*.

Before we begin a deeper analysis, it would be useful to briefly review the theoretical assumptions that we will draw from existing treatments of the concept and, subsequently, the contribution this chapter makes. . First, media are *generalized symbols* and thus have been commonly described as a specialized language, form of communication, as manifest in themes and texts, and as symbolic bundles. It is through language that the symbolic bundles are most clearly discerned by observers, and become cues to others that the person using the medium accepts the rules of exchange. We will take this point to its logical conclusion and posit that each medium becomes the indigenous source of a specialized institutional language that is learned by any and all actors pursuing or acquiring media in its various forms. There is a vocabulary of economy that is significantly different from that of religion or law. To be sure, institutions are never hermetically sealed and thus conversations and discourse within any given situation within any given institution can be governed by a single medium, the interplay between indigenous and "foreign" media, or corrupted/polluted and dominated by foreign media only. Second, and perhaps the biggest advance this chapter makes toward a theory of generalized symbolic media (or, GSM), is that media are not just a language or symbolic bundle but manifest in what we call *external referents of value*. The dollar bill is an example of the *objectified* form of economic GSM, but every medium can imbue objects with value and can become desirable goals for actors: the Christian cross; the doctor's white lab coat; a trophy; or a book shelf full of dense, intimidating books. The "big point" is by also conceptualizing GSM as tangible things, the abstractness of acquiring language is replaced by the very concrete pursuit of things that are desirable; this implies a more concretized source of normative social exchange, as well as a clearer marker of a person or group's position in the domain; and, finally, similar to a dollar bill, it can be "exchanged" as currency within the context of institution-specific interactions. Moreover, as totem-like objects, we can draw Durkheim's (1912) work on rituals into a theory of institutional culture, while also integrating the insights of Randall Collins' (1988, 2004) interaction rituals and stratification and Jeffrey Alexander's (1988d, 2003, 2004) work on cultural pragmatics, performance, and hermeneutics because the use of GSM, whether as symbols or as objects, requires the tacit acceptance of, at the very least, the basic normative framework of exchange, as well as can become "currency" in social exchanges.

Third, it is essential to keep in mind some GSM are "hotter" than others, which means they carry particularistic cultural realities that are anchored in socioemotional moorings. *Love/loyalty*, or the kinship GSM, is a good example: it is far less convertible across boundaries, as it is often exchanged in local, face-to-face relationships; although the medium itself carries generalized meanings across families and relationships, its particularistic coding (Luhmann 2010, 2012) and highly moral evaluative loadings (Abrutyn and Turner 2011) reduce its perceived transposibility. *Money*, on the other hand, is a cool medium with universalistic, impersonal meanings and is easily transferred across boundaries and is highly valued. Fourth, because of the variation in "temperature" and value, as well as the reality that media circulate differently and inequitably, meanings are not going to be uniformly held even if objective values and conversion rates exist. Sixth, GSM are unevenly distributed as symbolic resources, and as such, are a source of intra-institutional stratification (see Chapter 6, this volume; also Abrutyn and Turner 2011; Turner 2010c, 2012). Language, of course, can be a resource scarcely distributed across interactions (Goffman 1981), across corporate and categoric units (Turner 2010b), and within and across fields and niches (Bourdieu 1991).

Eighth and final, GSM *make institutional domains real*. As actors begin to use GSM, and pursue, acquire, invest, and sometimes try to hoard GSM, they come into contact with the macro world. Vandenberghe (2007:312) visualizes GSM as the

> conveyer belts that link the global system to the local life-worlds . . . [as they] construct systematic linkages between social positions and ideas on the one hand, and interpersonal and intergroupal relations on the other . . . [Ultimately, they] allow people and groups that are not physically co-present . . . to enter into contact and communication.

Such powerful imagery taps into the importance of GSM as a resource, and as the basis for cultural reality within autonomous institutions; they are what allows one institution to be "treated as separate [from other domains] for analytical purposes as well as in *situations of daily life*" (Luhmann 1976:511; emphasis added).

## MEDIA AS CULTURE

### What Are Generalized Symbolic Media?

Throughout the book, it has been stressed that institutional domains are, in one sense, a sphere of generalized exchange and communication. According to Edward Lawler (2006:257), generalized exchange "fosters higher levels of interdependence among actors" because it shifts the attribution of rewards—especially those undergirded by emotions—from the exchange partner to a larger social unit such as a collective, the system, or society. In many ways, this was one of the central tenets of Durkheim's (1912) *Elementary Forms of Religious Life*: the ritualization of certain types of social exchanges, led to the production of powerful emotions he called *collective effervescence*. Given the human need to identify, label, and attribute various phenomena, especially emotions (Shott 1979; Turner and Stets 2005; Robinson and Smith-Lovin 2006), actors look for the source of these good feelings. Durkheim assumed that these collective rituals often led to individuals attributing the emotions to something other than specific individuals, as the emotions were produced within a group setting, and thus could easily be attributed to collective representations such as totems or supranatural beings (Collins 1988). Generalized systems of exchange are effective in creating trust and meaning between strangers by standardizing roles and expectations, abstracting value-orientations and norms, and legitimating the distribution of resources by institutionalizing the assumption that everyone gives and everyone gets while delimiting direct, reciprocal exchanges that do draw individuals. Two problems, however, plague generalized systems of exchange. First, free riding must be prevented somehow; preferably through normative regulations, which are less costly. Second, because actors are distributed throughout a system and have inequitable amounts of resources, a generalized mechanism facilitating exchanges, or communication, is necessary to standardize values and generate an objective, or intersubjective, understanding of social exchanges.

As noted earlier, the most common use of generalized symbolic media comes from analysis of economic transactions and *money* (Polanyi 1957; Collins 1990; Turner 2004). Simmel (1907) argued that capitalism worked because of the transformation of money into a generalized symbolic medium of economic exchange. It is generalized because (1) its value is standardized and enforced by legal-rational authority; (2) as a token instead of a commodity like cattle or salt, it is portable and durable over geographic distances and time; and (3) when labor becomes a commodity, its value is transferable across a series of institutional domains in ways that allow the economy to penetrate myriad institutional cores by exchanging wages or salary for highly specialized services. It is symbolic because it cannot be eaten or consumed as other commodities can, its value is subjectively understood based on past and present experiences with *money*, and it is a collective representation and totem of a whole bundle of economic cultural dimensions. That is, the pursuit and acquisition of *money* implies the acceptance of a set of basic values, ideologies, beliefs, and norms regarding what *money* is, why it is worth pursuing, what having more of it can do, and the tacit, and often very basic, rules of exchange. It is for this reason, in part, that Luhmann (1976, 1979, 1982, 1995, 2012) has come to stress the communicative dimension of media: it is the mechanism by which texts become self-reflexive and close various types of systems and its use in conversation narrows choices in themes and forms of talk. Parsons (1963a, b), of course, had long recognized that economics were a specialized language with *money* as the overarching theme, whereas politics was about *power* (cf. Baldwin 1971). The pursuit of either medium implied the internalization of some aspects of the language such that the person could signify to themselves and to others his/her intentions, successes, desires, goals, and negotiate the terms of exchanges appropriately.

But, should we analyze all media as if they were analogous to *money*? There has been a temptation to do so, which has led to vexing questions focused on how exactly one can exchange *power* if it does not manifest into currency (Coleman 1970) or how one could trade *love* or *sacredness*, which seem impossibly quantifiable and, therefore, standardizable. The exchange of *money* seems obvious and makes complete sense given we buy and sell things with utility all the time using *money*. Are other institutions really marketplaces of GSM? And can we exchange non-remunerative GSM the same way as *money*? I believe the answers to both of these questions are yes if we shift away from the overeconomized view of social exchanges predicated on being socialized in capitalist moneyed economies. Most exchanges are not instrumental (Lawler et al. 2009), even those that are economic and use *money*. Economy is a cultural domain like law or sport, and thus obeys many of the same principles as these other domains. Furthermore, economy evinces dynamics specific to economic action or exchange that are not transposable to other domains. For instance, whereas power does not have a standardized value like money, "politics as an exchange process" makes sense as *power* does have exchange-value (Abrutyn 2013b) in the form of "generalized support [being] exchanged directly for policy-making responsibility" (Baldwin 1971:588–9). The entire patron-client system of exchange is an example of a system of generalized *power*: entrepreneurs pursue "clients" who will vote for them, their ally, or their party and in exchange they "promise" to make collective binding decisions favoring their constituencies; in other cases, with elected office comes the ability to offer some clients "power positions" that make them further dependent on the entrepreneur, while providing them with access to greater amounts of power (cf. Eisenstadt and Roniger 1980). In turn, entrepreneurs gain or retain "political power positions" while also enhancing the general assessment of their "expertise," or the real or perceived "recognition of [the entrepreneur's] knowledge about a problem and/or area" (Paine 1963:73). It is through the accumulation of patronage positions and (the scope, depth, and uniqueness of) perceived expertise that political entrepreneurs invest their *power*, or engaging in what Baldwin (1971:607) calls *political banking*, or actively working to "increase the amount of power in the polity" available to themselves. Political banking suggests the ability to *save and invest power*, which Eidham (1963) argues is possible as patronage implies future obligations and commitments (illiquid power) that can be rapidly made liquid in times of need (cf. Baldwin 1971:611).

If we suspend our cynical belief that most motivation in America is underscored by *money*, is it not the case that academics pursue *learning* and *intelligence* in various symbolic and material forms? To be sure, academics are paid salaries and often need grants to secure promotions, but do they not measure their self-worth vis-à-vis other academics through educational and scientific criteria? The discourses and texts that shape their daily realities and annual rituals, their student-teacher relationships revolve around themes of *learning* and *knowledge*? In its purist form, sports—when autonomous—is about *competitiveness*, and thus we evaluate performances and teams based on their level of *competitiveness*. *Money* in the form of salaries, disputes between owners and players, are a part of the domain, but they are a "necessary evil" (Leifer 1998). Ultimately, a player or teams "historic worth" is judged by objectified forms of competitiveness—e.g., stats or championships—and not their net earnings. In other words, *competitiveness* and sports are not *money* and economics, hence the logic of exchange are not the same. One involves market-based transactions for goods and services with utility, while the other involves the visceral social exchange of victory, success, morale, bragging rights, and strength/gracefulness for fame, prestige, salaries, and greatness. One cannot deny there is an exchange, regardless of the less than utilitarian aspects of sport or art, or for that matter, politics which is rooted in expediency and compliance.

In sum, institutional entrepreneurs facilitate and constrain action, exchange, and communication within an autonomous institutional domain through the production and distribution of special generalized symbolic media that circulate along the structural linkages discussed in Chapter 4. They are the *source* of institutional culture, and, as such, they help entrepreneurs try to deal with exigencies surrounding integration, regulation, and legitimation. On the one hand, these media, as symbolic bundles containing the various institutional cultural elements valued by entrepreneurs, actors internalize specialized languages and therefore intra-institutional culture in varying degrees according to the rule of proximity. By doing so, a certain level of cultural equivalency is imposed and accepted throughout the domain, enhancing trust and meaning, and legitimating entrepreneurial claims to power. In this sense, action, exchange, and communication come to be controlled and coordinated by both normative and taken-for-granted forces: some actors come to orient themselves to the values of the institutional core by internalizing various cultural elements of the symbolic medium, whereas others simply pursue the medium and, by doing so, cannot but help to follow the formal and informal rules governing action, exchange, and communication. On the other hand, media are also manifest in *external referents of value*, which act as markers or cues indicative of a person or group's position within the domain, as well as tools or instruments for action, exchange, and communication. An instrumental-rational side of media must also be acknowledge, as they may be ends in themselves and means to other *global* (and not *intra*-institutional) rewards such as wealth, power, prestige, privilege, influence, and so forth. Because the *rule of proximity* shapes the distribution of all resources, and media are an essential resource of autonomous institutions, media then are both cause and consequence of intra-institutional stratification.

There are two key axes of GSM which we must focus: first, media are both symbolic and material resources, and second, media are both integrative mechanisms and sources of stratification (and therefore, potential strains, tensions, and conflicts). Although we will touch on the second axis throughout this chapter, it will receive far greater treatment in Chapter 6. That leaves this chapter to focus on the first issue—the dualistic nature of GSM. Before we can take up this problem, it is worth providing a list of media and the institutions they are generally embedded and circulating within. This list is not closed, as the list of institutions can and will likely grow.

## An Inventory of Media

As institutional domains grow autonomous, and entrepreneurs secure a monopoly over the production and distribution of media—or, the creation and imposition of a discrete institutional culture—action, exchange, and communication become *thematicized*, as Luhmann would say. Put another way, economic action comes to be distinguishable from political action—in the ideal and, to varying degree in practice—via the theme or underlying *ethos* or *logic*. The same is true of economic exchanges and modes of communication—discourse, texts—vis-à-vis their political counterparts. By no means does this assume that in practice, economic exchanges are *purely* founded on one medium, but that (1) as autonomy increases, so does the probability that any give action/event, exchange, or communicative moment is constrained by the institution's medium of exchange; (2) actions, exchanges, and communication often revolve around the use of media as well as the accumulation of more media; and (3) what matters most is that actors, the audience, and those imagining future actions, the institution's particular medium shapes the meanings behind interpretation, controls and coordinates the formulation of meanings as well as the motivation and decision making of actors, and finally, integrates potential and real actors and their audience into a cultural equivalent system of action, exchange, and communication.[2]

It is clear from the discussion above that *money* is the medium of autonomous economic action, exchanges, and communication, but what of the other institutions listed in Chapter 1? Some creativity and empirical induction is necessary here, but some consensus exists for a few other media. First, political actions, exchanges, and communication are about *power* (Parsons and Smelser 1956; Parsons 1963b; Coleman 1970; Luhmann 1982). Comparing *money* to *power*, Parsons remarks that the "use of money is a *mode of communication of offers* . . . to purchase, [or]to sell, things of utility," whereas *power* is a mode of communication of offers to either positively reward or negatively punish actions and thus generate compliance (1963b:236–7). It facilitates generalized exchanges in a relational system of commitments and obligations, and thus political action, exchange, and communication is *thematicized* around *power*, or the probability that an actor or group's command will be obeyed, even in the face of resistance. It is a language or way of orienting discourse—for example, novels and movies about politics are about the pursuit of power, the struggle or fight for power, the resistance against power, and the consequences for accumulating power; political actors' behavior or goals are interpreted as either using power as means or setting power as a goal; and political interaction is understood as dealings in power—for example, negotiations, compromises, patronage. It is often in the negative that the medium of an institution is thrown in sharp relief: when an actor's decisions are about, or interpreted as being about, say, *money*, observers label it corrupt because the expectation and obligation is that action or exchanges will be rooted in *power* first and foremost, and then other media may be involved.

From here, a little inductive theory building is necessary so that we can delineate a list of media and their respective institutions. Of the four remaining universal institutions, three are easily identified. Kinship is about love (Luhmann 1998) and also loyalty (Levi-Strauss 1969). Both media speak to the socioemotional anchoring of social relationships in kinship. Loyalty as a generalized medium may be older in that it tended to facilitate discourse and exchange between disparate non-blood social units (Malinowksi 1922; Radcliffe-Brown 1965; Levi-Strauss 1969). A language of love, however, is not as recent an invention as western scholars often assume. Texts as old as the Hittites or Assyrians use the language of love, as does the Gilgamesh; and, ethnographies of hunter-gatherers also speak of love. The specific romanticized themes of love (Luhmann 2010) are new. Religious action, exchange, and communication are invariably about sacredness and/or piety (morality). The first medium captures the most universal theme or logic of action, exchange, and communication in religious institutions, regardless of their level of institutional autonomy: the ubiquity of sacredness surrounding the existence of the supranatural (Durkheim 1912; Geertz 1966; Wallace 1966; Stark 1999).

The second medium reflects the appearance of moral and ethical imperatives monitored and sanctioned by a transcendent supranatural being or force, which in fact is not ubiquitous to all religions (Eidheim 1963; see also Spencer 1897), but rather is most prevalent as religion becomes increasingly autonomous during and after the Axial Age (c. 900–100 BCE) (Eisenstadt 1986a; Stark 2007; Bellah and Joas 2012; Abrutyn 2013a). Law is a little less obvious, but the legal institution is thematized around *justice* and *conflict resolutions* (Hoebel 1973; Black 1976; Bohannan 1980; Luhmann 2004). The former tends to undergird the ideological underpinnings of legal action and decisions, whereas the latter forms the functional, concrete reasons for making law autonomous in the face of heterogeneous societies. The two are

*Table 5.1* Generalized Symbolic Media of Institutionalized Domains

| | |
|---|---|
| Kinship | ***Love/Loyalty***: language and external objects facilitating and constraining actions, exchanges, and communication rooted in positive affective states that build and denote commitments to others |
| Economy | ***Money***: language and external objects related to actions, exchanges, and communication regarding the production and distribution of goods and services |
| Polity | ***Power***: language and external objects facilitating and constraining actions, exchanges, and communication oriented towards controlling the actions and attitudes of others and obeying superordinates |
| Law | ***Justice/Conflict Resolution***: language and external objects facilitating and constraining actions, exchanges, and communication oriented towards adjudicating social relationships and invoking norms of fairness and morality |
| Religion | ***Sacredness/Piety***: language and external objects related to actions, exchanges, and communication with a non-observable supranatural realm |
| Education | ***Learning***: language and external objects related to actions, exchanges, and communication regarding the acquisition and transmission of material and cultural knowledge |
| Science | ***Applied Knowledge/Truth***: language and external objects related to actions, exchanges, and communication founded on standards for gaining and using verified knowledge about all dimensions of the social, biotic, and physico-chemical universes |
| Medicine | ***Health***: language and external objects related to actions, exchanges, and communication rooted in the concern about the commitment to sustaining the normal functioning of the body |
| Sport | ***Competitiveness***: language and external objects related to actions, exchanges, and communication embedded in regulated conflicts that produce winners and losers based on respective efforts of teams and players |
| Art | ***Aesthetics***: language and external objects related to actions, exchanges, and communication founded on standards for gaining and using knowledge about beauty, affect, and pleasure |

*Note:* These and other generalized symbolic media are employed in discourse among actors, in articulating themes, and in developing ideologies about what should and ought to transpire in an institutional domain. They tend to circulate within a domain, but all of the symbolic media can circulate in other domains, although some media are more likely to do so than others.

*A version of this table was originally published in Abrutyn, Seth and Jonathan H. Turner. "The Old Institutionalism Meets the New Institutionalism." *Sociological Perspectives* 54(3):283-306. © 2011 by the Pacific Sociological Association. Published by the University of California Press.

nearly inseparable, as *justice* tends to undergird conflict resolution in most cases (Lloyd 1964; Stone 1965). Finally, the last of the six universal institutions is education, whose currency and medium of exchange is *learning* (Turner 2010a). Education is about the transmission of knowledge, and the stratification of students is determined by the amount of *learning* they supposedly have acquired. It is this medium, and not knowledge per se, that is traded for other goods and services.

Of the remaining institutions, far less empirical work can be drawn from because these institutions have only recently been classified as such. Science, for instance, is about *truth* in the abstract (Luhmann 1976, 1995) and *applied knowledge* in the concrete (Abrutyn and Turner 2011). These two are often found alongside *learning*; and *truth*—once a medium of religious exchanges—is often found side-by-side with *sacredness* (Abrutyn 2013a). It was noted above that *competitiveness* is the mechanisms of sport actions, exchanges, and communication (Werron 2010), whereas *health care* is the medium of medical transactions (Starr 1982). Finally, *aesthetics* and *beauty* find their home inside of art (Luhmann 2000a).

## EXAMINING THE DUALISM OF MEDIA

### Specialized Institutional Language

As a medium through which actors choose between lines of action and goals, indicate to others what their choices are in addition to who the actor is within the institutional domain, and engage in social transactions of myriad nature, media are vital institutional forces. And as the source of institutional culture, one dimension of generalized media relates to its symbolic-cognitive side. Parsons was fond of referring to media as *specialized languages* that (1) *signified* the *value* of the goods or services it was a placeholder for; (2) clearly demarcated actions, exchanges, and communication between actors and these goods and services; (3) provided the cultural assemblages necessary to define institutional situations—for example, knowing which objects were worth acquiring, where and when these goods and services were attainable, and the basic conditions surrounding the acquisition of these objects; and, finally, (4) embedded action, exchange, and communication within a *normative framework* in which a *bare minimum* of shared meanings and understandings of the rules was implicit (Parsons 1963a:39–41; T. Turner 1968). Media channel action and interaction by restricting or delimiting the framework with which actors set goals, make decisions, choose strategies, and make sense of the other's actions. According to Luhmann media are "a code of generalized symbols" (1979:111), or "meaningful constellations of combined selectivity which can be signified by words, symbolized and codified legally, methodologically or otherwise . . . [and which] transmit contingent selections . . . [from]

past performances" (Luhmann 1976:512) so that "choices which linguistically remain open" can be narrowed (ibid. 511). Its normativity comes from the fact that its use, in conversation or action or exchange, signifies we accept certain conditions.

Consider, for instance, the polity and the circulation of *power*. Structurally, political autonomy entails the construction of a "highly centralized government with a professional ruling class, largely divorced from the bonds of kinship which characterizes simpler societies . . . [by instating] residential patterns often based on occupational specialization rather than blood [and in which political entrepreneurs attempt] to monopolize force" in addition to creating "public law and controlling markets" (Flannery 1972:403–4). But structural changes cannot proceed without concomitant cultural changes; the newly demarcated physical, temporal, and social spaces must be undergirded by symbolic meanings. That is, polity *is more than government or a state, a bureaucracy or an army*: autonomous polities are spheres of action, exchange, and communication that links a constellation of individuals, groups, and clusters of collectives together into "an institutional *power system*" defined by a "relational system within which certain categories of commitments and obligations . . . are treated as binding" (Parsons 1963b:244). These relationships are understood and talked about through the discourse of *power*; interaction, exchange, and communication between super and subordinates is facilitated and constrained, in the ideal, by values, ideologies, and norms related to the symbolic language of *power*; the resource gained or lost is *power*. To be sure, the relationship is not one-sided, but rather reciprocal in some cases, generalized in others: a king may reward his general by giving him land in exchange for greater political *loyalty* and strengthened compliance, or, through an annual public ritual, a king may lay the first brick of a new temple as a ritual act of power (Reed 2013) that becomes his signature on a "contract" signifying his commitment to the prosperity of the people and the city in exchange for the loyalty to his commands—as expressed in public law, the provision of tribute, corveé labor, and taxes, and, of course, willingness to fight against invaders or through conscription. In both cases, the discourse of *power* shapes the social relationship, gives texture and color to it. In addition, it delimits the themes with which actors understand events and people, as well as how observers would write about the events. Institutional autonomy and the circulation of a specific medium, then, implies a certain amount of self-reflexivity to symbolic reality. Political goals, for instance, become (gradually and relatively) divorced from other types of goals in people's minds and in their formulation/execution: they become "governed mostly by political criteria and by consideration of political exigency" because they are "different from other types of goals or from goals of *other spheres or groups in society*" (Eisenstadt 1963:19; emphasis added).

To be sure, how dominant a medium is depends on (1) how autonomous the institution is, (2) how autonomous other institutions are, and

(3) how hot or cold the indigenous GSM is in relationship to other foreign GSM. Furthermore, entrepreneurs and other actors near the core, which is the production and distribution "hub" for GSM, are more *self-aware* of the meanings of the symbolic bundle and are under more pressure to constrain their action, exchange, and communication through the mediation of the indigenous GSM. But, make no mistake, GSM circulate throughout a domain and thus carry and transmit the vision of institutional reality, or at least a partial vision intentionally or unintentionally parceled out for one strata or another. Thus, as political actors view reality, act, and talk through the specialized language of *power*, their political values, ideologies, norms, and strategies are reinforced and diffuse throughout the population (Lenski 1966; Rueschemeyer 1977; Scott 1998).[3] And as other institutions become autonomous, they develop ways of talking about *power* because it circulates across boundaries: in the scientific domain, "power is to political scientists what money is to the economist" (Baldwin 1971:578).

Of course, this discussion underscores the fact that media are more than just a specialized language. In a sense, GSM are cultural assemblages or toolkits through which institutional reality comes into focus. At their most abstract, media circulate value-orientations, or general assumptions of good/bad and right/wrong, which are funneled into less abstract cognitive lenses—*ideologies*—that explain, justify, predict, and interpret past, present, and future actions, exchanges, events, and issues. As such, media do not circulate as complete or total bundles, but rather in *parcels* that offer different ideologies to different locations within the institutional domain. *Parcelization* may reflect fractures among entrepreneurs in which competing ideologies—e.g., *progressivism vs. conservativism*—over the meaning and use of GSM unevenly circulate; pacelization also mirrors the intra-institutional class system in which actors closer to the core have different types of knowledge and advantages, especially greater diversity and amounts of parcels, than those further from the core. Some parcels simplify more complex ideologies consumed by those closer to the core, while others are contradictory. Through ideologies, and the concrete norms they suggest to the actor, generalized symbolic media frame the institutional setting and, because media are portable across domains, can effect action, exchange, and communication across domains.

In sum, economic actors talk about *money* and are oriented toward accumulating *money*, whereas religious actors talk about *sacredness* and/or *piety* and are oriented toward accumulating *sacredness* and/or *piety*; they are the worldview among actors in the economy or religious sphere—and can often affect their conception of other domains; they are the basis for the ideologies of economy or religion that inform individual and collective actors of what is right and wrong, good and bad, appropriate and inappropriate; and they are the symbolic medium through which the evolution of institutional and organizational norms within a domain and its constituent corporate actors are facilitated and constrained. As we shall see, in addition, they are the valued resources exchanged within the economy and religious spheres respectively; they can often be exchanged for media from other domains—for example, *money* in the form of campaign donations in exchange for *power* in the form of the right to influence the political party, political patronage, or favorable collective binding decisions); they are also the valued resource unequally distributed within and between domains and, hence, one pillar of the stratification system. As a specialized language and a symbolic bundle, generalized symbolic media give shape and texture to "discourse and theme-building in exchanges of actors within [collectives] and between [collectives] in different domains, while also providing a somewhat shared legitimating ideologies, institutional norms, and specific norm-regulating behaviors" (Abrutyn and Turner 2011:293).

## The Material Side: External Referents of Value

The material side of GSM deserves equal attention as the symbolic-cognitive side. It is the transformation of abstract symbolic bundles and notions of value into real tangible substance that act as external reference points for action, exchange, and communication. Although people *talk* about *money*, it is the physical form of *money* that is easily "called up" in their head; although people think about accumulating *money*, it is often a wealthy person or status object that act as reference points indicative of having "made it"; and although *money* facilitates generalized exchange that directs emotions toward collectives or the system, people often attribute their emotions to real objects around them. In short, the *objectified* form of GSM is important for a few reasons: (1) tangible objects are more easily imagined and sought after; (2) their acquisition brings immediate, visceral, sensate satisfaction that is more diffuse in the symbolic form; (3) as *external referents* of *value*, the *objectified* form of GSM signifies to the possessor and the observer or interactant relative position and privilege in an institution and what type of deference and demeanor each actor should take; (4) the *objectified* form sets up the possibility that a person may have objects but not possess the requisite knowledge or symbolic language with which to talk about or use them appropriately, thus allowing for discrepancies and inauthentic performances—e.g., a discrepancy between their sign equipment and their competence over using it (Goffman 1963a; Bourdieu 1986); (5) the *objectified* form creates manipulative strategies in which actors try to shape the objective world to their advantage; and finally, (6) *objectified* forms (a) can become central foci of important *institutionalized* patterns of GSM exchange or interaction, that (b) intensify the emotion surrounding their use or possession, consecrate and sanctify the object and, thereby, the GSM itself and the person who can touch or use it, and finally, (c) have the consequence of making the *institutionalized* ritual an *external referent of value*, that is a cue of the actor(s) position in relationship to the flow of GSM.

Thus, the *objectified* form, or the material manifestation of a generalized symbolic medium, becomes a force of action, exchange and communication. Like Durkheimian totems, *objectified* forms can become the focus and background authenticating performances meant to communicate solidarity (Alexander 2004) or domination (Collins 2004). Or, as Goffman (1959, 1963a) and later Bourdieu (1977, 1984) pointed out, the appropriate, official, or deviant use of objects are cues to others and our self of the dispositions we possess—that is, *embodied* forms of GSM. Put another way, the use of GSM to authenticate claims and generate trust or, to reinforce power differentials through "the ways of looking, sitting, standing, keeping silent . . . [that] are silent and insidious, insistent and insinuating . . . secret codes" will be called *embodied* forms of GSM, and are equally important external referents of value. Finally, *objectified* and *embodied* forms require some standardized rituals or paths that are both cause and consequence of the transfer of value from the symbol itself to the object. The *institutionalized* form of GSM, then, refers to the public and private rituals that denote the formal acquisition of GSM, the legitimate claim to using it, and the presumed special knowledge about how to use it across situations. Graduation, for instance, indicates to the graduate, the university, and the public that person "A" should have standardized amount of *learning*, which should be transferable in routinized ways across a set of situations. To be sure, it is the *institutionalized* form that often confers legitimate rights to the *objectified* forms as well as socializes and internalizes the symbolic-cognitive side of media such that the person gains access to the *embodied* form.[4] Before examining more closely each form, a few caveats are in order.

First, not all forms are equal. Acquiring the *institutionalized* form of *learning* by going to Harvard versus going to a two-year community college underscores the qualitative differences in both graduates' understanding of their accomplishments as well as for the impersonal stranger familiar with American education. Though these qualitative differences are not quantifiable in analogous ways as comparing salary or net worth, they have phenomenological consequences as well as concrete ramifications; moreover, it would be dubious to claim that Harvard degrees do not have noticeable effects on future educational exchanges or communication. Thus, there is a double-distinction we must identify in most *institutionalized* forms of GSM. On the one hand, "the essential effects of rites [is] that of separating those who have undergone the rite . . . from those who will not undergo it in any sense, and thereby instituting a lasting difference between those to whom the rite pertains and those to whom it does not pertain" (Bourdieu 1991:117). On the other hand, the rites are not evenly distributed in access, significance, or conferral of status. Bourdieu's quote, then, can be applied just as easily to the Harvard graduate and all non-Harvard graduates. The quantity and quality of *learning* varies based on the collective and the niche in which the actor pursues it. Second and closely related, the quantity and quality of the *objectified* and *embodied* forms vary concomitant to that of the *institutionalized* form. The bachelor's degree, as an *object* that hangs on a wall and acts like currency, means something very different when it says "Harvard" as opposed to "So-and-So State School." Third, the *institutionalized* form *does not* necessarily lead to acquiring the matching *embodiment* of the medium, and thus a person may graduate Harvard or any college and not be able to genuinely act in ways indicative of their assumed amount of *learning*. Moreover, having expensive art or a big house may not be coupled with *knowing* what it means, how to act around it, and so forth. It's the discrepancy between *objectified* forms and *embodied* forms that capture the problematic nature of impression management Goffman (1959, 1963a, 1963b, 1967) was so interested in, in addition to the problems Alexander (2004) identify inherent in inauthentic performances. What's more, having the object versus having the object and the embodiment of GSM is the very difference between ownership and entrepreneurship. Being able to transfer *money* into *beauty* (buying expensive art) does not turn someone into an artistic entrepreneur, though being a serious patron in the artistic community can shape the production of aesthetics and beauty (Luhmann 2000a). Fourth, all three external referents are resources in that they are means to other goals. The uneven distribution of access to any form of media is parallel to the uneven distribution of access to the symbolic-cognitive side and, thereby, variation in skill, size and diversity of strategies, the number and type of values, ideologies, and norms one adheres and is committed to, and the external form the individual, collective, or cluster of collectives take.

### *The* Objectified *Form*

The most obvious external form generalized symbolic media can take is the *objectified* form. Objects may include be tokens of actual exchange (coins), symbolic currency within varied markets (e.g., a college degree), formalized positions (e.g., titles in a bureaucracy), restricted identity equipment (e.g., a gavel or white lab coat), or permanent/temporary possession of demarcated physical space (e.g., a professor's office). *Objectified* forms can also be things that individuals cannot necessarily possess, but which can confer special meaning: an entire city, state, or region can be an *object* that groups struggle for. Israel, and especially Jerusalem, is considered by Jews, Christians, and Muslims to be *sacred*: the land, the buildings, the water, everything. But, for our discussion, the objects people come to pursue and acquire are of paramount importance to large tracts of geographic territory.

Thus, these objects become tangible rewards for following the rules, interacting and exchanging in legitimated fashion, and as placeholders of symbolic value. They are indicators of a person or group's relative value vis-à-vis other actors; according to the rule of proximity, we would expect those closer to the core to have greater access and shares of the objectified form. To be sure, in many institutions, certain objects are entirely restricted to entrepreneurs. The PhD is restricted to educational-scientific entrepreneurs, whereas the white coat that doctors wear is restricted to medical entrepreneurs. In other cases, these objects can be "franchised" to support actors, such as nurses having access to special medical "equipment" that is indicative of their elevated medical status, but maintains the broader medical stratification system. In all cases, however, the subjective and objective quality varies relative to the actor and objects distance from the core.

Think back, for instance, to the example of hanging a degree on your wall from Harvard as opposed to one from a small, state school. The subjective, and to some degree objective, quantity and quality of *learning* conferred on the graduate is a function of the types of educational-scientific entrepreneurs he or she would have access to. Professors in departments at prestigious universities are more likely to have greater quantity and quality of *objectified* forms of *learning* than those at less prestigious schools—for example, journals and books with their author name, lines on their curriculum vitae, and so forth. And even in the case where the state school graduate have more *learning*, that is was smarter and better prepared to apply these skills, observers might still evaluate the difference between her and another actor from Harvard based on the two universities' respective distance from the educational core and the site of GSM production.

### *The* Embodied *Form*

Possessing an object is one thing, knowing what it is, how it works, how to orient oneself to it, where to place it, and why it is important is an entirely other thing. *Embodied* forms of media come out in the conscious and unconscious dispositions of actors, the strategies—depth and diversity—they have access to and employ, and the way they use the objects (as well as the symbolic aspects of media); *embodied* forms produce greater levels of trust as authentic performances indicate a person's assumed competence may in fact be actual competence (Alexander 2004). The difference in attitudes and relationships between Old Money familiess and *money* is thrown in sharp relief against the so-called Nouveau Riche—for example, owning a piece of expensive art does not make one aristocratic so much as the well-rounded education that teaches one how to "interact" with the art work itself. Some aspects of *embodiment* are directly associated with the *institutionalized* forms of media. Becoming a doctor, lawyer, or professor involves an *institutionalized* process in which the length of training, the relative separation between neophyte and laity, and specialization lead to a discrete process of socialization that makes people into doctors or lawyers by imposing a certain level of media on these actors (Freidson 1994). Other aspects of *embodiment* are learned through the actual *practice* of roles, whether entrepreneurial or their counter-roles (Bourdieu 1977). A final source of *embodiment* comes from imitation and social learning, in which actors look to role models for information about how to act. The catch, of course, is that humans are avid "checkers" in that we constantly monitor each other to ensure we have an accurate definition of the situation, which in the negative means we are often quite sensitive to inauthentic performances and discrepancies between what is explicitly said and what is implicitly expressed through dispositions, exhibition of skills, and when we "let down our guard" (Goffman 1967). Ritualized performance reduce some of the problems associated with inauthentic performances as it standardizes certain institutional exchanges and communication (Alexander 2006), but that should not detract from the fact that not every actor who should have high levels of *embodied* media has high levels.

### *The* Institutionalized *Form*

*Institutionalized* forms are vital to the reproduction of the normative framework in which exchange and communication occurs (Bourdieu 1991; Alexander 2004). Patterned rituals as well as standardized "paths" toward identity-role transformation codify the acquisition of regularized levels of a medium. "Getting a college degree," as noted above, is a clear example in which a baseline level of *learning* is assumed to have been acquired, even in objective cases where it is not.[5] The same incongruities can emerge in other cases such as "climbing the corporate ladder" where an individual does indeed gain access to greater amounts of *money*, especially in its *objectified* form, but they may have lied, cheated, or been promoted to the point of their incompetence, and thus lack the *embodied* form complimenting the *objectified* form. *Institutionalized* forms are simply external referents to assumed levels of value, which can then be more easily converted into other types of media in other institutional domains. Of course, they often change over time and across space, although they often have very different subjective meanings attached to them based on the person undergoing the ritual and his/her relative position within the institutional domain as well as the collective's relative position. "Getting a college degree," then, likely means something different to a person whose parent's have professional degrees, and therefore, they are more likely to *embody* certain aspects of *learning* beforehand, while someone from a family with no previous college experience will understand the experience and go through the ritual in sharply contrasting ways.

In sum, media can be symbolic or material in its form, although the two are tightly linked. When we talk about economics, our discourse is framed by *money*, whereas talk within the family is delimited by themes of *love* and/or *loyalty*. The *objectified* forms of GSM further thematize the situations and collectives by externally representing the underlying institutional culture as contained within the GSM. These external referents confer value on the possessors, and like trying to master a language so that a person can become mobile, actors pursue the acquisition of *objectified* forms of media. Non-linguistic communication is also conveyed through the *embodied* form, or disposition centered on using and displaying *objects*, as well as carrying oneself in interactions or exchanges. And, finally, the well-worn paths that lead to rituals and rites of passage that confer special status on the actor or the group legitimately allowed to regulate said rites can also become external referents of GSM value—or the *institutionalized* form. To be sure, the symbolic dimension of GSM gives meaning to these material or external forms, whereas these external forms make the symbolic dimension realized in objective, or intersubjective, reality. Either way, the pursuit, acquisition, use, accumulation, and hoarding of GSM leads to the normative acceptance of some basic rules (and thereby integration), the regulation of behavior as there are legitimate and illegitimate ways of exchanging and communicating, as well as tacit assumptions that some people have more GSM and thus deserve more deference, and finally, create cultural equivalencies that become taken for granted as myriad people talk about the same things, act in the same ways, and habitualize the social space.

## SOME DYNAMICS OF GENERALIZED SYMBOLIC MEDIA

### Temperature, Penetration, and Meta-Markets

One of the central dimensions along which media are differentiated from each other are there *temperature* (Abrutyn and Turner 2011; Turner 2011). A continuum of sorts, some media are "hot" and others "cool." The hotter a medium is, the more particularistic the constellation of symbols comprising its bundle. Moreover, hot media tend to be anchored in socioemotional and evaluative/normative moorings, coating action, exchange, and communication in personal, meaningful tones. In the U.S., three media tend to be hot: *love/loyalty*, *sacredness/piety*, and *aesthetics*.[6] Notably there are no guarantees that these three are hot in every case. Religious domains had become firmly ensconced in their respective polities throughout the urban revolution 5,000 years ago, creating a political market for *sacredness* that substantively cooled the medium down. Additionally, as media are parcelized, some parcels may combine hotter or cooler symbolic elements for various sociological reasons. Cool media, then, combine universalistic constellations of symbols in their bundle and are generally not anchored in emotion or evaluative/normative moorings. Instead, they tend to be more instrumental-rational symbolic components, texturing actions, exchange, and communications as less personal. Media, like *money* or *power*, are seminal examples in the contemporary U.S. institutional complex, but only historical analysis can reveal the temperature of a given medium

As media cool down, they are more easily converted into a broader swath of goods and services and, thereby, circulate more freely across more institution domains. It is not strange, for example, to find *money* circulating besides *health care* or *learning* as doctors and educators are not paid in kind, but rather in salary. Because medicine and education possess labor markets, then, we find their "indigenous" media competing with "foreign" would-be colonizers that are the "coolest" of all—*money* and *power*. In a sense, cooler media have a wider variety of uses and can easily be grafted onto other media in ways that expand the themes available to institutional actors. Academia is about *learning* and in many cases *applied knowledge* and/or *truth*, yet professors need grants, seek royalties from book writing, and consult to acquire more *money*. Some of these strategies are sanctioned in the positive by academe, whereas others call into question the professor's motives. Conversely, hot media are less readily transferable across boundaries, owing to their tendency to be exchanged in greater face-to-face settings and in encounters linked together by shared history, experience, and strong cultural and structural equivalencies. *Love*, for example, does not easily convert into *money*. And when it does, the narratives surrounding it are often questionable such as a parent "buying" their child's affection or a man seeking affection by purchasing time with an escort or even a prostitute.

The way media circulate has consequences for the way institutions affect those individual, collective, or clusters of collectives embedded within them. Hot media tend to erect powerful homogeneous internal markets of both direct and generalized exchange and communication. Action in these environments tends to be closely monitored and norms far more stringently enforced through informal mechanisms of control. Furthermore, actors who are predominantly oriented toward the cores of hotter media tend to have parochial, sharply bounded lenses through which they perceive reality; they also tend to have lower-levels of socially desired resources like power and prestige, though their situational levels might be in fact high. Entrepreneurs from these domains have less influence over the "steering" of society, and must cultivate different strategies if they are to influence a greater proportion of the population than the local one they tend to frequently and intensely exchange and communication with. Cool media, on the other hand, tend to cross-cut institutional domains much easier, raising the profile of entrepreneurs propagating these types of media, giving them a greater share of socially desired resources, and expanding their influence across a much larger proportion of the population. As has been the case throughout, the process of *interpenetration*, or the degree to which one medium enters and circulates within other domains, has a double effect. It promotes the formation of inter-institutional (or societal) trust and shared meaning by linking disparate autonomous institutional domains and, essentially many of their constituents who act, exchange, and communicate with actors outside of their institutional domains frequently. As cool media circulate, the values, ideologies, and norms of the entrepreneurs who produce and distribute these media enters into the life-world of other autonomous domains and the pursuit and acquisition of these media implies (1) the tacit acceptance of the normative framework governing the cool medium's exchange and communication and (2) some degree of cultural equivalency *across* institutional domains and their collectives. The use of *money* across myriad institutional domains integrates a large, geographically and socio-culturally "distant" population because it gives even the most marginal actors some common language with which to communicate or exchange.

That being said, the interchange between institutional domains also threatens the coherence of encounters. If media are mechanisms for narrowing choices which linguistically remain open, then multiple circulating media re-open some of these choices and call into question ontological security, trust, and meaning. As new actors encounter each other, media can provide a "narrow world of common understandings, complementary expectations, and determinable issues" (Luhmann 1976:512), but this world is not so narrow when motives, strategies, and the like can belong to different symbolic bundles; or, in some cases, the individual's novel combination of indigenous and foreign media. And as we shall see shortly, foreign media can pervert, pollute, replace, and colonize indigenous domains in ways that have serious ramifications.

Finally, cool media are easily fused together to create meta-markets of generalized *inter*-institutional exchange and communication and *meta-ideologies*, which are akin to societal *ethos* or essence. Recall in Chapter 4, *boundary overlaps* occur across institutional cores in ways that link certain entrepreneurs in exchange and communication networks. The configuration of these networks comes to shape the construction of structural linkages across institutional domains and, thereby, the circuits along which meta-markets of cool media are built. In the U.S., for instance, *power* and *money* are the coolest media and are fused together as part of the American *ethos* in that elements from their respective symbolic bundles color the narratives, themes, *mythos*, values, ideologies, and norms considered "American."[7] Political and economic entrepreneurs, however, do not just fuse their media as they draw from the well of other domains: *power* and *money* are generally fused with diffuse notions of *justice* (e.g., civil rights, "rule of law"), *competitiveness* (e.g., politics and economics are often described in war or athletic metaphors), and *learning* (e.g., political or economic success is attributed to achieved status and not ascribed). These five media are fused into an American *meta-ideology* that penetrates *all* institutional domains in varying degrees, integrates disparate collectives across institutional boundaries, legitimates the social order and gives a sense of shared meaning, and regulates action, exchange, and communication. No matter how autonomous an institution and its actors have become, it is hard to escape the meta-ideology or meta-ideologies circulating, because the creation of "foreign" markets tends to be ubiquitous. That being said, the right to combine or recombine elements from media of exchange is often a key site of struggle in every society. From subcultures like minority ethnic populations seeking to self-determine to aspiring secondary elites looking for a seat at the table or for the whole table, the construction of oppositional meta-ideologies is quite common in modern nation-states, especially those with autonomous polities where every group can become politically oriented.

## Pollution and Colonization

The circulation of foreign media has the effect of "polluting" the purity of the institutional domain. It threatens coherence and ontological security and improves the probability of "corrupt" action, exchange, and communication. In most cases, where an institutional entrepreneur has succeeded in securing a relatively high level of autonomy, the effects are tolerable and minimal. *Money*, for example, is a necessary evil in most institutions as it is the basic means to all goods and services requisite for biological sustenance in capitalist societies. Institutions remain as pure as they can where a significant proportion of the population orients themselves toward the indigenous medium, and it shapes the vast majority of actions, exchanges, and communication. The professionalization process of legal entrepreneurs in the U.S. ensures the codification and internalization of the normative framework regarding the production and distribution of *justice*. Although the most egregious examples of legal encounters (e.g., court cases) that are "corrupted" by *money* or *power* may make one wonder just how autonomous law is, it is the thousands of cases tried every day and decisions guided by legal principles that sustain the legal domain's symbolic reality. Across time and space, we find variation in the U.S. system and its autonomy, such as the low autonomy of Chief Justice Taney's court (1836–1864; most notably in its decision in *Dred Scott v. Sanford*) and the relatively high levels in the Warren court (1953–1969) (Irons 1999). Moreover, we find powerful pressures for judges to make legal decisions based on legal values and norms and not on religious, political, or economic: in a recent high-profile case (*Kitzmiller v. Dover Area School District*), an avowed evangelical judge decided that intelligent design could not be taught in Pennsylvania schools, noting that he believed in creationism but the legal arguments for creationism were not enough to overturn constitutional law. Thus, foreign media often circulate besides indigenous ones, creating distinct, illegitimate markets as well as having minor and sometimes major effects on goal setting and decision making.

In some cases, a foreign medium can *colonize* an institutional domain, or set of domains. The idea of colonization comes from social philosopher Jürgen Habermas (1985), who may have exaggerated the degree to which institutions, or life-worlds in his terminology, could be colonized, yet who provides useful imagery for talking about the subversion of indigenous media. Colonization can occur one of two ways. First, a foreign medium can completely usurp the function of an indigenous one. In the former Soviet Union, legal decisions and legal entrepreneurs were guided by *power* and *political loyalty* as they were Communist party members first and jurists second (Berman 1955, 1968). *Justice* existed, and in cases that were of no interest to the state, it likely was a prominent factor in decision making, yet the currency exchanged in law and discourse surrounding it revolved around *power*. Second, entrepreneurs can usurp a hot medium by "cooling" it down. Political entrepreneurs often use the language of *loyalty* to extract alliances and legitimately obfuscate power-dependent relationships; Bourdieu (1989:16) calls these efforts *strategies of condescension* in which "agents who occupy higher positions . . . symbolically deny the social distance between themselves and others, a distance which does not thereby cease to exist," but which allows them to profit from the "symbolic denegation of distance." *Loyalty*, typically hot, retains its socioemotional anchorage in phenomenological terms, yet becomes a form or extension of *power* and the subset of modes of action, exchanges, and communication revolving around political *loyalty* are far cooler than in kinship; yet, political *loyalty* remains far hotter than *power* because *loyalty* remains predicated on face-to-face, direct exchanges. Entrepreneurs in subordinate institutional domains become merchants of superordinate domains, unconsciously acting as proxy entrepreneurs imposing meta-ideologies. As we shall see in the following section, institutions with hotter media are more likely to resist colonization as they often offer strategies of resistance rooted in emotion and morality. There are feelings of duty and obligation to real exchange partners that often govern relationships and reduce the chances of *power* or *money* mediating exchanges and communication. Nevertheless, cool media are attractive as they can be converted into broader, more global social rewards like societal prestige and influence.

From a value-neutral standpoint, colonization tends to be dangerous as it imposes singular solutions to a wide swath of human concerns; solutions that are often incompatible with satisfactory resolution. Some media, for instance, facilitate action or exchanges deeply rooted in meeting or resolving some biological concerns. *Love*, obviously is linked to our amygdala and our most primitive emotion centers. Less obvious, however, are biologically rooted needs like *justice* and *morality* (Gospic et al. 2011). Where kinship mechanisms can no longer secure *justice,* other institutions must resolve the problem in ways perceived by significant portions of the population as fair (Black 1998; Yoffee 2000). Moreover, it will force the polity to find other sources of legitimation for its authority, as the legal system will be seen as an extension of *power* as opposed to a potential check through the "rule of law." From an evolutionary standpoint, powerful selection pressures are likely to exert themselves on society's in which one or two autonomous institutions reign supreme and subvert the logic of myriad other domains. How long they survive is anyone's guess, but eventually change will become necessary or collapse, disintegration, or conquest from without probable. For the same reasons, once autonomous law has been established any real or perceived corruption of *justice* engenders outrage by many groups.

## Subjectivity, Resistance, and Conversion

Up to now, we have overemphasized the macro-level dynamics of generalized symbolic media, and must now turn our attention to other levels of social reality. In particular, we are interested in the subjectivity of media circulating, as well as the strategies of resistance employed against would-be colonizers. Locally, the meaning attributed to a given medium is highly variable across populations, communities, niches, collectives, and individual actors. Some of this variation is structurally determined: the *rule of proximity* from Chapter 3 posits that a series of actors will be differentially distributed within the institutional space and thus a variable amount of access to symbolic media, unevenly distributed *parcels*, and disparate quantity and quality of media across settings and actors is the norm. Other reasons for this subjective variation are more idiosyncratic: biological variation in the population—for example, random distribution of certain skills, morphological advantages, and cognitive abilities, socioeconomic differences, and so on. Whatever is the case, one cannot ignore the very real differences in what *love* or *money* means to individuals or collectives found within the same niche or field. For sure, a generalized system of exchange reduces the complexities and incoherence of subjectivity by erecting a baseline normative framework for giving and getting *love* or *money*, but this framework does not take away from the fact that there are phenomenological dynamics that make kinship or economy irrational in the Weberian sense (Garfinkel 1964).

Phenomenological dynamics are what give color to the individual experience, and what makes humans human. *Money*, for instance, does not have the same meanings, in the U.S., for many women as it does for men (Zelizer 1997). Actors alienated from an institutional domain, or who simply frequent one domain more than another, naturally combine familiar elements from indigenous media they have most access to with elements of foreign media. By doing so, they make a cool media warmer. This process, of course, can be exploited by entrepreneurs for both moral and amoral motives. A good example of this can be found in the American religious institution in which pluralism encourages fierce competition for human resources (Berger 1969; Finke and Stark 1988). Because religious entrepreneurs produce *sacredness/piety*, they have historically had to figure out ways to convert this into material resources necessary for each individual entrepreneur's biological survival as well as the survival and expansion of the collective enterprise (Weber 1922); ironically, the relationship between *money* and *sacredness/piety* has been far more ambiguous and antagonistic across time and space than it has been complimentary. Yet, churches need *money* to survive. Recent research has isolated the "conversion" strategies used by religious entrepreneurs in some churches, as they attempt to heat the cool medium of *money*. That is, they "*sacralize*" money (Belk and Wallendorf 1990; Mundey, Davidson and Herzog 2011), and reconfigure the phenomenological meanings their specific, local population has toward *money* by anchoring it in socioemotional and evaluative moorings tied to the success of the community, its relationship with the supranatural, and the "good" that *money* can do for the will and desire of the supranatural (Singer 2008; Smith, Emerson, and Snell 2008). This conversion does not change the objective value of *money*, although if enough religious actors reoriented their actions and attitudes regarding *money*, it could have broader, more global consequences such as specialized economic exchange within certain religious niches or fields. Yet, *money* remains objectively cool, impersonal, and instrumentally rational. However, the subversion of a foreign would-be colonizer into an extension of the indigenous medium reconfigures what it means and how it can and is used.

In part, subjectivity and the dynamics of local resource flows is predicated on the reality that GSM do not circulate *en toto*; that is, entire bundles are not, however, accessible by most actors. Instead culture is parsed into

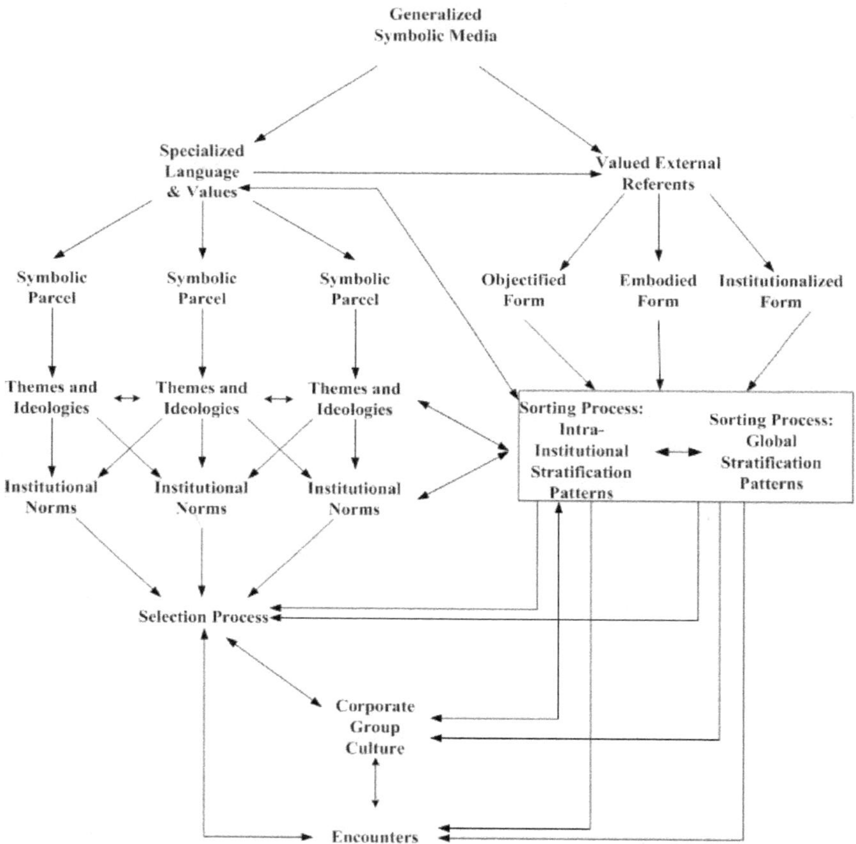


*Figure 5.1* Model of the circulation of generalized symbolic media.

smaller *parcels* that may reflect simplifications of more complex aspects of culture, purposeful/unconscious ideologies of subordination, 'loyal' oppositional segments, and so forth (see Figure 5.1 for a visual model). Polity, for example, is governed by some basic abstract values centered on *power* and its use, yet is parceled into smaller chunks that split along progressive-conservative ideologies, and is parceled even further as some parcels are for the laity, others for loyal party members, others for the opposition, and so on. In other cases, parcels are commensurate with patterns of stratification in which racial or gendered parcels are circulated that differ in content from the dominant cultural parcels. Notably, parcelization has two key facets. First, as would be expected, the closer an actor finds themselves relative to the core, the greater the number of parcels they have access to and, therefore, the more "complete" a picture of reality they can access. Second, even though culture is parcelized, cultural equivalencies are still produced as all parcels derive from the same parent bundle and ultimately reflect slivers of the institutional culture as propagated by entrepreneurs.

As we shall see in the following chapter, it is the process of parcelization that leads to the possibility of unique intra-institutional stratification. On the one hand, parcels reflect the inability of any one actor or group to know or possess total information. On the other hand, parcels reflect the very real uneven distribution of symbolic and material resources associated with GSM. This uneven distribution can and does lead to inequalities that are institution-specific, as well as potentially global or society-wide stratification patterns.

## CONCLUSION

As the source of intra-institutional culture, and when fused with each other a powerful source of societal culture, generalized symbolic media of action, exchange, and communication warrant far more attention than they receive in contemporary sociology. Perhaps a remnant of the eradication of Parsons, it is curious that more sociologists are not interested in perhaps the most important cultural concept Parsons employed. The discussion above offers a framework for thinking about the circulation of media, and when combined with the insights from the ecological and structural dynamics of institutions (Chapters 3 and 4, this volume), a coherent view of institutional space has been offered. What remains, however, is a discussion of the intersection between institutions and stratification. Specifically, the analysis in Chapter 6 will focus on the way global patterns of stratification penetrate the structure and culture of institutions, as well as how institutions create unique patterns of stratification as well as become sites of global social change. The latter two insights are entirely new, as most sociologists underscore the "holy trinity" of stratification—wealth, power, and prestige—while ignoring the structural and phenomenological consequences of institutional patterns of stratification, especially the phenomenological differences in having less access to *love* or *sacredness* as opposed to *money* or *power*, when the former two are deemed central to an actor's self-worth and self-efficacy. What's more, collectives and/or niches can become experimental laboratories in which the way media are distributed among incumbents can spread throughout the institutional domain and, through extant and newly erected structural patterns of mobility and boundary overlap, can affect the global stratification system. Institutional domains offer individual and collective actors the potential resources to be used in changing the larger social world. In many cases, this is a slow process, yet as in the example of religious entrepreneurs converting or *sacralizing money*, these changes have ramifications for those subject to them.

# 6 Intra-Institutional Stratification

## The Uneven Distribution of Media and Other Resources

> Take two kids in competition for their parents' love and affection. Add to that the envy that one child feels for the accomplishments of the other; the personal frustrations that they don't dare let out to anyone else but a brother or sister, and it's not hard to understand why in families across the land, the sibling relationship contains enough emotional dynamite to set of rounds of daily explosions
>
> —Adele Faber

Up until this point, the way institutions produce and reproduce stratification, as well as become centers of domination and arenas of conflict, has been primarily peripheral to the various structural and cultural concerns germane to each chapter. Make no mistake, despite and because of the best efforts of entrepreneurs to integrate disparate social units institutional domains remain sites of tension, struggle, resistance, and conflict. Moreover, stratification systems are merely abstractions that only become realized within the confines of institutional domains (see Figure 1.1).

The originality of this chapter stems not from some overarching theory of stratification, as there are plenty of good ones to choose from (Lenski 1966; Collins 1975; Turner 1984b). Rather, this chapter looks to highlight a key dimension of social stratification currently undertheorized in sociology: intra-institutional patterns of stratification. For many social scientists, there are only three key *graduated* parameters that inequality hinges on: power, prestige, and wealth; and four key *nominal* parameters that intersect with the "holy trinity": race, class, gender, and sexuality.[1] There is no doubt that these parameters are important, because macro-level stratification systems do tend to feature these parameters in most contemporary nations. There are other resources, however, that are essential to understanding tensions, conflict, inequalities, and how people experience their reality; and, situational stratification can be just as relevant to understanding how inequalities effect reality for people as the larger, more invisible global patterns that sometimes are impactful, and other times less important to explaining micro- or meso-level dynamics (Collins 2000a). The stratification of emotions, for example, have recently become central to explanations of micro-level inequality within and across interactions (Summers-Effler 2002, 2004) and corporate actors like groups or communities (Turner 2010c; also Turner and Stets 2005).

In this chapter, then, we seek to build off a small but growing literature that examines the unique patterns of stratification that emerge within institutional domains (Abrutyn and Turner 2011; Turner 2010a, c, 2012). Three contributions to this discussion and the broader sociology of stratification are made. First, the ecological dynamics (Chapter 3) and structural linkages (Chapter 4) of institutions are examined as the central structural forces of intra-institutional inequality. Indeed, the number of cores, their level of discreteness from other cores and the environment, and the diversity and type of structural linkages from the core to the environment shape the texture of intra-institutional stratification. Second, how generalized symbolic media become the axis along which unique intra-institutional classes are created and through which meaning and legitimacy maintaining the institutional social order are elucidated. In this second section, we will look at (1) the status hierarchies that form around a given GSM that make institutional reality a powerful orienting force, (2) the way foreign GSM can also build status hierarchies that lead to contradictory orientations, and (3) the way two or more GSM can fuse together in ways that lead to *inter*-institutional status hierarchies and inform existing theories of societal stratification. Third, institutions can also become "laboratories" of social change that have consequences for broader patterns of societal stratification. That is, structural linkages and the distribution of a particular GSM can shift as thresholds are reached that lead to a cascade of change in resource distribution; this change can remain locked within a domain, or through inter-institutional linkages, can spread across boundaries.

## THE STRUCTURAL FOUNDATIONS OF INSTITUTIONAL STRATIFICATION

As institutions grow autonomous, a natural stratification system emerges between those who are inside the core, those who have ease of access and are near the core, and a series of gradations as actors or clusters of actors find themselves further from the core. Following the rule of proximity, a second rule can be posited—the *rule of institutional distribution*: *the further are an individual, collective, or cluster of collectives from the core, the weaker the flow and access to institution-specific resources, the greater the need for external agents of authority and coercive force, and the greater the likelihood that categoric distinctions associated with core distance will be discriminated against based on institution-wide status beliefs and expectations.* Put another way, inequitable access to institutional resources—including the core itself as well as GSM—generates institution-specific class systems that may or may not intersect with broader patterns of stratification like gender or race. The rule of institutional distribution is important to understand the efficacy of institutional control and the variation across institutional environments in terms of commitment.

In essence, distance from the core equals fewer resource opportunities. In medieval Europe, because of primogeniture, second-born sons were cognitively "distant" from the kinship core and were given far less resources (Goody 2000). Although children of privilege were better off than their poorer counterparts, it was expected that they were to make it on their own and not through inheritance of status or wealth. One could speak of this structural element of kinship as having less access to *loyalty*, and perhaps even *love* as it is plausible to suggest that there were resentments given the archetypal motif of fratricide found in numerous myths and stories across societies (e.g., Cain and Abel). When conventional sociological accounts talk about these in terms of power or economic wealth, they miss the very real emotional side of these events and narratives (Zelizer 2013).

Distance from the core also shapes the quality of the GSM one has access to, as well as the content of the parcels or slivers these actors have access to (see Figure 5.1). Distant actors often have only vague understandings of the goings-on of the core, because they have only incomplete parcels of GSM to work with. Moreover, the physical core may only be an image on television they have seen, and in cases where they do go—for example, poor people attending a court date—to the physical location, it is likely that the symbols and external referents do little more than cue up some very basic stereotyped behavior and diffuse emotions. Rather, as one moves further from the core, compliance becomes spottier, commitment to institutional identities, values, ideologies, and norms inconsistent, and actions and goal setting regulated only in so far as external agents are monitoring and sanctioning. There is just so little material incentive or normative internalization that institutional agents become the central symbol of the institution. Hence the reason they are often the target of anger and aggression in times of institutional unrest.

Finally, where institutional distance correlates highly with (1) specific distinguishable nominal parameters like race or geographic location, (2) distinct positions within one or more divisions of labor, and/or (3) other global parameters of stratification, then institutional stratification systems will become even more powerfully salient. Thus, the deepest layer of institutional stratification emerges around access to a given GSM. Educational stratification, at its heart, revolves around how much *learning* an actor has, or whether he or she possesses the appropriate external referents indicative of high amounts of *learning*. The same point goes for economic stratification and *money*, scientific stratification and *truth*, and so forth; where institutions have become autonomous, the most important axis of stratification across institutional situations is access to GSM, with the pinnacle of institutional privilege being the legitimate right to produce and control the distribution of a GSM. Institutions, however, do intersect with global patterns of stratification that add layers to institutional domains, making things like gender and *learning* or race and *money* salient intersecting parameters. The contours of institutions changes based on these intersections, as does the contents of fields and niches, collectives and role-positions which may or may not reproduce the larger institutional or global stratification system.

## Some Ecological Dimensions

A few important ecological dimensions shape the way GSM are produced and distributed, and, thereby, the structure of intra-institutional stratification. First, the composition of the core(s) matters a lot. To best illustrate this, we will use the Catholic religion in western Christendom as an example. In the wake of the Roman Empire's collapse, Catholicism gradually became the central integrative force across what could only loosely be called Europe at the time (Chadwick 1967; Southern 1953, 1970). Though political unification was attempted several times, most notably during the Carolingian kingdom, Europe remained politically decentralized as an entity unlike its Chinese or Islamic counterparts which managed to have an imperial center and several smaller provinces or suzerainties. Although each political sphere, whether local or regional, demarcated a set of people who had local religious practices, it was a monolithic religious institution with a centralized physical and cognitive core that shaped European history (Abrutyn 2013a, b). Thus, local religious institutions were never able to develop discrete cores, because the Catholic Church put lower-order physical cores into every village, town, and city in the form of parishes; symbolically, they allowed local religions to survive through the creation of local patron saints (cf. Sharot 2001) and, through legal innovations, created a powerful centripetal force that "drew" kings and peasants alike toward the religious center by controlling personal status rights and responsibilities—for example, making marriage a sacrament, determining adoption conventions (Berman 1983; Gies and Gies 1986). The singular core meant rigid control over the flow of *sacredness/piety*, which reached its zenith during Henry IV's challenge to Pope Gregory VII's reforms that gave the Pope sole control over religion's GSM (Clagett, Post, and Reynolds 1966; Wood 2012); the struggle ends, of course, with Henry's famous walk from Canossa and the five centuries worth of papal control over religion and *sacredness/piety*.

Compare this institutional arrangement with the modern U.S.'s religious institution: there is not one hierarchically arranged set of cores, but several competing cores that reflect the pluralism of U.S. religion (Berger 1969; Finke and Stark 1988). Although religion remains relatively autonomous, the stratification system is less clearly defined, the circulation of religious GSM less monopolized by a single entity, and hence, struggles over which religious "parcel" is the truest or most valued underscore religious competition. Heterodoxies are both dynamic for social change via competition (Eisenstadt 1984) and less psychologically coercive for the laity, yet are problematic for religious entrepreneurs seeking to have a "seat at the larger societal table" and have a hand in "steering" the trajectory of human societies; hence the fluctuation between religious political mobilization and its ebb in the wake of pushback from other status groups in American society (Marsden 1990; Brint and Abrutyn 2009). As such, we can propose that institutional stratification systems are, in part, structurally affected by (1) the degree to which one set of cores are tied together through a singular structural linkage of domination and embedding, (2) multiple cores compete for this monolithic status, and (3) cores are free to emerge in horizontal space and compete for resource flows.

In addition, the degree to which a given core is discrete from other local or regional cores matters, as it determines just how much variation may exist across an institution. If, for instance, small towns in the U.S. have monolithic religious cores physically located in a downtown area near the city hall, the most powerful merchants, and the courthouse, we would expect a strong overlap between these domains, a blurring of institutional boundaries that leads to the formation of elite networks that find more elites sharing more in common than not, and the reality for the small town folk will be very different. The centers of domination will merge into a center of domination that is very different from the larger U.S. institutional system that sees economic cores as being physical differentiated from political or legal cores. There will also be differences across local levels as a big city like Los Angeles or New York will make these spaces physically and cognitively distinct enough that the centers of domination will not merge, but remain somewhat autonomous. The bigger city actors will understand the U.S. institutional system better in the sense that it will make more sense and seem more familiar to them. Indeed, the divisions and tensions between town and country are just as much a product of the massive chasm between small town institutional arrangements and bigger city ones. In the case of the former, GSM will often be fused together and circulate within a single elite making economics and politics deeply linked to religion and kinship, whereas in bigger cities unique circuits of *power* and *money* will often be too cool and incommensurate with *sacredness/piety* and *love/loyalty*.

## Some Structural Dimensions

In addition to ecological dynamics, it matters how the core and the environment, and how social units in the environment are linked to each other. Typically, the way cores are linked is replicated in non-core niches and fields. If exchange is the basic linkage, as it is in the economic institution (Collins 1990), then horizontal relations will denote the way GSM flow and structure social relationships and reality accordingly. If embedding and inclusion is the primary structural linkage, then this will be replicated across groups as it is in education and science (Barr and Dreeban 1983). The point is that GSM flow along the structural linkages which shape the divisions of labor, and thus structure resource distribution and inequality.

No structural force may be more important to understanding institutional stratification than *mobility*. Mobility refers to networks of linkages that regularize and standardize the flow of human, material, and, of course, symbolic resources. Networks may exist within and between institutional domains. These networks vary in terms of how closed they are, with true cultural reproduction being reflected in hermetically sealed networks. But networks also can shape the intra-institutional stratification system as fields reveal networks linking the flow of resources across some niches and not others; although these networks are rarely truly closed, they have real consequences. Recent research on the flow of political science PhD's from their graduating department to assistant professorship positions found a powerful multi-tiered system of inequality: 11 total departments were filling 50% of the open jobs, leaving over 100 departments and their matriculating students to fill a very small set of leftover positions (Oprisko 2012); a similar study found related patterns in history departments (Grafton and Townsend 2008). To be sure, these networks are not constructed or necessarily closed for nefarious reasons, but rather human nature: resources, like job openings, are always scarce, and GSM, especially the external referents, act as signifiers of the amount and quality a set of actors should possess. And, like a path through a field, the more resources flow across a network, the deeper its imprint becomes and the harder it becomes to break it.

## THE SYMBOLIC FOUNDATIONS OF INSTITUTIONAL STRATIFICATION

As a rule, stratification is *always* about resource distribution (Lenski 1966; Turner and Hanneman 1984; Collins 1975, 2000a). As noted above, the uneven distribution of GSM leads to structural consequences that affect how committed actors are to the institutional core, how important external agents become in regulating behavior, and how legitimate the core and its entrepreneur's vision of reality is perceived as being. GSM and access to it also undergirds the formation of intra-institutional status beliefs and expectations (Berger, Cohen, and Zelditch Jr. 1972; Ridgeway 1991, 2006), which have ramifications for interaction, exchange, and communication between social units. Status beliefs give shape and texture to

> [p]erformance expectations, which are often unconscious, are members' guesses about the likely usefulness of their own contributions to the group task or goal compared to the contributions of another. The lower an actor's expectations for her own contributions . . . the more likely she is to hesitate in presenting her ideas, to ask the other for suggestions, to react positively to ideas the other presents, and to accept influence from the other. In the self-fulfilling manner, each member's expectation disadvantage (or advantage) compared to others shapes her participation, evaluation, attention, and influence, creating a behavioral power and prestige order. (Ridgeway 2001:325)

Thus, status beliefs have powerful effects on how actors go about organizing their social reality. Generally speaking, sociologists conflate the macro-level stratification system—that is, the sum total of nominal parameters and their relationship to graduated parameters—with the way it plays out on a daily, situational basis (Collins 2000). This belies a number of unique dynamics that emerge across institutional domains that warrant further attention. Although being a woman in most societies constrains action across a wide swath of institutional domains, it does not *mean* the same thing in every domain, nor is it experienced the same way because each autonomous institutional domain has its own cultural system relatively discrete from the global one. This leads to divergent patterns of stratification and the manifestation of status beliefs, their interpretation, and consequences.

Thus, it is GSM that ultimately become the "lynchpin" in the intra-institutional stratification system. Phenomenologically, it is through the *medium* of the institution that people *talk* about and *experience* their position, advantage, or lack thereof. As the epigraph above notes, spurned children talk about a lack of *love*; congregants or adherents to a specific religion talk of non-religionists as lacking access to the *sacred* or being *impious*; the discourse and evaluation of athletes, coaches, and teams falls within the realm of *competitiveness*; and those in disadvantaged minority categories speak of their "disprivilege" in the discourse of *power* and *money*. And when certain institutional categoric units (e.g., students, doctors, mothers) find their role-status position highly correlated with access to multiple media via a particular institutional domain, the discourse reflects the status beliefs regarding students and *learning* or mothers and *love*.. This is not to say that other media do not influence the conversation. Sport is about *competitiveness*, yet teams are businesses, which must find the balance between discourses of competitiveness and those of *money*: some teams, like those in bigger markets, have access to greater amounts of *money* thus shaping the distribution of *competitiveness* and leading to ideologies of the "advantaged teams" (e.g., "Big Market Teams") and those of the "disadvantaged" ("Small Market Teams") (Leifer 1998). Yet, familiar themes perpetuated by sports analysts, fans, and other actors like former players and coaches revolve around things like the decline in *competitiveness* as players age, the uneasy tension between a free agent looking to be paid commensurate to his/her perceived *competitiveness* balanced against the team's budget, perception of his/her skills, the broader market, and the notion of a "hometown discount."

On the one hand, control over the production and distribution of GSM is akin to Bourdieu's *symbolic power* and *violence*, which gives entrepreneurs "the monopoly of legitimate naming . . . [or the] imposition of the legitimate vision of the social world" (1985:731) and which act as "the gentle, invisible form of violence, which is never recognized as such, and is not much undergone as chosen" (1977:192). To be sure, control over a medium is less totalistic or objective as Bourdieu seems to imply, yet dominating a medium means shaping the discourse with which actors in the institutional environment are sanctioned to use as well as the dominant procedure of interpreting and using texts; it means defining what is considered valuable or valued for those pursuing and acquiring the medium; it means formally and informally denoting evaluations of external forms of media; and, most importantly, it means having the advantage of coordinating the flow of media within the institutional domain, including the withholding of media as a possible weapon against usurpers, competitors, or enemies. That is, the "official language," in Bourdieu's (1991:45) terminology, is the "generalized codification and imposition" of reality that becomes "known and recognized throughout the whole jurisdiction [of the institutional sphere, and which helps] reinforce the authority" system.

On the other hand, because media circulates unevenly, and because it is both a symbolic and material resource, institutional stratification emerges around the *rule of institutional distribution*, which shapes how distribution works within a domain. Having greater access to a medium means being more *fluent* and adept at communicating, as well as indirectly speaks to the number and diversity of strategies a person or group has access to in using, saving, investing, accumulating, and converting media. It also means possessing the types of objects that act as symbolic markers indicative of a person's assumed position within the domain (Goffman 1963b, 1971), even if objectively he or she has little *embodied* or lower-status *institutionalized* forms. The visibility of *objectified* forms indicates to others where a person stands and the type of deference he/she are owed (Goffman 1967), even while observers constantly look for authentic performances that demonstrate congruence between *objectified* and *embodied* forms (Alexander 2004). And, finally, it makes the *institutionalized* paths to access sanctified, which are acts "of communication . . . [that signify] to someone what his identity is . . . in a way that both expresses it to him and imposes it on him by expressing it in front of everyone (Bourdieu 1991:121).

From a structural perspective, we would expect that the closer an individual, collective, or cluster of collectives is to the core of an autonomous institutional domain, the greater is the degree to which they will have access to a disproportionate share of media and, therefore, the greater the correlation between the categoric unit they belong to and the medium of exchange. Hence, as noted above, the structure of intra-institutional stratification is founded on generalized symbolic media. It comes to shape the experiences and understanding people have, while also legitimatizing the social order as defined by entrepreneurs who control its production, distribution, exchange, and consumption. The independence of *objects* from *embodiments* and, less prevalently, *institutionalized* forms points to the variation in claims to institutional privilege and the problem of authenticity. In addition, symbolic reality becomes as equally important a dimension of stratification, as it is not just about having lots of resources or prestige, but it also has to do with the types of values, ideologies, and norms people access and use, the strategies they can choose from, and the forms of talk they can mobilize in conversations, textual discourse, and the like. It is because of these points, and others, that each autonomous institution becomes its own unique "life-world" with a distinct set of narratives about inequality, and from a phenomenological standpoint, a relatively discrete social reality. Again, this by no means implies gender no longer matters; quite the contrary, it matters all the more! But it becomes distinctly manifest across domains, and in some domains it may not be the most salient category of distinction. This point becomes particularly salient when the temperature of a given medium is considered, the domain's autonomy and the degree to which other media circulate within it, and the broader institutional complex and how it is arranged—for example, is polity and *power* cool, or are they localized and hot.

## Institutional Categoric Units

Autonomous institutional domains generate their own categoric units beginning with the creation of an entrepreneurial unit and the bounding of an institutional core. Whereas gender or race are categoric distinctions which have real and perceived biological roots, institutional categoric units are "coated" or "drenched" in meanings derived from the circulation of generalized media, control over the production and distribution of media; they are purely sociocultural constructions that become structural components constraining the reality in which incumbents view the social world. That is, doctors, lawyers/jurists, CEOs, and scientists are categoric distinctions that carry status beliefs and expectations that shape the reality of non-entrepreneurs who are interacting, exchanging, and communicating with them. In a sense, then, the abstract role-status position's title "doctor" or "scientists" are *objectified* forms of *health care* or *truth/applied knowledge*, respectively. Hence the struggle, often times, over the definition of what a doctor or scientist is and who should have access to these roles. "Possessing" the title, again, does not imply having *embodied* forms of a medium, nor does it indicate whether the person acquired the title legitimately or through the acquisition of *institutionalized* forms, but rather it simply acts as a categoric distinction that carries a series of codes and beliefs about what other actors should expect, the types of obligations the incumbent has, and their authority and relative social distance (Goffman 1963a).

The construction of a generalized role-status position like doctor requires a corresponding "subordinate" role-status position with minor membership criteria and, therefore, available to as wide a swath of people as possible.[2] The conscious and unconscious identification and orientation toward the subordinate categoric role reinforces the claims of superordinates, makes real the distinctions, even small ones, based on access to a

GSM, and becomes the foundation for a complex, institutional stratification system. Whereas the heart of institutional stratification begins with the entrepreneur-consumer (or client) social relation, the institutional domain becomes very complex as gradations of entrepreneurs emerge around each collective's relative access to a medium, as well as its role in the production and distribution of the medium. For instance, professors generally are educational entrepreneurs are they are either involved in the production of *learning*, the distribution of *learning*, or both. Those that are involved in both stand to be in firmer control over constructing the legitimate vision of educational reality, whereas those who simply disseminate the medium are reinforcing the former group's claims—for example, academics at research universities produce the knowledge, found in textbooks, that state school professors teach. But the lines of stratification do not just stop at producers and distributors, as there are several different levels of *learning* "quality" rooted in objective and subjective evaluations. Peer-review, for instance, is a procedural tool meant to ensure quality *knowledge* is produced and integrated into *learning*; however, individual members of entrepreneurial units are not simply judged by objective standards, but their affiliation with a prestigious collective, networks, relative standing in a field or discipline, and ability to articulate their ideas are all subjective forces driving the construction of *knowledge*. Thus, within the producers and within the distributors of a given GSM there are gradations that have important effects on how institutional media circulate and why.

The same divisions within the entrepreneurial class emerge within those actors found within the environment, as well as those who enter the institutional domain in order to access its goods and services. Based on the *rule of institutional distribution*, we can surmise that some collectives and clusters of collectives not involved in production or distribution, but rather in support or liaison activities are closer than others to the core and, thereby, have greater access to media and are more influential. They are also likely to be perceived by others as being sources of high-quality media, and are more likely to exchange and interact with those seeking access to the core. "Consumers" also vary in terms of their distance from the core (Abrutyn 2012), access to media in terms of quality *and* quantity, and of course their likelihood of being able to acquire more or better media. Two academics meeting each other at a conference immediately examine each other's name tags in order to determine where the other stands in the institutional domains of science and education via name recognition and/or organizational affiliation; two fans meet in a sports bar and "size each other up" by rattling off statistics and evaluating each other's claims to being "authentic" followers of the sport and team and not just "fair weather" fans.[3] The distances between them, ultimately, come to shape the expectations each has of the other, the trajectory of the encounter, and the chances more complex interaction, exchange, and communication emerge.

## Consolidation, Centralization, and Hoarding

If institutional categories are constructed along the lines of correlation between some types of actors and high levels of access to media, then one of the central dynamics of interest across institutional domains, as well as within the smaller clusters of collectives like fields and niches, is the degree to which any one specific collective or cluster can *monopolize* the production and distribution of GSM. That is, how consolidated and centralized are the resource flows in an institutional domain, and, closely related, are global and institutional patterns so correlated that we can identify patterns of media hoarding? The first dynamic is not necessarily linked to the second, as centralization does not always lead to hoarding, although it is a necessary condition of hoarding. Let's examine the first dynamic by using two examples of entrepreneurs who have very different levels of consolidation and centralization.

## Institutional Power vs. Field/Niche Power

The American Medical Association (AMA), or the official board of medical entrepreneurs charged with monitoring and sanctioning the production and distribution of medical media, is quite different than any given academic field and its "official" association—for example, the American Sociological Association (ASA). The former has consolidated and centralized institutional power within a specific core, whereas the latter has consolidated and centralized power within a field in the overlapping environment of education and science. Within the field of sociology, specific forms of *learning* and *truth* circulate alongside *applied knowledge* that relate to the study of societies, social action, and social organization. Some sociological entrepreneurs interact and exchange with entrepreneurs from other fields. Yet, the structure of science is not hierarchical, but rather linked via exchange and less so through embedded/inclusion. There are no truly centralized boards or committees that regulate sociological entrepreneurship like that of the AMA, as science and education are constructed by sets of overlapping cores based on discipline or field. Medicine, on the other hand, is founded on domination and inclusion/embedding, with the AMA having the ultimate right to decertify an individual or, in extreme cases, an entire collective for malfeasance and illegitimate behavior (Starr 1982). What are the consequences for the circulation of media?

Both the symbolic and material elements of *health care* are carefully regulated, and thus there is far less variation across individual settings.[4] Medical universities control medical forms of *learning*, *applied knowledge*, and *truth*, and although there are variations in techniques and the use of technologies, what passes as *health care* must be certified by the center. Encounters with medical entrepreneurs—whether producers, distributors, or both—are highly regularized and standardized and, thus, more constraining (Freidson

1962; R. Turner 2001). Furthermore, the encounters are sharply differentiated along the lines of access to *health care*. The ASA, as an example of any academic discipline, does not have an official board whose function is to certify its entrepreneurs; indeed, the ASA merely facilitates the official annual meeting of American sociologists and tenuously shapes the national discourse. Lacking the legitimate right to strip a sociologist of his or her status, or a department of its right to provide degrees, the ASA has very little control over what one might consider sociological *learning*, *knowledge*, or *truth*, hence the proliferation of schools and traditions, perspectives and paradigms. There are myriad languages considered legitimate, with some sociologists unable to even communicate with each other. There are also numerous paths to sociological "prestige," as sub-group formation ensures fractured status hierarchies. To be sure, the most prestigious departments and scholars continue to shape the meaning of *learning* through control over journals, the most desired academic appointments, and other formal positions. Thus, sociological "power" remains centralized to some degree, but unable to truly control the certification and application of sociological knowledge. On the one hand, sociologists can secure mobility in prestige markets in different ways, yet, on the other, old patterns of stratification are reproduced throughout sociology in terms of control over power and, to a lesser extent, sociological "wealth." Sub-groups competition becomes asymmetrical, even if the use of phrases like "big tent" conceals the underlying inequality of sociology as an organizational field of *learning*.

## Intersecting Parameters and Hoarding

Where the control over the production and distribution is centralized and consolidated, the potential for *hoarding* emerges. Hoarding occurs when global nominal parameters intersect with institutional nominal parameters and together correlate highly with institutional graduated parameters. There are two consequences of note when hoarding occurs. First, institutions reproduce global status beliefs about gender or race. Second, the lack of access to a specific institution's medium adds to the global status beliefs in ways that make them more oppressive. For instance, if women lack *power* and *money* because political and economic entrepreneurship intersects with masculinity as a central criteria for incumbency, then part of the meta-ideology of the larger society will revolve around the narrative explaining and justifying why women do not belong in politics or business. This meta-ideology becomes increasingly complex as gender becomes a criterion for other entrepreneurial positions, such as education or sports, leading to narratives that provide compelling logic: women lack *learning* and the requisite *competitiveness* to run and defend a country, whereas business becomes a sport that requires cunning, intellect, and the ability to win at all costs. There is no need for empirical evidence to support these assertions as they are ideological and rooted in conscious and unconscious observations as well as the symbolic bundles themselves which are internalized through their pursuit and acquisition. Indeed, the very language of economics or politics, sport or education, become gendered.

This same process can, and quite naturally does, occur within a specific field, as certain niches can hoard the flow of generalized media in ways that constrain the construction of reality within subordinate niches. For instance, if an "elite" niche emerges within a specific field such as the sociology field discussed previously, informal control over sociological *learning/applied knowledge/truth* may occur along with the strategies of *misrecognition* meant to hide entrepreneurial power and position, and deny privilege (Bourdieu 1977:172–92)—for example, scholars in these niches study inequality and often are at the forefront of criticizing its reproduction throughout society, despite their own tacit participation in the reproduction of academic inequality.[5] In addition, these niches and their collective perpetuate field/niche inequalities and the reality of hoarding by employing strategies of condescension, or

> those strategies by which agents who occupy a higher position in one of the hierarchies of objective space . . . deny the social distance between themselves and others, a distance which does not cease to exist, thus reaping the profits of the recognition granted to a purely symbolic denegation of distance which implies the recognition of distance. (Bourdieu 1989:16)

Despite these reproductive strategies, it is impossible to objectively deny that these niches hoard the generalized symbolic medium, and informally control how resources flow. As noted in previous chapters and above, studies in political science and history have revealed gross inequities in terms of graduate student placement in open professor positions, with a tiny minority of top schools dominating, and therefore reproducing position, placement leaving a huge majority of PhD-granting departments to compete over the leftovers (Grafton and Townsend 2008; Oprisko 2012).

However, as institutional domains become autonomous, caste-like intra-institutional stratification patterns become difficult to protect. Educational entrepreneurs begin to operate on their own value-orientations and ideologies, and it becomes less likely that global patterns will simply be reproduced because entrepreneurial factions are more probable. To be sure, global patterns do not just fade away or become replaced, but they can become increasingly challenged and specific institutions can employ achievement based criteria to reconfigure the way social relationships are constructed and the way stratification exists. Coupled with potential social movements from the peripheries of institutional environments that are not destructive or focused on usurpation but rather reorienting the flow of resources, and institutional domains can become sites of social change; sometimes radical social change.

## Institutional Power, Wealth, and Prestige

We are finally in a position to talk about sociology's "holy trinity" of inequality and the production and distribution of symbolic media. That is, although global power, wealth, and prestige remain interesting to inequality research, institutional domains erect their own social orders that place a premium on institution-specific power, wealth, and prestige. Admittedly, the global and institutional forms, as we will see shortly, have key relationships with each other. Therefore, when we talk of institutional power, wealth, and prestige we are talking about the right to monopolize production and distribution of media (institutional power), access to and the amount of media one possesses (institutional wealth), and those who have the right to determine the standards by which media are evaluated and deemed qualitatively better than other manifestations (institutional prestige). These three axes are independent of each other, but are clearly interrelated. Having a lot of *learning* means one is "wealthy" in an educational sense, but does not speak to their relative educational power or prestige. Indeed, they might be a trivia whiz, yet have no control over producing *learning*, or no influence over others because their *learning* is not qualitatively distinct. Of course, entrepreneurs, by definition, possess institutional power as they are the producers and distributors of media, and, as such, they likely are wealthy as well, but they may or may not be considered prestigious as media vary in terms of quality. Additionally, the discussion on hoarding underscores the fact that institutional prestige and standards of quality are not always the same as power and wealth, although it is true that they overlap.

One of the key reasons for distinguishing these three types of axes of institutional stratification speaks to the different motivations actors have in pursuing a particular medium (see Gerth and Mills 1953:19–34, 165–91, especially, for a lost, yet fascinating discussion of institutions, motivation, and character structures). Some actors are interested in the accumulation of media as either a means to accessing another institution's medium or as an end itself. Knowing a lot might be edifying, even to someone outside of a formal academic field or collective. Other actors desire authority and power, which often brings wealth. Being able to command an audience or make collective binding decisions is gratifying to some people, while scary to others. Finally, influence and status seeking is a universal feature of all groups/subgroups (Lenski 1966; Boehm 1999). There is something special about being an influential person or group, as it gives you the unique right to steer things without using material incentives or the threat of possible force. Instead, prestige brings the bearer self-worth and self-efficacy, those around him/her pride and residuals of prestige, and for observers positive affect linked to being near the source of social esteem.

A second reason draws our attention to the situational side of stratification (Collins 2000a). When social science focuses only on global patterns, we miss the trees in the forest; after all, it is the trees that mean the most to actual individuals experiencing each situation. People do not ordinarily see global patterns because they are too busy living their lives (Turner 2010b). When a man enters an economic firm or religious congregation that is led by women and the staff is predominantly women, his experience is very different as are theirs from the more global patterns of resource inequality. Pointing this out neither minimizes the effects global patterns have on those women's life chances or that man's opportunities, nor ignores the way he may try to carry these global status beliefs into daily encounters. What it does is speak to the reality that institutional settings offer numerous combinations of stratification rooted less in global patterns, while creating miniature life-worlds or ephemeral encounters that conform as much, if not more so, to institutional standards than strictly global ones (Goffman 1967; Luhmann 1995; Collins 2004; Summers-Effler 2002).

An essential distinction should be made: institutional power and the generalized symbolic medium of *power* are not the same. The former refers to specific actors in specific situations using their position to control and coordinate the behavior and attitudes of subordinates. It relies on direct exchange, personal relationships, and the like. To be sure, when these actors have greater access to *power* as a symbolic medium, then their position is enhanced and they enter a broader normative framework of exchange. *Power*, as a generalized symbolic medium, assumes a universal system of social relations founded on generalized commitments and obligations, and which is governed by a "code of generalized symbols which guides" choices by delimiting selections across a range of settings "abstracted from the initial contexts" of power relations (Luhmann 1979:111). The same distinction can obviously be made between institutional wealth and the economic medium *money*. A father, for instance, may say he is "rich" because he has lots of *love* and his family is *loyal*, but this says nothing of his position within the economic world and his relative access to *money*. Of course, as we shall see access to media overlap and intersect in ways that create matrices that define a person or group's basic societal position.

## INTER-INSTITUTIONAL STRATIFICATION

In the following section, the way intra-institutional stratification "bleeds" through structural linkages connecting myriad institutional domains is explored. This discussion begins with an analysis of the transformation of institutional power, wealth, and prestige into inter-institutional power, wealth, and prestige. This will be followed by a close look at the dynamics of cool media in the construction of broader stratification systems by using *power* and *money* in the U.S. as examples. Finally, the importance of media across institutional boundaries will be addressed in terms of conflicts over who has "ownership" over one medium or the other; this particular conflict tends to symbolically undergird most conflicts that manifest themselves in material and structural ways. It is really a struggle over the definition of the situation and who propagates the legitimate vision of reality.

## The Diffusion of Power, Wealth, and Prestige

What are the wider implications given the development and centrality of intra-institutional forms of power, wealth, and prestige? Given the dynamics of media, especially their temperature, the tendency for cooler media to penetrate other domains and fuse with other cool media, and the prevalence of meta-ideologies that give added texture and shape to all institutional domains in an institutional complex, intra-institutional power, wealth, and prestige can be transformed into *inter*-institutional forms. Indeed, when possessing the right to produce or distribution a particular institution's medium of exchange has consequences across institutional boundaries, institutional power becomes increasingly diffuse and meaningful beyond the boundaries of the institution in which the medium is created; or, when possessing a lot of one medium allows the possessor to exchange and communicate more easily and frequently across institutional boundaries that institutional wealth becomes diffuse and the medium becomes a key form of inter-institutional currency; and, finally, it occurs when one medium becomes highly valued and its possessors influential in other institutional settings that institutional prestige becomes inter-institutional prestige.

In hunter-gatherer societies and horticultural chiefdoms, kinship *loyalty* was a key medium of inter-institutional power, wealth, and prestige. That is, the greater the number of people *loyal* to a chief, the more his commands would be followed, the more likely he was to possess signs of wealth like land, wives, and yams or other staple crops, and, finally, the more influential he became as others looked to him as arbiter of disputes and so on (Earle 1991). Moreover, *loyalty* became a currency across domains as he had political and economic rights that others did not; he or a close relative was typically the principal religious actor; he was often given temporary authorization to make legal decisions. *Loyalty* became a mode of inter-institutional stratification, and the loss of *loyalty* had serious ramifications for an individual's ability to sustain the social order. In modern nation-states, *loyalty* still has some inter-institutional consequences as impersonal social relationships in autonomous polities and economies often develop norms of reciprocity and obligation in ways akin to kinship relations (Blau 1964). *Loyalty* becomes key to expanding *power*, as well as obtaining *power*, and it is *loyalty* that often contributes to "climbing the ladder," although with less equivalence than in polity.

## The Problem of Cool Media: *Power* and *Money* in the U.S.

Some media, particularly cool media, can become generalized sources of inter-institutional power, wealth, and prestige in ways that create meta-markets, or inter-institutional exchange systems that regularize certain types of transactions and which overlay the unique realities of a given institutional domain. In the modern U.S., for instance, power and money are generalized sources of institutional power and wealth, and thus create meta-markets, which shape the actions, exchanges, and communication within most other institutions. Luhmann (2012:213–4) speaks, for instance, of the "legal coding of power," or what Weber referred to as the emergence and institutionalization of legal-rational authority. As the polity becomes the domain in which the legitimate use of coercive force is monopolized, the medium of power—which again is a normative system of social relations founded on commitments and obligations—becomes a highly coveted source of authority across other institutional domains in which entrepreneurs look to link the core to the environment, in part, through domination. Instead of legitimating the use of violence, which would be destabilizing anyway, political entrepreneurs create meta-markets of power transformed into franchised authority (Abrutyn and Turner 2011). Political entrepreneurs give franchised authority to kinship entrepreneurs in exchange for loyalty to the state and its laws and money in the form of taxes; the same type of exchange goes to legal entrepreneurs in exchange for legitimation of political claims through independent judicial decisions and the continued legal coding of power; economic entrepreneurs give money in the form of taxes and campaign contributions, as well as indirectly through the provision of employment positions that facilitate money in taxes from kinship actors. These exchanges become standardized in ways that erect normative frameworks for exchange and communication across domains (Parsons and Smelser 1956). *Money*, like *power*, builds links between the economy and other domains through meta-markets. Because *money* becomes the primary source of acquiring goods and services necessary for subsistence in societies with autonomous economies, all other domains become tightly linked as all other actors *need* money to survive as humans. Legal entrepreneurs provide *justice* and *conflict resolution* for *money*, medical entrepreneurs *health care*, sports entrepreneurs *competitiveness*, and political entrepreneurs *power*. As such, all actors see part of their daily actions, exchanges, and communication affected by the value-orientations, ideologies, norms, and strategies revolving around *money*. Thus, more professors are oriented toward educational and scientific norms than not, which gives a sense of predictability and stability to everyday encounters in either domain while also giving observers a keen tool of evaluation to judge real or perceived corruption in behavior or attitudes. Nevertheless, it would be naïve to think collectives like Harvard or Yale, which have far greater access to *money* in the form of grants or alumni contributions or *power* in the form of political ties to think tanks, are not affected by having better position in these meta-markets; moreover, it would be inaccurate to think that many of their incumbents are not motivated, in part, by their greater access to these extra-institutional resources.

In essence, on the one hand, through these meta-markets and interchanges, autonomous institutional domains are further integrated and a shared cultural reality, via meta-ideologies, is imposed across domain. On the other hand, the imposition of meta-ideologies and the construction of meta-markets serves as a reminder of the global stratification system and the sources of true societal influence. Those in the polity or economy, in the modern U.S., are in a unique position to shape the reality of a larger swath of the population than any other institutional entrepreneurs. Their media, currently, are the most valued and desired, and thus they have the special ability to "steer" the society in one direction or the next.[6]

## Struggles Over Ownership

One final dynamic of inter-institutional relationships is worth examining briefly. Institutional entrepreneurs and other types of actors do not reside within a static system that they simply accept. Resistance, in the form of subjective conversion—for instance, the example in Chapter 5 regarding the *sacralization* of *money* (Belk and Wallendorf 1990; Mundey, Davidson, and Herzog 2011)—is one strategy. But entrepreneurs are often engaged in much broader "campaigns" for position. What is at stake is a seat at the table in ways that "steer" society, thus the rewards are great when attainable. Continued relevance is a secondary concern entrepreneurs have, especially those who feel what is or was their domain is being usurped. Kinship entrepreneurs—for example, parents—often feel threatened by the penetration of political entrepreneurs who can delimit their kinship counterpart's authority by legislating the scope of their power.

Throughout, a particularly salient struggle has been alluded to that has manifested itself over the last two centuries between what we might call *cosmological competitors* (Abrutyn 2013a). Cosmological entrepreneurs are principally concerned with *truth*, and symbolic and emotional bases of power. They look to construct a normative framework of action, exchange, and communication in which "the selection of information is attributed to *none of the participants*," but rather to some transcendent or external force (Luhmann 2012:203). Religious entrepreneurs, for example, look to the sacred and supranatural to provide *truth*, positing they are merely the perceptive medium through which *truth* is interpreted, or, more accurately, professed to the masses. Conversely, scientific entrepreneurs look to the scientific method, the five senses, and appeals to reason/logic to "discover" knowledge that is universal and has nothing to do with the value-orientations of the scientist. Both, at one time or another, were labeled "they" by the laity and referenced as a collective body of experts and authority. Over the last 200 years, scientific entrepreneurs successfully secured their independence (for a review, see Gaukroger 2006) and because of their objective track-record (e.g., cars start, planes land correctly, weather is predicted somewhat accurately, and so on) have temporarily won this battle in the eyes of most economic and political entrepreneurs; the former use them for new products, technologies, accounting, and so on, whereas the latter use them as experts to develop policies (or counter-policies) as well as enhance military capabilities. For the vast majority of humans in the U.S., and throughout most of the non-European world, the general lack of access to *power* and *money* and the inability of scientific *truth* to speak to the metaphysical problems of suffering, evil, and impending mortality have contributed to the rise of religio-kinship movements that fuse *loyalty* to *sacredness/piety* in the struggle for greater moral authority and *truth*. Not surprisingly, many of these battles are being fought in the language of science given its success and persuasiveness (e.g., creationism became *intelligent design*). Make no mistake: this is a struggle over the legitimate monopoly over the production and distribution of truth, and although this is a particularly salient struggle it is neither the only one nor, at all times, the most important one.

## LABORATORIES OF SOCIAL CHANGE

Institutions also become sites of potential global social change. Thus, despite there being more centers of domination as Weber feared, as the number of autonomous institutions increases, the overall level of societal stratification and inequality decrease as (1) the *number, type, and quantity of valued resources* increases; (2) *intra-institutional patterns of stratification* grow more salient and situational than broader patterns; (3) more *boundaries overlap* and create more complex corporate units and individual identities; (4) more *paths or channels of mobility* emerge; and (5) more *parameters intersect* as categoric units previously segregated interact more frequently (Abrutyn and Turner 2011; Turner 2011). Each of these dimensions are relatively independent of each other, while none of them is guaranteed owing to the fact that autonomy is uneven and resources can clearly be hoarded. As the institutional complex of a given society gives way to a greater number of autonomous institutions, tremendous pressures and opportunities for previously oppressed groups to at least join the dominant society arise, while also generating powerful integrative forces predicated on these groups having access to some channels or paths instead of none. Let's take a look at each piece of the process and flesh out the argument a bit more.

### Growth of the Pie

For many sociologists, resources like power are thought of in terms of a "zero-sum" game: if someone gets a certain amount of a given resource, someone else must lose some access to that resource. Michael Mann (1986) argued against this simplistic view, noting that as societies have gotten larger in terms of territory, political complexity, and population, a resource as scarce as power grows concomitantly. There is more of it to go around, and there are more groups potentially ascendant as a result (Eisenstadt

1963). In previous chapters, it was argued that institutional autonomy is a process by which an institutional domain grows relatively distinct from other domains, formulates an intra-institutional structure and culture organized around and by the circulation of a generalized symbolic medium of exchange, and regulates this circulation via a discrete system(s) of authority. By definition, then, autonomy generates an expansion in the available resources in a given society, as well as diversifies the type of resources that are valued. To be sure, a resource may derive the lion share of its value *inside* the institutional domain and, hence, is limited in terms of who one can exchange, yet this delimitation does not detract from the fact that there are simply more resources to attempt to secure.

The cynic would argue that this expansion of resources means more forms of inequality and domination; he or she would be right to some extent. I caution, however, that the question of inequality is not as simple as an "it exists or not" answer. More resources mean less "zero-sum" monopolies, and greater distribution. And although the possibility of correlations between being white or male and having disproportionate access to a given (or myriad) resource(s) is real and sometimes the case, it is also clear that stratification in most "developed" nations has declined from what many experts considered the golden age of inequality (Lenski 1966). This trend has been affected most by the growth in the number of autonomous institutions and, thereby, the number of media circulating increases as does the number of goods, services, and other resources that actors can acquire or, at the very least, pursue.

Consider, for example, the contemporary U.S. versus, say, ancient Rome. In Rome, the primary media of exchange were *power* and *loyalty*, with *money*, *sacredness/piety*, and perhaps *justice* being less valued, but important resources. *Learning* was deeply embedded in *sacredness*, and lawyering was really a side gig for Senators—a pastime, as strange as that may seem (Kunkel 1966). Most often, *power* was the dominant medium for valued positions, influence (prestige), and wealth. In the U.S. today, *power* retains its value, but is buttressed and perhaps surpassed *money*. But, there are other paths of mobility such as legal entrepreneurs monopolizing *justice*, athletes *competitiveness*, or doctors *health care*; all of these latter types of media can be converted into salaries to survive and, in some cases, greater amounts of societal power. At the same time, media once valued as high as *power*, such as *sacredness/piety*, has become localized and embedded in religious or kinship exchanges, and rarely, other domains.

## Why Intra-Institutional Patterns Matter

In small communities, which church you belong to (and, therefore, the amount of *sacredness/piety* you have access to) matters far more than a person's *power* or *money* in determining the amount of *influence* they can acquire; in the economy, *money* is the most relevant distinction between individuals and groups, as is *power* in the polity. Lawyers are ranked in terms of their success in court as much if not more so than their money, and judges based on their legal knowledge and court record more than power. Artists are evaluated based on their aestheticism, whereas athletes ranked by their competitiveness. There are obviously other media that help shape these evaluations, but superstar basketball players like Kobe Bryant or Michael Jordan are considered above their peers not because of their salaries, but because of their competitive drives—which, incidentally, bring higher salaries.

As the focus shifts to intra-institutional patterns, broader patterns do not disappear, but often fade into the background. In sports, the specter of race occasionally becomes salient, though its importance is always an open question. Black athletes are predominantly paid by white owners, meaning the relationship remains tinged with racial dimensions, but *money* is the great leveler as players are increasingly in a position to buy in to ownership or, in Michael Jordan's case, become a majority owner in a team. Jordan has shifted his alliance to ownership, as the recent National Basketball Association's lockout (2011) clearly illustrated.

## The Ambiguity of Boundary Overlaps

As the number of autonomous institutions increases, so does the likelihood of more complex and diverse boundary overlaps. In Chapter 2, I examined the dynamics of institutional environments due to overlapping boundaries. Two key consequences derive from overlapping boundaries. First, those corporate and individual actors found in the interstices of institutional environments are less monitored and sanctioned because the rules are vague. Moreover, commitment to a single institutional domain becomes complicated because of the ambiguous reach of authority systems. Second, these actors are further "protected" by the fact that multiple media circulate rapidly within the overlaps and are often fused together in unique ways. Social movements, novelty, and new entrepreneurs often are found in these overlaps first because of the opportunity to mix and match values, norms, and ideologies.

It is here, then, that movements pushing for greater rights, more mobility, and greater resources are likely to appear. Using the ideologies available in new ways creates one of the key mechanisms necessary for social change: a counter-narrative meant to expose the weaknesses of the existing dominant narrative of social inequality, while positing a better, more fair vision of reality (Snow and Soule 2010). Moreover, boundary overlaps increase the chances that a higher proportion of heterogeneous interactions (what Turner 2010a means by "intersecting parameters") will replace their homogeneous counterparts and encourage the disconfirmation of status beliefs and the declining salience of certain types of categoric distinctions (Blau 1977).[7] Furthermore, overlapping boundaries become conduits of meta-ideologies that can be altered to reflect the changes on the ground:

if women increasingly succeed in non-traditional roles, and groups advocating and pressing women's success further emerge, meta-ideologies will begin to incorporate these changes. It is likely a gradual change, which may make it seem as if it is not happening at all, but the U.S.'s political or legal system looks a lot different today than 30 years ago. Sandra Day O'Conner's legacy is embedded in the fabric of the legal narrative of this nation as much as Albright, Pelosi, Rice, and Hillary Clinton's impacts as Secretaries of State will likely be deeply ingrained in the story. These gains predate what will most likely be a threshold that brings about much more rapid change, but until that threshold is reached status expectations change at what seems like a snail's pace.

## Paths to Mobility

As the number of autonomous institutions in a given society increases, the number of paths to mobility grows parallel. Becoming a doctor may not net someone much *power*, but it brings a fair amount of *money* and even more society-wide *prestige/influence*; professors lack *power* and *money* (generally speaking), but the PhD is generally regarded as prestigious and, thus, *influential*. Where there are two paths, such as those found in Rome or Mesopotamia, the frequency, intensity, and speed of mobility is curtailed. Achievement was either secured through political mobility or kinship mobility on the village or neighborhood level. The latter was predicated on ascriptive characteristics: one's lineage, their age, their perceived wisdom, and the number of rivals; the former type of mobility was restricted, in part, to lineage as well, but was far more achieved: success on the battlefield, loyalty to the king, the purchase of titles, ownership of land, and so forth. Ultimately, either path was narrow and limiting.

In the U.S., it is obvious that there are greater numbers of paths that bring happiness, feelings of self-efficacy, situational and local prestige (*influence*), varying degrees of wealth, and situational and/or local *power*. This is a tremendous pressure release on the polity in particular, because it ensures a degree of stability in the masses conferring legitimacy on the ruling elite. Even if political *power* is beyond the reach of most, at least medical or legal paths remains open for *money* and *prestige*; at least artistic, athletic, media/entertainment, and scientific paths exist for *prestige* and some *money/power*; and at least educational attainment ensures some basic mobility for even the most negatively privileged status groups in the U.S.

The key to mobility causing larger social change in stratification comes from credentialism, or the standardization of requisite criteria of mobility (Abrutyn and Turner 2011; Turner 2010a). Indeed, the power of media such as *money* or *learning* is their *generalizability* across domains in their objectified forms. A dollar bill, especially with the advent of the Internet, is a dollar bill regardless of race or gender. The more *money* a person can secure, the less salient their categoric distinctions become.[8]

The same point is true about college degrees as sources of *learning*. There may, indeed, be some remnants of institutionalized barriers to mobility for, say, black Americans, but the degree holds the same value for a white or black graduate of Harvard. That black Americans hold these degrees, and that these degrees (or those from similar prestigious universities) have translated into blacks securing better positions, demonstrates the changes. Has the civil rights movement reached its ultimate goal of equality? Absolutely not; however, the degree's value stands and the fact that we can point to some successes is indicative of the mobility of some black Americans. The more this happens, the more heterogeneous interactions become, the less salient these categoric distinctions are. It takes time, but it has already begun.

## Intersecting Parameters

I have discussed how intersection of parameters affects inequality in previous chapters, and throughout the discussion. Essentially, as Abrutyn and Turner remark, the extent to which mobility, boundary overlap, and the increasing salience of intra-institutional patterns of stratification

> promote intersection of parameters marking categoric unit membership across the full spectrum of the division of labor in corporate units and across all institutional domains, it (a) reduces the potential tensions inherent in inequalities of resource shares, (b) reduces the salience of stigmatizing status beliefs derived from the meta-ideology legitimating the stratification system, and (c) increases the salience of institutional ideologies and norms relative to status beliefs about members of categoric units. In so doing, intersection increases the common culture regulating actions among diverse individuals at different locations in the divisions of labor of corporate units across differentiated institutional domains. (2011:293)

In other words, the blurrier the correlation between a given categoric distinction (e.g., sex or race) and a graduated (or set of graduated) parameters become, the less clear the stratification system becomes in terms of ascriptive markers. First, perceptions change as meta-ideologies concerning the importance of *learning* or the "color-blindness" of *money* circulate across boundaries and through multiple corporate actors. These ideologies nearly always reflect some sliver of reality, as minorities do become increasingly mobile, if only on a case-by-case basis; as noted above, these seemingly small gains eventually lead to thresholds that turn into rapid change. Second, as success stories grow more visible, status beliefs become tenuous in the face of massive disconfirmation. Has race become inconsequential because Obama was elected? Of course not. But that is not really the correct question. The better questions should be (1) did Obama's election change the black community's aspirations, belief in the system, and motivation to seek mobility, and (2) how has his election effected the white community? If the answer to the first question is in the positive, then we should see some effects over time regardless of the answer to the second question. If the answer to the second question is even slightly in the positive—for example, some proportion has become more supportive of black efficacy—then, again, we should see gradual intersection of parameters and a retreat of previous status beliefs about laziness, inferiority, and so on.

At the same time, it shifts the focus from the salience of categoric units rooted in general patterns of stratification, to achieved categories such as "college graduates." Again, I caution that the change has been slow, and black college grads have been declining over the last three or more decades, as have the number of white male grads. Yet, the distinction has become salient enough that the Obama has been campaigning on a policy that sees businesses tightly linked to community colleges in hopes of providing the skills necessary to meet a rapidly changing technological environment. As the salience of intra-institutional categories dwarf broader nominal distinctions like sex or race, these latter types produce fewer problems. To be sure, the distance between the success the Italians or Jews have enjoyed since the 1950s and that of African Americans is still quite wide. But, any honest assessment would have to conclude that strides have been made towards closing this gap; and, barring unforeseen catastrophic events, this trend should only continue into the 21st century as the U.S. becomes less white in general.

## CONCLUSION

In essence, a unidimensional view of institutions or structural/cultural spheres as stabilizing forces of cultural reproduction and changing only under evolutionary pressures for adaptation is no longer tenable. To be sure, they do reproduce culture, but one cannot take for granted who controls the production of culture, the self-interested side of cultural production, and the way stratification matters in institutional analyses. That being said, a one-dimensional analysis of macro-level reality that relies on outdated monolithic notions of inequality and power is also problematic. Thus, a robust theory of institutions requires consideration of (1) the way intra-institutional stratification forms and becomes central to the reality of those regularly or only occasionally inhabiting the institutional core or environment, (2) the sources of intra-institutional stratification and how these often are more salient than global patterns, (3) the dynamics in which some institution's patterns of stratification spread across boundaries and (4) often become grafted onto more global patterns, and, finally, (5) how institutional stratification systems can become sources of change that reconfigure how societal stratification systems look and feel. This chapter elucidated these dynamics in hopes of fostering a more judicious, complete institutional analysis; one that takes into consideration power and conflict in a serious manner while acknowledging that institutions do contribute to phenomenological feels of stability and ontological reality; even in the face of sometimes massive inequalities and discrepant objective realities.

# 7 Considering the Consequences of a New Theory of Institutions

A theory is only as useful as its explanatory power. Thus far, we have gone as far as possible in positing a theory of institutions and their autonomy, the actors responsible for carving out autonomy, the ecological dynamics, and a more descriptive examination of the internal structure and culture of autonomous institutions, including the emergence of a stratification system. The questions we now turn our attention to concern the consequences autonomy has for explaining and understanding the various levels of social reality. Some of this discussion has been touched on briefly throughout the previous chapters—some in explicit ways and others implicitly. Other pieces will be entirely new and, hopefully, insightful to sociologists in a wide ranging set of fields. Hence, when possible, the analysis will draw clear links to other traditions or areas of sociological theory that complement each other.

## MACRO-LEVEL CONSEQUENCES

### A Slightly Different Evolutionary Sociology

Old structural-functionalist analyses have long relied on evolutionist analogies to think about society—for example, the organismic analogy (Spencer 1897) or differentiation-integration-specialization (Parsons 1964; Radcliffe-Brown 1965). The underlying argument, of course, was that *societies* have needs and certain structures have to "evolve" to help the *supra*organism adapt to environmental changes; religion, for example, was a key integrative cultural system that had to keep pace with environmental and, eventually, other subsystems' changes (Bellah 1964). Neo-evolutionary social scientists have strongly critiqued this type of evolutionism by rejecting its teleological progressivism (Sanderson 2007), noting its strong affinity to developmental biology and not biological evolution (Blute 2010), and offering, instead, a revivified and rehabilitated functionalism through emphases on selection and the multilinearity of sociocultural evolution (Turner and Maryanski 2008; Turner 2010a; Abrutyn and Lawrence 2010). Political evolution, then, is not about a societal need for goal attainment but rather occurs when certain exigencies emerge that create selection pressures that may *or may not* be responded to adaptively (in the short or long run); specific political evolution does not assume a direction, *per se*, as it is subject to numerous sociocultural and historical conditions impossible to predict. From a general standpoint, political evolution is the process by which the political institution becomes the autonomous physical, temporal, social, and symbolic space for political entrepreneurship and increasingly distinct political decisions and goals (Abrutyn 2013b). That is, the macro-level of social reality is reconfigured as polities evolve such that, in the case of the first polities some 5,000 years ago (Eisenstadt 1963), macro-level political spheres emerge side-by-side kinship domains. The theory of institutions posited in previous chapters, then, presupposes a slightly different historiography that considers general evolutionary trends in light of historical moments in which one institution or another becomes autonomous for the first time, marking a qualitative change in human organization and culture (Abrutyn 2009b). At the same time, the theory forces us to consider how institutions evolve within a given society over time, as *specific* sociocultural is, in part, a process by which institutions expand or contract in their autonomy and, thereby, have consequences for the case one is studying (cf. Abrutyn 2013a, b).

In addition, the process by which political, or any type of institutional, evolution occurs is driven by the efforts of institutional entrepreneurs who undertake institutional projects aimed at institutionalizing new frameworks that supposedly resolve problems they identify (Eisenstadt 1964b; Colomy and Rhoades 1994; Colomy 1998). Eisenstadt originally conceptualized entrepreneurs as the sociocultural analogy to biological mutations, hence they are the source of evolution *variation*, in that they are the innovators, articulators, and architects of *qualitative* structural and cultural transformations (Abrutyn 2013a).[1] Selection, which is separate from variation, comes via two types of process: *Spencerian* and *Durkheimian* (Turner and Maryanski 2008). The first type of selection is closely analogous to Lamarckian selection and occurs when exogenous and/or endogenous forces put enough pressure on existing structural and cultural configurations—or, the pressures are perceived as real—that an individual or set of individuals begin to innovate, or those who had long been innovating, but had generally gone unnoticed, become salient (cf. Abrutyn 2013b). Put another way, in the face of pressures—that is, when those pressures are perceived as being real, or at the very least proxies to these pressures like the threat of or real decline in standard of living—extant structural and cultural solutions, posited by real actors, require adjustment or new ones need to be created to resolve these pressures (Nolan and Lenski 2009; Turner 2010a). With every solution, new problems emerge that further push the group toward potential collapse. The second type of selection mechanism, *Durkheimian*, is closer to Darwinian natural selection in that *competition* is the central force underlying qualitative changes: in the face of scarce resources within a given niche or field, some collectives are better fit in terms of being better positioned for resource appropriation, better skilled in terms of producing superior goods or services, or just luckier (Durkheim 1893; Hawley 1986). The ensuing competition between collectives leads to some either becoming more specialized within the niche as a strategy of survival, diversifying to more dynamically compete, seek out a new or join an existing niche, or risk "extinction" (Hannan and Freeman 1977; McPherson 1983, 1988). Spencerian evolution tends to capture entrepreneurship in terms of creating new autonomous institutions, whereas Durkheimian evolution tends to capture entrepreneurial innovation and quantitative growth *within* institutional domains as new fields and niches form.

In either case, we see a dual logic to institutional projects that moves evolutionary sociology away from progressivism and a belief that change is adaptive and equilibrium is desirable. Projects and entrepreneurship both have a self-interested dimension and collective orientations; although neither can be parsed out from a given project, projects can be primarily oriented towards one or the other. Thus, *adaptivity* and *fitness* have less to do with a society's adaptivity and more to do with a group or set of interrelated groups trying to preserve and expand their cultural base by building discrete spheres of social action, exchange, and communication which reproduce and reinforce their cultural practices, while sustaining their existence over the course of numerous generations (e.g., Wilson 2002; Abrutyn 2013a). Institutional evolution is the process by which entrepreneurs and their new or recombined cultural patterns become the backbone in the "formulation of an innovative project" that, through a concerted effort to institutionalize it, carves out enough "free space between the entrepreneurs' actions and the macro environments in which they are pursued" and, thereby, imbues "the innovators efforts with a degree of creativity and voluntarism" by the attainment of some degree of independence (Colomy and Kertzmann 1995:194). The unit of selection, then, is the *group*, or entrepreneurial unit and their cultural innovations; the level of evolution is the *institutional domain*, and adaptivity is judged by the degree and length of time with which the entrepreneurial unit's structural and cultural elements survive and the entrepreneur can sustain their newfound position.

This type of evolutionary sociology is not entirely new. Some social scientists studying religious evolution have moved toward an explicit or implicit "entrepreneurial" group selectionist argument (Eisenstadt 1982, 1984, 1990; Stark 2006, 2007; also Stark and Bainbridge 1996; Abrutyn 2013a, b). David Sloan Wilson (2002), for example, provides a brilliant reexamination of Weber's classic Protestant Ethic thesis by applying a group selectionist argument to Calvinists and their doctrine as the cultural "meme" that powerfully integrates adherents in ways that improve the chances of their survival in the threat of extinction from competitors or threatened elites; this theoretical strategy may seem familiar, as Weber (crudely) applied it to the implausible survival of Jews despite numerous attempts to eradicate or assimilate them (1917–9 [1952]). Additionally, this strategy elaborates a synthesis of Durkheimian (1912) concerns with how close a moral community is drawn to each other through repeated ritual encounters that crystallize a *conscience collective* by imbuing it with *collective effervescence* (cf. Collins 2004) and Weber's (1922) interests in a charismatic cultural carrier group's struggle against competitors for power and prestige (cf. Eisenstadt 1989). The path to entrepreneurial success is a product of their being in the right place at the right time and the skill they possess in articulating cultural resonant and persuasive frames of interpretation (Snow and Soule 2010). Moreover, their success depends on existing elites "aiding" in their selection by "elevating" their status or trying to destroy it (Colomy 1998).

### *Institutions and Evolutionary Problems*

The question, then, is what types of exigencies lead to institutional evolution and greater or lesser autonomy? Some basic macro-level dynamics help us understand institutional evolution (Turner 1995; Nolan and Lenski 2009): exigencies surrounding population growth and density (and the often overlooked rapid *de*population) have clearly been prime movers in some historical cases of evolution (Adams 1966; Tainter 1988; Yoffee and Cowgill 1988; Stein and Rothman 1994). As have problems rooted in production, distribution, and reproduction (Boserup 1965; Cohen 1977; Hawley 1986), and, of course, problems centered around power (Spencer 1897; Carneiro 1978; Mann 1986). These are macro-level forces because they create specific exigencies, sometimes exogenous and other times endogenous to the group, that put pressure on individuals as well as the group to innovate or face potential demise, collapse, or conquest. While innovations often solve these problems, they also transform the social organization and relationships of a group that put pressure on innovators to begin to find new ways to integrate the social and functional divisions of labor formed through innovations, legitimate their claims to power or authority, and regulate the flow of resources.

Institutions become the "warehouses" of these past solutions and present adjustments, and the laboratories in which entrepreneurs try to resolve the macro-level exigencies and intra-institutional exigencies related to integration, regulation, and legitimation. Their adaptivity, again, has less to do with making a society more "fit," but rather has to do with an entrepreneur solidifying its innovations, spreading or imposing them on a significant proportion of the population in order to control or reconfigure the flow of human and material resource so that they can sustain their existence, and, finally, creating enough independence to be able to monopolize their practices and knowledge, the right to develop and disseminate them, and the training of new entrepreneurs. Evolution occurs as institutions become more autonomous and the social landscape is changed, for better or for worse, for all or most humans within the political, geographic, and cultural boundaries of the society.

Understanding adaptivity, then, is more complicated then structural-functionalists have often made it seem. Thus, political evolution *was not* really adaptive for the entire population, but rather for the ruling elite and the growing landed gentry, and to a lesser extent, the remaining free farmers who were often used by the ruling elite against the aristocracy to maintain their autonomy and break or weaken ascribed ties (Eisenstadt 1977; Eisenstadt, Abitol and Chazan 1987). Indeed, it was *adaptive* for a small segment of the population (Fried 1967), yet it did have the collective benefit of allowing for larger populations as risk and economic management (Lipinski 1979), as well as centralizing defense against external threats (Adams 1966), and public works like irrigation and canals were coordinated (Postgate 1977).[2] As an institution becomes more autonomous, the question of sociocultural evolution takes on an interesting dimension. It forces the historical social scientist to consider the difference between the unit of selection, the entrepreneur, and the unit of evolution, the institution. Adaptivity is measured in three ways: the degree to which (1) the entrepreneurs succeeds in spreading their cultural patterns across a population, (2) they and their cultural pattern survive, and (3) the population benefits versus is harmed.

### *Adaptivity*

What makes institutional autonomy adaptive for the entrepreneur and, potentially, the larger society? For the entrepreneur, autonomy means greater freedom from external interference in their pursuit and realization of goals. The construction of an institutional core ensures some independence against other entrepreneurs, and gives them the physical and temporal space necessary to reproduce their practices as well as continue to develop new ones or hone old ones. It is also by carving out "free space" that new entrepreneurial project can be constructed that focus on expanding the domain's boundaries or, in many cases, adjusting and adapting to environmental changes. Theologians like Thomas Aquinas or the Pharisees in ancient Israel do not look to build new institutional domains, but rather adapt existing ones to changes in the environment that threaten the entrepreneur and the cultural patterns viability (Abrutyn 2013a). Their efforts may result in gradual changes that eventually add-up and reach a threshold in which the domain is qualitatively transformed, or as is often the case, their innovations are radical but couched in "conservative" ideological frames that link their projects to the immediate or ancient past, thus justifying massive changes.

How, then, does an entrepreneur's adaptivity and the growth in institutional autonomy lead to a more adapted society? Through three interrelated routes: differentiation of space, greater potential for creativity and innovation, and reduction in competition. In Luhmann's (2004) elucidation of law, he underscored the importance of subsystem formation and autonomy for the differentiation of temporality. By handing the problem of conflict resolution over to a distinct institutional domain (law), time becomes structured more complexly in ways that are beneficial. A conflict that does not have an immediate solution, but which generates powerful emotional reactions as it violates numerous moral and legal norms, is potentially dangerous for stability, as people are liable to act in unpredictable and impulsive ways that subvert the logic of *justice*. By subjecting it to a distinct procedural process that stretches out the time from the point of the conflict to its resolution, it reduces the complexity of the environment by structuring the internal temporal world of law and giving people time to "cool off." By the time a decision is reached, the immediate intensity of emotions are less inflamed, and although people will judge how fair or unfair, just or unjust the legal decision is, the probability that unpredictable, system-threatening behavior will occur is greatly reduced.

This same effect occurs as institutions differentiate physical, social, and symbolic space in ways that reduce environmental complexity by structuring systems more clearly and, by way, enhancing trust and commitment and assuaging ontological insecurity (Giddens 1984). Physical differentiation allows for the compartmentalization of roles and status that have a double function: it increases the probability of successful interaction, exchange, and communication by delimiting the expectations and behavioral repertoires needed in a given situation while also allowing certain expectations and behavioral repertoires to be generalized across situations, as subordinate generalized roles like student, client, or patient do carry some basic status beliefs across performances.

A greater number of autonomous institutions also means more centers of creativity, which increases the chances that exigencies will be perceived by one entrepreneur or another. Though there are no guarantees that problems will be identified, or identified correctly, or that once identified appropriate solutions will be found or can be found, it goes without saying that the more entrepreneurs and distinct cores, the more likely someone will perceive a problem as salient; the more ideas will be posited and dialectically lead to potentially novel solutions. Therefore, the structural and symbolic independence entrepreneurs are afforded in autonomous institutions gives them a decent chance of addressing these problems. In the negative, this was Mills' (1959) warning in *The Power Elite*: giving a small, homogenous categoric unit the ultimate right to make decisions for a rather large population increased the chances of failure and, possibly, collapse. One may very well point to the former Soviet Union as the realization of Mills' analysis: a tiny proportion of the political elite were making decisions, while their economic, legal, religious, and scientific counterparts had little freedom—both real and perceived—to address problems they were likely aware of. The lack of creativity probably doomed the Soviet Union long before its eventual collapse, which attests to the paradoxical adaptability of the political entrepreneurial unit and the maladaptivity of the political institution. Yet, where entrepreneurs are competing against each other, they often become highly creative as a means to expanding their influence (Eisenstadt 1982, 1984, 1990). This creativity can make a society more elastic and flexible in the face of new or amplified old exigencies.

The last source of adaptivity comes from Durkheim's (1893) *Division of Labor* thesis, which supposed that organic solidarity—or solidarity founded on mutual interdependence born of specialization in skills and niches—reduced conflicts and, to some degree, competition. In many ways, Durkheim was correct, but not because it leads to normative mechanisms of control, but rather techno-rational mechanisms of control. More institutional domains mean more specialized actors dealing with human concerns more efficaciously than a small set dealing with a greater number of problems. We become dependent on each other for the types of goods and services we provide, as do institutions become interdependent on each other for the types of things they do for the society at large (Parsons and Smelser 1956; Turner 1997). Moreover, each autonomous institutional domain has its own status hierarchy erected around the generalized symbolic medium that circulates throughout; in addition, secondary, foreign media come to form complementary and, sometimes, independent status hierarchies within these domains that increase the number of paths of mobility and resource attainment available to a significant proportion of the population. Where political *power* is the only path, or one of the only paths, fewer actors will be mobile and the amount of stratification will be sharply constructed. But, as Lenski (1966, 1970) has argued throughout his career, industrial and postindustrial societies are far less stratified than their agrarian counterparts precisely because there are more routes to power, prestige, and wealth. Becoming a professor may not bring a person as much power or wealth as the president or a CEO, but it does present more people with paths to getting some power and wealth, and certainly prestige. Regardless, then, of the degree to which stratification and inequality remain problems in modern societies, it is difficult to disagree that if societies were pyramids, societies with highly autonomous institutional complexes are much wider in pyramidal shape than those that lack autonomy.

## Domination and Conflict

Institutional autonomy, however, is not always beneficial to all humans, and it is the tenuous balance between costs and benefits that often dictate the degree to which a society is on the precipice of collapse or disintegration, in addition to the prevalence of what Durkheim would call pathologies. Two costs seem most essential to this balance: the number of sites and forms of domination and the amount of conflict between discrete entrepreneurs. The former weighs on the willingness of non-elite strata to participate in civil society and be motivated to engage in pro-social behavior, whether regulated by the polity and economy, or normatively sanctioned. The latter reflects the unity or lack thereof between elites and, therefore, the amount of stability a society will have in the face of various types of exigencies. Both of these dimensions have to be understood in *degree* and not kind, as elites are never fully in lockstep, nor are they in total disarray.

Weber (1946a, 1946b) wearily predicted that the future was rife with greater numbers of rationalized social spheres, each imposing a different, yet interrelated form of domination on the population (see also Habermas 1985). Perhaps an over-exaggeration, he was correct in positing the additive or multiplicative consequences of institutional autonomy: each new domain added another differentiated social sphere in which overlapping and unique rules constrained the actions and attitudes of social actors. The advent of the medical institution in the U.S. at the turn of the 19th century saw the gradual march toward specialists monopolizing *health care* to the point where medical entrepreneurs monopolize, to some degree, the right to medicines, the definition of what medicines are the legal or legitimate ones to take, and so forth. Previously, *health care* was the domain of the family, religion, and a whole host of medical actors competing for attention with each other (Starr 1982). It is, then, a new center of domination in that people unconsciously pursue medical experts for sickness, and when actors want to take their own lives because they are old or terminally ill, it is *against the law*. The same process led to legal entrepreneurs monopolizing law, *justice* and *conflict resolution*. Previously, kinship *justice* provided self-help for grievances (Black 1976; Yoffee 2000), as did religious entrepreneurs through various trials, whereas law as a weapon used by the rich against each other was a hobby for political entrepreneurs like the Senators in Rome (Kunkel 1966). With each new domain, come new entrepreneurs vying for all sorts of resources ranging from attention to material resources to human resources. Domination ranges from distraction, such as the allure of sports for fans who spend their *money*, strain their marriages, and live vicariously through their favorite athletes, all the way to restrictions in mobility, use and appropriation of resources, access to positions, and so on.

In addition to domination, Weber (1946b) also analogized these rationalizing spheres of social order as the domains of gods who jealously protect their boundaries while also looking to settle scores. Again, Weber is probably overly sensitized toward the conflicts between entrepreneurs, but his point remains important to understanding societal viability predicated on autonomous institutions. Where elites become bitterly divided, either within a single institution or between jealous entrepreneurs, societies become unstable and susceptible to all sorts of endogenous and exogenous forces (Skocpol 1979). Constant efforts to undermine each other, or in the worst cases, suppress autonomous cores to the logic of one domain and usurp the monopolies rival entrepreneurs have leads to inflexibility as problems are either ignored or ill-perceived, or insulated elites lack the creativity or freedom to innovate successfully or adapt on the fly. To be sure, it is the rare case in which we find anything approaching perfect harmony between disparate entrepreneurial units, yet tenuous power-sharing agreements are part and parcel of sociocultural evolution. Ambition or powerful external threats can ruin this precarious balance quite rapidly and lead to shaky social stability.

## Historical Phasing

One final point about macro-level social reality mentioned above, and worth elaborating a little bit more, derives from the idea that there is an historical "phasing" of institutional autonomy. Again, a clear distinction exists between general and specific sociocultural evolution, with the former referring to trends or patterns seen over the *longue dureé* versus the multilinear and historically contingent processes that shape individual cases in time and space (Sahlins 1960). The old evolutionisms in the social sciences generally posited a stage-model to capture the general path societies were on (Marx 1845–6 [1972]; Tylor 1878 [2008]; Parsons 1966). Although there is sometimes utility in looking at the *a posteriori* trajectory of humanity in terms of changes in subsistence technologies (Nolan and Lenski 2009) or abstraction of religious systems (Bellah 1964, 2012), these stage-models of societal development often ignore the specific and unpredictable *evolutionary* paths many societies take, as well as the possibility of retrogression, dedifferentiation, and contingencies (Steward 1955 [1972]; Yoffee 2005; Sanderson 2007; Turner and Maryanski 2009). Thus, recent neo-evolutionary efforts have focused on (1) identifying the general theoretical mechanisms like selection pressures or sources of variation while noting evolutionary research should consider multilinear contingencies (Lenski 2005; Richerson and Boyd 2005; Abrutyn 2013a, b), and (2) looking for general processes instead of general pathways (Chase-Dunn and Hall 1997; Turner 2010a), or offering historiographies bereft of stage-models (Sanderson 1999). These advances have been central to a more cogent and robust theory of sociocultural evolution.

In this spirit, the theory of institutions posited throughout suggests another direction sociocultural evolution can take that blends the general and specific analyses. On the one hand, it has been suggested implicitly and explicitly throughout that there is an historical phasing on autonomous institutions (see also Turner 2003; Abrutyn 2009b). For instance, polity appears to have been the first *autonomous* institution apart from kinship about 5,000 years ago (Eisenstadt 1963; Adams 1966; Johnson and Earle 2000). The conditions for parallel evolution have already been posited elsewhere (Sanderson 1999; Abrutyn and Lawrence 2010), which indicates an interesting point of general evolution. Yet, although the same types of conditions and pressures appear to have pushed polities to emerge as distinct spheres before other domains, the five or six cases—Egypt, Mesopotamia,

China, Mesoamerica, Peru, and perhaps the Indus Valley—all develop their own idiosyncratic polities, move in very divergent paths, have political entrepreneurs and other types of entrepreneurs create unique projects, and so on. The specific evolutionary stories are extremely different. The two stories, however, need not be contradictory as they both inform contemporary analyses of institutional autonomy and political evolution. The nation-state is the convergent form of organizational and normative political structure and culture (Meyer 1987), yet the path to the nation-state varies as does the actual content of each polity—for example, Iran is different from the U.S., which are both different from Japan. To use essentialist categories like "capitalism" or "democracy" or the "nation-state" is only useful in so far as we are identifying general institutional trends, but these categories lose much of their utility and interestingness when we consider specific cases (cf. Arrighi 2007).

The fact that there is possible historical phasing requires much more attention than we can give in this space. It alludes to some basic dynamics about humans that reveal the types of problems we are likely to face under similar conditions, as well as the creativity in and limitations to resolving them; the historical phasing of institutional autonomy offers a compelling and different, yet complementary story about human evolution. Moreover, it offers a fascinating frame for reinterpreting history as it pushes us to think in terms of patterns and convergence, while forcing us to consider ideographic, contingent divergent social change. It puts emphasis on agency, especially entrepreneurship that temporarily extricates itself from the problem of embedded actors being constrained in strategizing, being creative, and exhibiting volunteerism (Emirbayer and Mische 1998; Leca and Naccache 2006). But this historical phasing is not just predicated on the emergence of certain macro-level forces are in some sort of historical ordering, but also on the meso-level exigencies summarized by Eisenstadt (1977, 1985): *integration*, *legitimation*, and *regulation*.

## CONSIDERING THE MESO-LEVEL

### Addressing the Three Sociological Problems

At the meso-level of social reality, new exigencies become central to institutional entrepreneurs' projects—mainly, *integrating* disparate social units, *legitimating* entrepreneurial claims to monopolies over various aspects of the institutional domain, and *regulating* the actions of social units found within the institutional domain and those entering in search of access to whatever goods and services entrepreneurs provide. That is, the macrolevel of reality is the institutional domain, but its autonomy shifts the "drama" to internal struggles, which are necessarily mesolevel because they include collectives and clusters of collectives interacting, exchanging, and communicating. Through the structural and cultural mechanisms discussed in Chapters 4 and 5, entrepreneurs attempt to stabilize and regularize this interaction, exchange, and communication. No matter how incomplete these solutions tend to be, entrepreneurs settle on them because they are perceived to work or are, at the very least, the best available given the sociocultural and historical constraints entrepreneurs tend to face. These solutions delimit choices, while giving color and texture to the organizational cultures that form, the meanings individuals employ to understand and navigate the institutional sphere's universe; they also shapes the way actors, collectives, and clusters of collectives interact, exchange, and communicate with each other.

More than anything, the consideration of these three sociological problems has been absent in most contemporary meso-level analyses. In particular, interest in integrative problems has been replaced by either overemphasis on taken for granted, so-called cultural-cognitive mechanisms of social control (Scott 2001, 2008), which unfairly bias phenomenological, Berger-Luckmannian (1966) forces over normative and regulatory dynamics that cannot be ignored. When normative or regulatory forces are considered, over-simplified references to "professionalization" (Sutton 1984; Sutton et al. 1994) and "legislation" (Edelman and Suchman 1997; Dobbin and Sutton 1998) replace serious consideration of the structural and cultural linkages erected by entrepreneurs. Indeed, it is almost as if power, conflict, and struggle (see Fligstein and McAdam 2011, 2012 for a critique) in addition to the social division of labor (Rueschemeyer 1986) cease to exist in many contemporary meso-level accounts of organization and social action. And, when they are mentioned, it is again in the service of cultural reproduction or unintentionality (for critiques, see Emirbayer and Mische 1998; Colomy 1998; Leca and Naccache 2006). Revisiting integration and regulation as *problems* that organizations must contend with, and whose solutions by entrepreneurs affect organizational action and adaptation could push a whole new line of research.

## Depth in the Environment

In part, our institutional theory presses sociologists to lend some credence to the importance of the structural and material dimensions of the social world. Most new institutionalisms have adopted the language and concepts of cultural sociologies at the expense of thinking about the real world. Thus, when describing institutional environments, or fields as Bourdieu (1993) prefers, ambiguous concepts like "rules of the game" (Giddens 1984; North 1990), "cultural myths" (Meyer and Rowan 1977), or isomorphic forces (DiMaggio and Powell 1983) are used in place of structural analyses. To be sure, these metaphors or conceptualizations have their utility, but are also limiting. Most recently, two new theoretical perspectives have emerged that have pushed hard on the "old new" institutionalism (cf. Powell and

DiMaggio 1991): institutional logics (Friedland and Alford 1991; Thornton, Ocasio, and Lounsbury 2012) and *strategic action fields* (Fligstein and McAdam 2011, 2012). Both press new institutionalists to stop taking the environment for granted, yet the former continues to make the mistake of ignoring structural aspects like the division of labor in favor of the use of a vague term *logic*, that has almost as many meanings as *institution* does. In some ways, *logic* is a way of saying institutional domains have intra-institutional cultures that vary across domains in time and space, and this variation goes a long way towards shaping the types of organizational dynamics revealed in new institutionalist analyses. Given the overreliance new institutionalists have had towards economic firms in post–World War II western (or westernized) nation-states (Aldrich and Ruef 2006), the institutional logics folk make great points about the need to discern different cultural constraints across different cultural spaces. The extensive theoretical treatment of generalized symbolic media in Chapter 5 offers the logics perspective some theoretical grounding that does not contradict their insights, but offers a bridge to engage in a more robust discourse with a greater body of institutionalists and macrosociologists.

The institutional theory posited throughout, however, goes far beyond the logics perspective, by firmly placing the macro-level in both symbolic *and* material reality, whereas institutional logics implicitly replicate Parsons' cybernetic model and the belief that culture belongs to the macro and practices and material stuff are found only in the meso or micro. Generalized media and structural linkages are macro in the sense that they come to reinforce and delineate the outlines of the physical, temporal, social, and symbolic spaces that are institution-specific, and which constitute autonomous institutional space. Again, our institutional perspective does not supplant the logics perspective, but rather adds different contours to their insights, and expands its rather limited historical frame beyond modernity and capitalist-democratic states.

Much of these conclusions can be said about the relationship between institutional theory and the strategic action fields (SAFs) theory of Fligstein and McAdam (2011, 2012). For them, fields are embedded within fields, are embedded within fields; a sort of never-ending series of bigger and smaller contests across time and space that lack any macro or historical anchorage. Institutions and institutional cores provide some anchorage: the level of autonomy, and the location of the SAF within an autonomous institution relative to the core clearly shapes the intensity, duration, and stakes of any given contest. Moreover, the unique structural and cultural dynamics of one institution will produce very different SAFs than institutions built structurally and culturally different. Again, there is no reason to supplant SAF theory, as it is a serious advance beyond new institutionalism and a much needed integrative project that offers a more powerful lens for understanding the emergence of conflicts and their ability to spread across a series of previously unrelated spaces. Yet, a more complete view of the macro-level world any given SAF emerges in will be able to answer questions they often ignore: why are some SAFs linked to each other and how are these linkages differ? Why are some SAFs unlikely to spill over into other spaces? What are the true foundations of social reality that go beyond "rules" and "interpretive frames" (White 1992)?

### *Historicization and Comparative Institutionalism*

One final way our theory supplements new institutionalism is in offering a more cogent framework to begin historical-comparative analyses of organizational dynamics. That is, do the dynamics new institutionalists identify extend to other institutional domains or other times and places, or are they constrained to the industrial/postindustrial western democratic-capitalist nation-states (for a critique, see Abrutyn and Turner 2011; also, Calhoun 1993)? Consider the categories found in new institutionalisms that restrict the historical generalizability and comparability across time and space. Instead of identifying polity or economy as institutional domains, scholars define *democracy* (Alford and Friedland 1985), the state (Meyer 1987), capitalism (North 2005), or, even more vaguely, Catholic/Christian churches/religions (e.g., Thornton, Ocasio, and Lounsbury 2012:54) as institutions. These historically bound terms present major problems for identifying generalizable elements of polities, economies, and religions, as well as comparing non-democratic polities to democratic polities. But even if we were to assume that there were complementary historical institutions like "empires," "socialism," and "Chinese religions," it is questionable how useful these historically bound distinctions would be in any analysis of comparative merit.

Further complicating matters is the essentialism inherent in a concept like "capitalism," which is unwisely applied to all states within the global world-system as meaning the same thing objectively, and subjectively. Yet, Chinese capitalism, if that designation is even accurate, does not look like American capitalism, and if it continues to trend toward free market economics, there remains no reason to assume it will eventually converge in form (Arrighi 2007). Ironically, new institutionalists have been "discovering" variation in organizational forms for some time (Ouchi 1980; Hamilton and Biggart 1988; Biggart 1991), yet have not bothered to build general theories surrounding economic institutions and then specific theories about variation across economies and reasons why this might be so. The same problems have plagued the "world polity" perspective (Thomas et al. 1987), in that mass education has been assumed to be universally desirable and uniform in form across space (Boli, Ramirez, and Meyer 1985; Meyer, Nagel, and Snyder Jr. 1993), as has the nation-state (Meyer 1987). Both of these characterizations grossly misrecognize the tremendous variation across nation-states or public schools in form, efficacy, underlying cultural and structural logic, and the relationships between institutions in each society. So, it is without a doubt correct to see mass public education and nations becoming prolific across societies, but it is the superficial spread of legitimate forms begs the question of how the unique local cultures interact and reconfigure the "cultural myth," as well as local entrepreneurs come to accept the myth and why they pursue its implementation.

Indeed, there is no reason for western social scientists to assume western blueprints or myths or "institutions" are the only ones, the last ones, or evenly adopted across cases. This remains one of the blindspots in contemporary Euro-American sociology as scholars continue to imagine something new came out of the west be it romantic literature and *love* (Luhmann 1998), the bureaucracy and the supreme rationality of Christianity (Meyer 1987), overly standardized official languages (Bourdieu 1991), capitalism (Alford and Friedland 1985)—when, in fact, Weber (1927 [2002]) had already identified numerous historical types and, as noted above, world-systems scholars like Giovanni Arrighi (2007), and others like Abu-Lughod (1989) have long questioned the wisdom of claims of specialness emanating from western social science. By adopting a more abstract, theoretical institutional analysis, these problems are much more satisfyingly dealt with. Polities exist everywhere, which means there are generic qualities that link all societies to each other, and which presumably will shape political actors in similar ways regardless of time and space. As polities become more autonomous, we should expect some unique collectives and meso-level dynamics to form around *power* that are not likely to appear within economy or religion, though some dynamics will be diffuse. Capitalism is a convenient term denoting some shared characteristics of a series of economies, but "economy" provides a broader landscape upon which to paint similarities and differences diachronically and synchronically.

## Talking About Modernity

A final point of interest derives from the fascination social scientists have had with the "rise" of the west vis-à-vis China, India, and Islam (Weber 1920 [2002]; Chirot 1985; Hall 1985). Though there is not enough space to go into great detail, using the tools developed within this book, a slightly different take can be offered about the changes in the west in relationship to those that "did not happen" in the east. In essence, the proliferation of autonomous institutions, first economy and law, then education, science, medicine, art, and sport in the west coincides with the emergence of *money* as a medium of economic exchange and communication, which provided aspiring entrepreneurs with a durable and portable means toward subsistence—one which can theoretically be expanded whereas old forms like land, cattle, or salt were necessarily scarce. With the formation of labor markets, non-productive, non-religious entrepreneurs like merchants, lawyers, doctors, athletes, and so forth could acquire enough material resources to aspire to independence and, thereby, carve out autonomous institutional domains.

On the heels of this transformation was the growth of the educational sphere (Rashdall 1936) to the point where aspiring entrepreneurs like lawyers or doctors could begin to link their burgeoning cores to the educational domain in ways that usurped some control over *learning* and sell it on a market for salaries or wages. That is, some legal entrepreneurs were also educational entrepreneurs, but their control was limited to *legal learning*; the same happened for medical and scientific entrepreneurs, as well as economic entrepreneurs who expanded the importance of the educational credential in the mid-twentieth century (Collins 1979). Less obvious, but no less important, has been the ways in which athletic and artistic entrepreneurs have monopolized specialized forms of *learning* (Bourdieu 1992; Werron 2010).

Modernity, if that label is useful (cf. Eisenstadt 2000), centers on the circulation of *money* across boundaries in exchange for things like *health care* or *justice*, whereas the monopolization of specialized forms of *learning* is freed from either centralized control by educational entrepreneurs—for example, the Confucian literati (Hsu 1986)—or its deep embedding in one institutional domain, like the case of the former Soviet Union (Gaworek 1977). There are some possible reasons for this, the most likely of which was the emergence of legal entrepreneurs due to the unpredictable intersection between a underemployed mass of second-born sons due to rules of primogeniture, a centralized religious collective's—the Catholic Church—decision to struggle against political counterparts through legal measures, and the integrative power of religion vis-à-vis the weak, decentralized conflict-ridden political entrepreneurs (Unger 1976; Berman 1983). These conclusions do indeed require more systematic treatment, but by reconceptualizing the circulation of media, the types of entrepreneurs and their successes, and, eventually, the manifestation of integrative, regulative, and legitimative problems and the successful/failed solutions offered by entrepreneurs, a fresh look at a seminal problem, like the rise of the west, can be approached with both the macro- and meso-levels of analysis considered.

## THE MICRO-LEVEL

### Establishing a Strong Macro-Micro Link

A weak, and perhaps insurmountable, gap exists between macro- and microsociological theory (Knorr-Cetina 1981; Fuchs 1989). Many sciences never bother to even "find" the link, choosing instead to treat each level as its own distinct level of reality with unique properties and dynamics. Sociologists have never been able to take this approach, choosing instead to look for metaphors and analogies that improve the way the two levels of social reality interact with each other. In Chapter 3, the ecological dynamics of institutions were posited and many of the propositions were drawn from the insights of social psychology. Although our discussion does not offer a definitive theoretical framework, it does add to the literature and suggests some ways to think about macro–micro bridges.

Let's begin with the basic consequences of institutional autonomy for real humans. First, institutions circulate media of interaction, exchange, and communication. Through their pursuit and acquisition, use and conversion, elements of the symbolic bundles are internalized in ways that delimit interaction, exchange, and communication. Thus, the baseline for understanding institutional domains is that they shape the way humans act and interact; the media facilitate and constrain goal setting and decision-making as they become both means and ends to action, exchange, and communication. The closer an actor is to the core of an institution, and its relative degree of autonomy, the greater is the probability that their actions will be predictable and stereotyped, their individual goals more closely aligned with collective goals, and their choice of means and ends more tightly monitored and sanctioned.

Institutions allow "individuals and groups . . . [to] engage in a mutual process of exchange in order to pursue and attain goals . . . Institutions devise collective goals, and make it possible for their members to pursue these goals in a systematic manner" (Eisenstadt 1971:10). Institutions, and especially their entrepreneurs, had to use structural and cultural mechanisms to *convince* actors that pursuit of some self-interested, instrumentally rational goals was bad or illegitimate, while also making it "possible for people to pursue their personal goals and still contribute to attaining the goals of the collectives" lodged within the institutional domain (Eisenstadt 1971:10). This type of reasoning led Parsons, in his posthumous *Prolegomena* on Social Institutions (1990), to employ an action "chain" metaphor: each unit act, or a single means-ends relationship, was merely an *intermediate* link in a much larger chain, whose terminus was an intangible, often abstract *ultimate* or *substantive* end (cf. Parsons and Shils 1951). One might easily swap out the ambiguous "ultimate end" and replace it with any number of human concerns we have discussed, or the attainment of the generalized medium. Parsons views social action as voluntaristic and overly determined. But by adding the ecological dynamics we can push this analysis away from seeing all chains of action as equal. To be sure, systems of generalized exchange (La Valle 1994) and communication (Luhmann 2012) give *texture* to a lot of institutional action, regardless of the location. That is, most of our action and attitudes are stereotyped across settings and actors, and despite our over-psychologized common sensical beliefs toward humanity, institutions sharply delimit what is possible and who we can be. And although Parsons was not naïve, he erred in explicitly making it seem as if (1) means-ends were objectively and subjectively the same across institutional domains, (2) a single ultimate end guided all institutional action, and (3) the mechanisms of social control, monitoring, and sanctioning were evenly distributed within an institution.

The first assumption is clearly false. Although humans are not "unique snowflakes," we are each a relatively unique product of the intersection of our biographical details and the historical context in which this biography is told. Not only do we have freedom to reject some ends, but how we perceive the ends is much more complicated than Parsons lets on. And, of course, it goes without saying that the means are highly stratified and access contested. The second assumption is less obviously wrong. In one sense, he is correct. Religion, for instance, is about communicating with the *supranatural* and obtaining *sacredness/piety* as currency for religious exchanges and communication. But the "ultimate" end is not as simple as communicating with a deity, but actually varies quite a lot across time and space. For instance, Anthony Wallace (1966:104–57ff.) identifies five ultimate ends that come to link cultic assemblages[3] together: technology (e.g., rain dances), therapy/anti-therapy (e.g., curing illness or cursing an enemy), ideology (e.g., explanation, justification, interpretation of natural order), salvation, and revitalization (e.g., Durkheim's rituals of collective effervescence). One could add religion offers anxiety reduction concerning, especially, the problem of death or mortality, as well as why there is suffering and evil in the world (Geertz 1966). The third assumption was challenged cogently in Chapter 3, when we noted distance from the core means everything in most cases. It is true entrepreneurs can marshal coercive force to suppress actors across the institutional environment and draw them closer to the core, but coercive force is costly and unstable over the long run. Thus, most of the time, distance from the core means less monitoring and sanctioning and more freedom to be novel and creative.

The micro world, then, consists of identities, roles, and statuses; dyads and triads and small groups; and encounters and exchanges (Turner 2010b). Each of these is a distinct unit of analysis that interest sociologists, but in most cases as we shall see in a moment, they are not abstracted from the broader structural and cultural environment in which they operate. But microsociologists, like their macro counterparts, tend to be less versed or less interested in the properties of the macro (or vice versa), and thus vague notions of the environment are used as backdrops for their more detailed elucidations. But we have already built the scaffolding for linking the two in Chapters 4 and 5. Structural linkages, some horizontal and others vertical, some miniature niches and others wide fields, provide the conduits along which resources flow from the core and from one space to the next, one actor to the next. They are the invisible, coercive social facts Durkheim was adamant about. The divisions of labor that exist in an institution as replicated, in part, in a collective embedded in a niche embedded in a field are the *real material sociocultural presence of the macro-world*; the role-status position a person occupies in a given division of labor, or in the cross-cutting of a series of social divisions of labor determines a large amount of his or her reality (Lenski 1966; Rueschemeyer 1986). Meanwhile, media circulate across these linkages in ways that coat or drench the role-status position in institutional and extra-institutional meanings, provides the actor with symbolic elements to talk to others as well as a normative and regulatory framework governing the rules of exchange and communication, and the resources necessary to claim privilege or to strive for it or to "know one's place" as Bourdieu (1977) was fond of saying. Media, through the structural conduits or circuits available to it, are the "*conveyer belts that link the [macro-level of social reality] to the local life-worlds*, they are the ideal tools to construct *systematic linkages* between social positions and ideas on the one hand, and interpersonal and intergroupal relations on the others" (Vandenberghe 2007:312). They allow actors who are present or not co-present to understand each other, to simulate exchange in their mind or in practice, and they link the macro to the micro (Luhmann 1976; La Valle 1994; Vandenberghe 2007; Abrutyn 2009a, 2012; Abrutyn and Turner 2011; Turner 2011).

## Reconsidering Current Social Psychological Theories

### *Micro Elements of Mind*

In thinking about the macro–micro link this way, we can make some suggestions for more concrete overlaps between institutional analysis and social psychological traditions. We begin with the most basic, simple micro elements: identities, roles, and statuses. Identity Control Theory (ICT) supposes that all actors carry an *identity standard* that acts like a ruler that "measures" feedback from the environment—for example, the way a person acts toward the individual—and determines how congruent ego's conception of him or herself is and alters perception of him or herself (Burke 1991; Stets 2006). A person has an identity that corresponds with each role-status position they fill, as well as what is often called a *person* identity, or a more global self-conception that transcends the constraints of situations. When an identity is not confirmed, that feedback over or under *verifies* ego's identity, we find that ego adjusts by under- or overcompensating to try to elicit expected feedback while also avoiding the negative affect generated by incongruence (Burke and Tully 1977; Burke and Harrod 2005; Stets 2005). These conclusions work nicely with institutional theory. First, the sticky question of social structure and macro-context remains hazy in ICT. To be sure, "capturing" the macro-level of reality using surveys and experimental designs is never easy, and rife with potential ecological fallacies, yet recent work on moral identity has identified some proxy measures (Stets et al. 2008). Nevertheless, an institutional theory would further bolster the claims made by ICT as well as offer new directions in understanding *which* identities should be activated in which situations, and so forth.

The logic is as follows: ICT gleaned from Sheldon Stryker (1980), the idea that a person's identities are embedded within what he called an *identity salience hierarchy*. Some identities were *prominent* to the person's self-conception and others were *committed* to because of the social networks he or she was tied to. The result of the often contradictory synthesis of *prominence* and *commitment* was *salience*, or the activation of one identity vis-à-vis all other possible ones. The hierarchy, then, was fluid as each situation tended to call out different role identities commensurate with the setting, the counter-roles present, and the expectations thrust upon the person. But, the person had some freedom to both choose the settings he or she was often in and to choose to emphasize identities not necessarily fitting of the situation. Both choices, of course, were constrained as short of living in a hermetically sealed environment, it is impossible to have complete will in, while activating an identity not commensurate with the situation could lead to various types of sanctioning and negative affect. Institutional theory would offer a few predictions that would help provide some context for ICT and identity salience. First, the closer a person is to a given autonomous core, the more frequent they will play the institutional role, the more rewards they will derive from that role as opposed to other roles they might play, the denser their networks activating that role will be, and thus, the more likely that role will be central or prominent in their global self-conception.

Second, when a role becomes that prominent, the symbolic content of the identity will come to shape their view of non-institutional interactions more often than not. A business man may come to view his family interactions, religious decisions, and political goals through the prism of *money*, and its requisite value-orientations and ideologies. He is likely to not only actively seek out interactions and exchanges that verify this identity, but his "father identity standard" will look *very* different than someone who is more committed to kinship, or perhaps more equally balanced across domain roles. Indeed, vignettes meant to hypothetically place a respondent in one world or another might be missing the point when it comes to the types of structural and cultural milieu a person inhabits frequently. Third, ICT can provide us with important measures of institutional autonomy, but shifting its focus from understanding how actor's feel when their identity is not verified, to elucidating more clearly, and on the ground, how institutional ecology shapes identity formation and the verification process.

Additionally, similar threads can be drawn to other social psychological areas: role theory (R. Turner 2001), affect control theory (ACT) (Robinson and Smith-Lovin 2006), and status construction—including status beliefs and expectations—theory (Ridgeway 2006). We have discussed roles quite extensively elsewhere, but let's look real briefly at the other two. ACT takes as its object of study the lexicons that people assign meaning and emotion to that shape how they interact. If symbolic media present to us *specialized language* and this language is unevenly distributed throughout the domain, then we can make a couple of assumptions that would support ACT and reciprocate the favor by further teasing out how these languages operate in micro encounter. Each institution should have a lexicon. The official lexicon would likely shape the realities and constrain interaction as actors find themselves physically and/or cognitively to the core; further away, we should find more diffuse meanings, as well as integrated lexicons that capture the overlapping environments actors find themselves. Finally, liaisons should be "fluent" in numerous official lexicons, and thus a whole set of interesting dynamics may be uncovered by examining them. In terms of status construction theory, much effort has been expended—for many good and convenient reasons—looking at global stratification systems and diffuse beliefs revolving around race, gender, and so forth (Berger, Cohen and Zelditch Jr. 1972; Ridgeway 1991, 2001). Presumably, their general principals would hold when looking at *intra-institutional stratification* and the discrete status beliefs that form within the domain. So, although gender continues to matter, it would be interesting to examine a single academic discipline or a hospital to uncover what institution-specific status beliefs govern conduct within these more circumscribed domains. What *learning* is favored among sociologists, and does this affect them in ways that gender affects people across situations? What type of *health care* matters most, and how does a medical status hierarchy look compared to other types? Not only would we likely find commensurate dynamics that further bolster status construction theory's assumptions, but it is just as possible we would find unique dynamics worth highlighting to better grasp the reality of different types of institutional life-worlds.

### *Encounters, Exchanges and Small Groups*

We will spend much less time considering how institutional theory relates to the interaction, exchange, and communication that occur when two or more people begin to interact. Luhmann (1995, 2012) dedicated his entire career to linking the social system to ephemeral interaction systems, emphasizing the way social and organizational systems delimited communicative action by way of various mechanisms like communication media, language, and thematicization. But other parallels can be drawn by social psychologists and microsociologists who were keenly sensitive to macro conditions. Goffman's (1974) *frame analysis* is an obvious candidate: an institutional frame constrains the definition of all situations, followed by field and niche frames, the frame or frames found within the specific collective the encounter may occur within, and, of course, the frame found in the specific situation predicated on the counter-role(s), the real person occupying these other roles, and the ecological setting itself. But this analysis could be extended to his work on stigma (1963b) and asylums, or what he termed "total institutions" (1961). As was the case in our brief discussion on status beliefs, we could add a form of stigma rooted in institutional definitions and stratification systems. Stigma could be defined by entrepreneurs or even those with authority in collectives based on the codes embedded within the generalized symbolic medium, and not just broader types like "tribal" (e.g., ethnic or gender), personal reputation, or physical handicap. But his work on asylums opens up interesting links to institutional theory. It raises the question, are there institutional domains, or niches within a specific institution, that is closed off from other media to the point in which it constrains behavior and attitudes? Clearly, mental institutions are an extension of the medical institution (Foucault 1988) and convents extensions of the religious sphere, but prisons find themselves in the overlap between the polity and law (Foucault 1995). Because of this variation in institutional location, there may be some differences Goffman failed to examine, or simply were of little interest. But this variation raises more questions about other spaces he did not examine like boarding schools (Cookson Jr. and Persell 1987). If anything, returning to some of Goffman's work on structural social psychology would be fruitful if it only reintroduced some dimensions generally omitted in social psychology today—for example, the degree to which a space is closed and roles highly circumscribed.

Perhaps the most overlap we find is in the exchange tradition (Blau 1964; Ekeh 1974; Cook, Cheshire, and Gerbasi 2006). The dynamics of generalized exchange, or indirect, collective-oriented exchange have been key to understanding heterogeneous solidarity since, at least, Durkheim (1912) and his nephew Marcel Mauss (1967; cf. Levi-Strauss 1969). The underlying problem of generalized exchange derives from the tendency of actors to attribute their benefits from the group, collective, or diffuse system as opposed to a real other; free riders become the extreme pathology, but coordinating and controlling action and exchange is complex. In Chapter 5, we offered one solution to this problem by focusing on the circulation of a generalized symbolic medium whose pursuit and acquisition assumed a baseline acceptance of some types of norms (T. Turner 1968; Carlson 1990) and, also, as Bourdieu (1991) would argue, becomes part of the habitus, or through the *embodied* form of media, internalized into our very dispositions. Lawler's (2001, 2006) work on affect and exchange can be further deepened by considering (1) how media enter into the exchange; (2) how the variation in media temperatures alter the way emotions are manufactured, attributed, and the problem of coordination is resolved or not; and (3) the relative distance from the core through which the exchange occurs, as well as (4) the differential access each exchange partner has in terms of media and other desired social resources. The exchange of media expands the definition of social exchange, while also underscoring the variation in texture and color of exchanges. Exchange theorists, whether those focused on direct exchange or generalized exchange, have tended to study exchange monolithically, and thus have had to continually argue against over-economizing social actors and their interactions (Granovetter 1985). Media offer an entirely unique social resource that governs social exchanges, even economic exchanges, in ways that move us further away from utilitarianism and rational-choice theory, without denying the fact that humans are conscious of what they think they want and how they think it best to get it.

## LAST THOUGHTS

Clearly institutional theory can and should supplement various areas of sociological inquiry across all levels of social reality. This begins by acknowledging that the macro-level of social reality, and especially institutional domains, are real things; milieus in which lower-levels of social reality are shaped even when they are sometimes able to do the shaping. The discussion in this chapter merely scratches the surface of how institutional theory can speak to the vast tracts within the discipline without making the Parsonsian mistake of positing a "totalistic," and impossibly parsimonious, theoretical framework that reduces everything to a four-fold deductive typology. Institutions are environments that facilitate and constrain interaction, exchange, and communication. In many ways, they are like ecological niches, but they are built by humans instead of natural givens to be dealt with by societies. Much of this theory cannot exist without the insights and dynamics offered by other traditions, many of which have been explicitly addressed above or mentioned in passing throughout. What is offered is a more coherent vision of the social world that gives sociologists and social scientists a baseline for engaging in discourse that pushes what we know further. It tries to be sensitive to other perspectives by not usurping their position, but rather building the scaffolding in which their framework is given deeper meaning and abstracted context.

The power of the theory derives from the fact that only a finite number of institutions have and do exist, because there are some very basic concerns humans have that can become salient over time and space, and only so many resources in a given society that can be devoted to these concerns. Thus, a thread that links humanity across time and space is offered. In addition, we know hunter-gatherers are *not* similar in many ways to postindustrial Germany, and this is because institutions vary in their level of autonomy and, thereby, institutional complexes vary in the number of autonomous institutions, their size and scope, and ultimately, the number of independent entrepreneurs specializing in dealing with one or more concerns. Modern societies are not better or more fit because of this, but rather we have come to physically, temporally, socially, and symbolically differentiate these concerns as the sheer number of people is too great for one or two institutions to meet their individual and collective needs. The darker side of this is that autonomous institutions present blueprints for aspiring and ambitious entrepreneurs looking to be mobile. Power and domination expand parallel to a societies capacity to handle ever-greater and more amplified exigencies; the probability that conflicts will emerge also grows geometrically, as there are more resources to fight over and as more autonomous institutions emerge, less constraints preventing heterodoxic competition exist and competing visions of reality threaten the stability found in institutions with a single, orthodoxic vision emanating from the core into the environment.

Thus, there is a middle ground in which institutions are defined *macro-level structural and cultural spheres composed of individual, collective, and clusters of collective actors whose action, exchanges, and communication are facilitated and constrained by their integration into divisions of labor and through the circulation of generalized symbolic media, regulated by the distribution of (material and symbolic) resources and authority, and given a sense of shared meaning through the linkages, pursuit of resources, and the legitimated vision of reality espoused by those actors with the greatest share of the resources* that accounts for many of the interesting insights of structural-functionalism, while also being careful not to ignore the powerful criticisms and theoretical advances made by conflict and cultural sociologies. Indeed, as Chapters 4 and 5 showed, structure and culture are tightly woven together as structure provides the conduits along which culture travels, is imposed and internalized, is manipulated and acquired, and is developed and altered. Restructuring an institutional domain implies altering the culture, while recombining the bundles or parcels of media implies having to reconfigure the structural linkages to some degree. That the life-world of institutions is structured and because culture shapes this life-world, it is impossible to deny the struggles actors go through to be mobile, to improve their structural position, to acquire more resources to pursue their own goals, and, ultimately, to gain access to positions of cultural production. Institutions *do stabilize* social interactions, exchange, and communication, but it does so at the expense of even distribution of resources. It carves the social world into smaller, inequitable spaces like fields and niches in which hierarchies govern relationships as much as horizontal exchange networks and functional interdependencies. Media, as the ultimately leveler, becomes the vital mechanism of integration and legitimation as its circulation presupposes some type of framework which dictates the terms of institutional exchange and communication, and thus produces cultural equivalencies while obfuscating structural inequalities.

In essence, the theory tries to strike the right balance between the stability and conflict dimensions of social life, the material/structural versus symbolic/cognitive side of social reality, and the objective/subjective divide. It may be imperfect, but it is an advance over previous efforts that purposefully avoid taking a side by walking back statements made and using highly abstract and arcane conceptual language to hide their biases. Meant to spark discourse, theory is never written in a vacuum and the work posited herein is intended to be further developed by colleagues. The goal was to return institutions to the forefront, or to a place commensurate with their historical value; as such, this book is call for revivifying institutional analysis and making room at the crowded table for one of the longest running traditions in sociology.

# Notes

## NOTES TO THE INTRODUCTION

1. There are too many institutionalisms to count. New institutionalists are not a single entity, with variation across disciplines (cf. Nee 2005), and tremendous variation within sociology itself (see Powell and DiMaggio 1991; Scott 2001). New institutionalists find themselves in continuity as well as in distinction to what is often called "old" institutionalism (Stinchcombe 1965), or more recently the "old new" institutionalism (Stinchcombe 1997; Fligstein and McAdam 2012), which further confuses the matter as there then must have been an "old" institutionalism by which the "old new" institutionalism came into existence. Thus, we are left with only poor choices in terminology, and have settled on historical institutionalism.
2. It may be worth noting, earlier than later, the problems with labeling traditions one thing or another. A large and loosely coupled body of research and scholars has been labeled the *new institutionalism*. It may be better to call it the new institutionalism*s* because there are widely divergent positions, methods, and theoretical frameworks being used; not just between economic and sociological new institutionalists, but within the sociological tradition there are divisions. Moreover, as I will labor to show over the course of this chapter and the book, new institutionalists are actually not interested in institutions, which they tend to take for granted as extant social phenomena not worth expounding upon. Rather, they are better labeled new *organizationalists* because nearly all of their efforts have been devoted to theoretical and methodological analysis of post–World War II formal, economic organizations and their environments. That is, with the exception of the focus on the modern nation-state (Meyer 1987) as an organizational unit and mass education as a cultural myth (Meyer et al. 1979; Meyer, Nagel, and Snyder 1993).
3. In later chapters, for example, Chapter 7, the meaning of "adaptive" will be posited. In essence, the term is not used as the old functionalists used it—for example, institutions do not make society adapt, but rather it merely has to prove adaptive for a significant proportion of the population, either objectively or intersubjectively.
4. Recently, some institutionalists have begun expanding this list, identifying five other institutions which may be ubiquitous, but which are often called "secondary" or late-differentiating institutions (Abrutyn 2009b; Abrutyn and Turner 2011): science (Ben-David 1965), medicine (Starr 1982), art (Luhmann 2000a), sport (Werron 2010), and media (Luhmann 2000b).

## NOTES TO CHAPTER 1

1. Of all of the concerns discussed thus far, creating distinctions may seem the most out of place. Humans, however, are naturally status seekers (Lenski 1966; Sanderson 2001), and thus creating distinctions can become important to humans. In the earliest hunter-gatherer societies, serious efforts and mechanisms were in place to prevent upstarts or, at the very least, reduce the amount of prestige and power an individual could garner (Boehm 1999; also, Lee 1989). But autonomous economies produce massive amounts of surplus, and where large amounts of surplus exist, self-aggrandizing goals are seductive. Moreover, to reproduce the boundaries of an autonomous economy requires the institutionalization of key values like progress, technological advance, amoral decision making, and accumulation (and reinvestment) of wealth.
2. The church claimed hegemony over personal status issues like marriage, birth, inheritance, divorce, and the like (Goody 2000).

## NOTES TO CHAPTER 2

1. Some caveats to consider as we explore the nature of entrepreneurship, institutional change, and the evolution of institutional autonomy. First, Weber drew from religious carrier groups and innovators to build his theory of charisma. It is far easier to conceptualize Mohammed or Buddha as charismatic leaders than, say Sargon of Akkad (Liverani 1993), Gratian (1582 [1993]) the great legal innovator of legal-rational western law, or Galileo (Gaukroger 2006). That is, the concerns of religious entrepreneur's strikes deeply at existential problems like evil or death, whereas political entrepreneurs deal in pragmatic problems, legal entrepreneurs in mundane conflicts, and scientists in jargon-laden research. Yet, one must not forget that an entrepreneur's task, if he or she is to erect a successful project, involves monopolizing claims to one or more universal human concerns: political entrepreneurs must not only exhibit brute force, but also innovate in ways that resolve anxiety concerning security; legal entrepreneurs do not just resolve mundane conflicts, but deal in justice which appears to have some biological roots (Gospic et al. 2011); and scientists, like their religious counterparts, are *cosmological* entrepreneurs struggling over the definition of and method to ascertain *Truth*, as well as answer the "big" questions (Abrutyn 2013a). Second, charisma is often less apparent in these latter groups as opposed to religious groups because their entrepreneurs do not necessarily use public displays or speeches or texts the principal dissemination of charisma, but rather rely on other types of signaling: political entrepreneurs have parades and such, but also rely on manipulating the environment to make themselves and their domiciles bigger and formidable looking; legal entrepreneurs stand on pomp and ritual, but also rely on the physical organization of space and the monopoly over special language—whether in the form of oaths said in ordeals or "legalese" that requires professionalization; and, scientists rely on objective proof—for example, curing diseases, cars starting on a regular basis, flying—that demonstrates their power, certainty, and prestige. Despite the subtle differences in charismatic demonstrations, they still marshal charisma and therefore find their claims legitimated by affect and substantive rationality. Ultimately, then, it is the differences in *substantive values* that come to shape the differences in institutional domains and, therefore, the differences in action, goals, and decisions by each entrepreneur and by actors found within these domains.

The differences in substantive values can be attributed directly to the differences in exigencies entrepreneurs contend with, seek to solve or meet, and their underlying interests. They are the builders, or architects of autonomy, the tenders to this institutional process, the aggrandizers seeking expansion of autonomy, and, often, the cause of the contraction in autonomy.

2. Contemporary humans take for granted the population of cities given the recent watershed moment in which more people live in urban areas than rural ones for the first time ever. But it was actually a problem populating cities as diseases often wiped out significant proportions of the population, cities were targets for barbarians or foreign invaders who sometimes sacked the entire city leading people to flee to the hinterlands, and recessions/depressions were just as possible then as today—except in the former case, people would simply leave the city and return to the farmlands where subsistence was easier to attain.
3. The reader may or may not be familiar with this type of analytic modeling. In the lower left hand corner of the model is a key denoting what each symbol means. The model moves from left to right, with each box-arrow-box being a distinct relationship between two concepts. The symbol "+" signifies a *positive relationship*—that is, for instance, if populations grow then exigencies should follow suit, whereas when populations *contract*, exigencies should also decline in significance. The "-" symbol indicates an *inverse* relationship; "=" stands for a lag that either denotes a threshold must be reached before changes occur, or that eventually there are diminishing returns and a plateau effect; finally, "+/-" or "-/+" symbols refer to curvilinear relationships. Thus, as entrepreneurship occurs, innovation should grow, but all things remaining equal, innovative activities will begin to decline as it is in the entrepreneur's interest to prevent innovations that threaten their position and privilege. However, *all things remaining equal* is rarely the case, as the model presumes dynamism and not stasis.
4. This list does not have to be definitive. These three types are obvious across historical cases, but I leave open the question whether they are the only types of entrepreneurs, or whether there are sub-types of important theoretical and empirical distinction.

## NOTES TO CHAPTER 3

1. In reality, the core and its environment is not likely as symmetrical as it is in this model. For clarity, we conceptualize the perfect institutional domain, but like most aspects of empirical reality, the lines probably zigzag and do not follow some geometric perfection.
2. In a later section below, we will examine the multiplicity of cores in terms of geographic space, proxy cores, and generally give depth to the concept as developed herein.
3. For much of the discussion below, my focus will be primarily on the individual actor and not a group or set of groups. This should not detract from the overall picture that institutions are comprised of both types of actors. Some of the theoretical work changes slightly to apply the principles to groups, but ultimately, it is more a shift in semantics and syntax than a shift in dynamics. When possible, I will try and explicitly address how groups operate.
4. Social psychology has needlessly been ambiguous regarding its concepts because of the overpopulation of theories and the lack of integrative theory meant to reduce the differences between each little research program (cf. Burke 2006). To avoid confusion here out, I would like to define the terms I

use. A *self* is the sum total of components that make up a person's personality and cognition; this term is synonymous with *person* in my opinion. *Roles* are behavioral and expectation sets that act as vehicles of social structure and are learned through interaction with counter-roles and through modeling those we respect that play the role. Of course, each role has a parallel *status position* that corresponds to the role's relative access to resources, power/prestige differentials with counter-roles, and its authority. *Identities* are the unique or specific way a given person plays a role. Thus, *student* is a role-status position, and each person in school has a student identity that differentiates them—within reason—from others; for some, being a student may be central to their self-conception, whereas for others, it may be situationally salient. The identity is a product of previous experiences that shaped the role and present experiences that create consistency in behavior, expectations and obligations premised on past performances, and success or failure. Although it is not perfect, for much of the discussion I will treat role and identity as synonymous because, in a sense, they are.

5. The same sort of role is played by sports writers who, in part, are entrepreneurs are the recently autonomous sport institution in many western nation-states, but who also play a vital role in translating concerns of athletes and owners into language fans can understand, and vice versa (Leifer 1998). Additionally, lobbyists are truly economic actors, but they find themselves communicating with political entrepreneurs and then back to economic entrepreneurs; political parties act as liaisons for most other institutions, as career party members "get out the message" to citizens, businesses, churches, and so on, while resending the messages of the people to politicians; nearly every house of worship has outreach programs meant to draw in community members, as well as associations that lobby on their behalf.
6. As societies get larger and denser, the probability that some fringe actors who reject the social reality will appear increases. Hermits, lunatics, revolutionaries, and the like are just a part of the social world.

## NOTES TO CHAPTER 4

1. To be sure, this discussion or the decision to examine the structural elements before the cultural ones (Chapter 5) does not imply the primacy of structure over culture, but rather is a matter of explanatory clarity and convenience. Culture can and often does shape structure, and more importantly, the subjectivity of culture can lead to the obfuscation of structural elements.
2. In *Behavior in Public Places*, Goffman (1963a:69–75) captures the perils of being "away" in an encounter—that is, being physically co-present and cognitively distant. As one moves nearer to the core, it becomes increasingly difficult to neglect expected performances as the stakes get higher (and the visibility and probability of social control mechanisms being used increases).
3. Admittedly, the literature is filled with myriad clusters, each with a unique connotation and usages—for example, organizational fields (DiMaggio and Powell 1983), fields (Bourdieu 1992), strategic action fields (Fligstein and McAdam 2012), market (Fligstein 1996), networks (Powell 1999), economic sectors (Scott and Meyer 1983), resource niches (Hannan and Freeman 1977), and so forth. For simplicity sake, the concept *resource niche* will refer to *intra*-institutional clusters of organizations and *field* will refer to *intra*-organizational clusters. There is a common sense logic behind this. Niches, in Hannan and Freeman's (1977) use, appear to be closed populations of

organizations competing for a set amount of resources. Autonomous institutions are relatively bound spheres of social action, exchange, and communication, and, therefore, it makes sense that they would be carved into niches with uneven access to institutional resources that shape the inside of the niche; furthermore, the core is a niche itself. Fields have been used in many different ways, but tend to imply a more permeable and diffuse space with greater diversity in organizational forms, or at the very least, diversity in institutional pressures—for example, *organizational fields* often encompass a bunch of similar organizations, but isomorphic pressures from other institutions penetrating and constraining their actions. Although this may not be perfect, the debates over what clusters should be called can be better resolved by choosing two types—one intra- and the other inter-institutional—and then, below, explaining how the structural linkages vary across institutions, hence the variation in clusters and their composition.

4. Size and density are relative. Small task-oriented groups of four members evince a prestige and power order quite naturally and rapidly (Ridgeway 2006). Formal leadership and authority, however, require greater numbers of members to emerge.
5. The fact that actors have recourse to other forms of self-help, like vigilantism, kinship revenge, and the like does not take away from the fact that significant proportions of the population regularly seek legal counsel for small claims, divorce, lawsuits and so on; indeed, the wealthier an individual or collective actor is, the more likely they are to pursue legal recourse to solve problems (Black 1976), create/sustain inequalities (Turk 1976), or improve their ability to strategize by "testing" or "discovering" law (Evan 1980).Thus, the conflict perspective is right to point out the way the use of law is unevenly distributed, and the way *justice* is often stratified, yet what is equally correct to posit is that where law has become autonomous, greater numbers of people believe law is the legitimate means to achieving certain ends; even if they cannot afford to do so themselves.
6. An interesting aspect of overlaps is the propensity for nascent entrepreneurs to appear in these spaces. Though it is beyond the discussion in this chapter, overlaps provide liaisons with the unique position to combine elements of multiple institutions in new ways. Entrepreneurs are often prevented from doing so, lest they "pollute" the careful vision of reality they have spent time crafting. Meanwhile, support actors, or those nearest to the core, are often looking to usurp entrepreneurial power or gain entry into the core themselves. Their strategies rarely involve radical value-orientations or ideologies, but rather instrumental-rational strategies aimed at enhancing their position. Liaisons, on the other hand, have leverage because they are needed by entrepreneurs in multiple domains, as well as environmental actors in multiple domains, while also having access to numerous types of institutional elements. Thus, it is not surprising that legal entrepreneurs in Europe in the 11th century found themselves between the polity and religious domains, and exploited it to their advantage (as did their economic and scientific counterparts). Moreover, liaisons have a degree of independence then, and can pursue their own interests which are not entirely bounded by a given institution. Lawyers, for instance, are legal liaisons, but are not necessarily beholden to the legal domain only. Some lawyers work for an economic actor, whether a person or a firm, and thus owe their principal allegiance to the economic institution; their activities will often be economically oriented as a result. Similarly, the Attorney General and his/her department are obviously legal actors, but are embedded deeply in the political realm.

## NOTES TO CHAPTER 5

1. Few scholars have used the term *generalized symbolic media* in a systematic way besides Parsons and Luhmann. Luckily, their use was overly technical and of course, overly abstract. Recently, a few people have returned to the concept and have begun to reconceptualize generalized media as the force behind institutional culture (Abrutyn 2009a, 2013a, b; Turner 2010a, 2011, 2012). As such, it is argued that "culture has to come from somewhere, and while it is certainly true that individuals generate culture as they act, interact, and organize, *they do so through the use of generalized symbolic media*" (Abrutyn and Turner 2011:287; emphasis added).
2. Later in this chapter, the way multiple media circulate within a given institutional domain, compete with each other, sometimes fuse into a larger meta-ideology, and, in some cases, corrupt and pollute autonomous institutions will be elucidated. For now, the discussion will treat institutions as pure systems of generalized exchange in which one medium shapes all action, exchange, and communication.
3. The reader should note that this discussion does not mean that *all* persons have access to *power* in all of its form. Again, the pursuit of *power* and its attainment implies adherence to a *basic normative framework* and nothing else. As we will see below, and especially in Chapter 6, every medium is a bundle, but it circulates in *parcels* that reflect slivers or segments of the broader culture. Thus, all actors are embedded within a system of power relations and are pursuing the medium of *power*, hence the imposition of cultural equivalencies. Yet, structural and cultural differences remain based on broader patterns of stratification as well as unique intra-institutional patterns founded on the *rule of proximity*.
4. It should be acknowledged that I am in Bourdieu's (1986) debt for the basic idea behind the three forms of external valued referents—*objectified*, *embodied*, and *institutionalized*. But the substitution of *media* for *capital* is, arguably, a major theoretical advance. For one thing, the cultural-economic capital dichotomy is a false one (Bourdieu 1993). Social spaces cannot simply be reduced to instrumental-rational and some vague "cultural" form that is an amalgam of aesthetic, moral, ethical, religious, legal, and other elements (for a more elaborate critique of cultural capital, see Calhoun 1993)—an unfortunate remnant from a Marxian perspective that sees the economic base as pitted against a superstructure filled with everything *not* economic. Moreover, the arbitrary appearance and disappearance of social capital only serves to reinforce the inadequacy of reducing all social spaces to types of capital. Second, whereas each institution develops its own medium with a material and a symbolic side, Bourdieu's (1989) model limits everything to three types of capital (economic, cultural, and social) and the legitimate forms of those capital, symbolic. This forces social scientists to, *ad hoc*, invent religious or political capital and assume they operate like the other types. Indeed, religion is not at all about capital, but rather about *sacredness/piety* and those two things are what form the basis of exchange and communication; not a vague and amorphous concept like religious capital. Third, by moving away from capital, we can avoid overeconomizing aspects of social life that are economic, while returning the economic sphere of exchange and communication to the sociocultural moorings it has in real life (Polanyi 1957; J. Turner 2004). In sum, media are more expansive and less limiting for analyses than capital, as we can discern clearly between religious and artistic spaces without falling back on a catch-all term like "cultural capital" and assuming economic capital is somehow *not* cultural or social.

5. Again, people and groups are always measuring congruence and authenticity.
6. As we shall see below in analyses of subjectivity, pollution, and colonization, hot media can be "cooled" down when they are transformed into placeholders for other media. Thus, corrupted *sacredness* means it becomes a placeholder of value for, say, *money*. Often overlooked by sociologists is the converse: cool media can be heated up.
7. Even in a "postmodern" era, if there is even a postmodernity, there remains an Americanness and a Frenchness, even if as Durkheim would predict, the values and norms are highly generalized and abstract. To be sure, what it means to be American has changed over the last forty years, yet one could argue the current struggle between ultra-conservatives in the U.S. and progressives *is about* Americanness and who gets to define it.

## NOTES TO CHAPTER 6

1. The term *parameter* was used by Blau (1977) to stand for the types of categoric distinctions that defined heterogeneous societies. *Nominal* parameters were horizontal categories, or those that lacked status distinctions, whereas *graduated* parameters stood for categories that varied vertically in terms of status distinctions. When nominal and graduated parameters intersect, stratification systems form along the intersections that correlate most with inequitable access to resources or distinct positions in divisions of labor. It is possible for multiple intersections to emerge as well. Hence, if being white correlates with high occupational prestige and wealth, and being black with the opposite, than the macro-level stratification system will be characterized, in part, by racial inequality.
2. As has been the case above, the argument does not belie the fact that incumbency in either superordinate or subordinate role-status positions, that is, being a member of an institutional categoric unit, may intersect with global patterns of stratification. Being a woman may prevent an individual from becoming a doctor or scientist. The goal of this chapter is not to examine patterns already well documented by sociologists of inequality, but rather to capture the unique dynamics of institutional stratification systems assuming all things being equal. Indeed, when a woman becomes a doctor or scientists, she might have "less" *truth* or *applied knowledge* then her male counterparts, but the title does carry certain meanings beyond her gender in interactions with *most* non-entrepreneurs. Her patients or students listen to her not as a woman first, but as a doctor or scientist then a woman. And though there may be patients or students who are consciously or unconsciously biased toward women, a significant proportion of people will generally orient themselves to her appropriately.
3. Interestingly, the process of establishing authenticity (Goffman 1959, 1963a, 1967; Alexander 1988, 2004) and its consequences (Collins 2004) has become a fascinating, but often ignored tradition in sociology.
4. Starr's (1982) phenomenal book on the rise of American medicine presciently ends with the deregulation of insurance companies in the 1970s leading to a hazy future for medical entrepreneurs and the gradual erosion of institutional autonomy. Years later, we can see the fluctuation of autonomy and its tenuousness, as alternative medicines and "McHospitals" have become real competitors with doctors, and their authority has become less trusted as it was in the height of their independence—for example, 1940s to 1960s.

5. When revealing or exposing the nature of structural relationships, it often appears polemical and perhaps self-serving. However, my point is merely (1) to illustrate how hoarding works and (2) to imply that it is somewhat natural to human institutions. Sociology is not the only discipline to be guilty of this, because resources are always scarce and thus collectives and clusters of collectives always are in competition with some winning and losing (Bourdieu 1990a). What is most interesting, however, are the strategies to deny this process: as if studying global inequality makes the sociological system of cultural reproduction better or more moral. Indeed, one need only look at the American Sociological Society's annual conference sites to realize that the mission is not to help disadvantaged urban economies given the fact it is not held in Detroit, New Orleans, Cleveland, Memphis, or other small cities hit hard by the recession as well as, in some cases, by natural disasters. Again, this is less a critique than making an important point about how stratification operates.
6. Steering as best they can, given the facts that unpredictable events often unfold, the contingencies that cannot be anticipated, the reactions and actions of other societies, and the fact that no actor has total information and, more often than not, is operating on incomplete understanding of the social world as refracted by one ideological persuasion or another.
7. The opposite, incidentally, may be true as well. If, for instance, religion-kinship overlaps become *gendered* (e.g., the heavy circulation of feminine exchanges) in reality or perception and politico-economic overlaps become masculine (in reality or perception), then these instances will uphold stratification patterns as I noted in previous sections above. The key is to remember each of these five aspects of the process of institutional change are interdependent, but independent of each other. Thus, for instance, where there are more resources available and more paths to success, and women gain traction in mobility, than overlaps will become sites of heterogeneous interaction and, thereby, feedback on mobility and resource access. These mechanisms become self-reinforcing and movements can drive change that spreads via overlaps and mobility.
8. And this does not mean rich African Americans or women escape discrimination. The fact that they are rich, however, underlies the mobility available to individuals. The greater the numbers of individuals from these categoric groups that become mobile, the more tenuous old status beliefs become. Women, for example, have reached a certain point in the U.S. where some basic rights once denied could never feasibly be taken away. The presidential candidacy of Rick Santorum (2012) has demonstrated the taken for granted aspects that have been established; that Nancy Pelosi or Hillary Clinton are in positions of power and can use these as megaphones decrying the rhetoric of misogyny reinforces this point and also changes the way status beliefs are constructed and maintained.

## NOTES TO CHAPTER 7

1. Without wading into the debate, it is worth noting that sociologists have been involved in a vigorous debate regarding the unit of evolution and the unit of selection. The revivified sociobiologists, or evolutionary psychologists as they prefer to be called, see the individual as the unit of selection, reducing everything to biological reproduction and the perpetuation of culture through a person's ability to reproduce (e.g., Sanderson 2001). Others emphasize the concept *memes* as analogous to biological genes, arguing that bits of cultural

information are transmitted through language and practices, with some surviving and others dying (Lenski 2005; Blute 2010). And, finally, some prefer group-selectionist arguments, positing that selection works on groups and it is group culture that proves to be fit in terms of the group's ability to survive and, perhaps, even spread or impose their culture (Turner and Maryanski 2008;Wilson 2002). Although this is an important debate, I fall on the side of the group-selectionist argument and, thus, see entrepreneurs are the sources of variation upon which evolutionary forces can work.

2. Admittedly, this is a chicken-egg argument as the creation of urban settlements became targets for raiders who were pushed into less habitable land, thus the need for defense was artificially or unintentionally created. On the other side of the coin, however, humans living near alluvial planes became highly circumscribed, in part, by rational calculations that the desert or mountains were ecotones less likely to provide sustenance for families or clans, and thus the decision to stay put was not as simple as a warlord forcing or coercing them to stay (Carneiro 1970). Or, consider the need for economic management: more people meant more surplus, which gave ambitious entrepreneurs the key resource necessary to set and realize self-interested goals, yet the threat of disease or famine or drought kept these actors from generally becoming entirely self-absorbed and, in many ways, circumscribed their appropriation of surplus (Service 1975). As such, they had to devote some resources to the collective lest they lose their entire urban population to a disease or engender a costly rebellion in the hinterlands. The balance between self-aggrandizement and collective goods production was tenuous, hence the near constant tumult of political entrepreneurship throughout history.
3. A cultic assemblage is a single ritual bolstered with its underlying belief, or theology. A religion comprises a series of cultic assemblages that generally have some common threads in theology, but also some highly disconnected elements that speak to the genesis of the cultic belief and the period of syncretic work that merged various cults into a single religion.

# References

Abrutyn, Seth. 2009a. "Towards a General Theory of Institutional Autonomy." *Sociological Theory* 27(4):449–65.

———. 2009b. *A General Theory of Institutional Autonomy*. Ph.D. Dissertation, Department of Sociology: University of California, Riverside.

———. 2012. "Toward a Theory of Institutional Ecology: The Dynamics of Macro Structural Space." *Review of European Studies* 4(5):167–80.

———. 2013a. "Reconceptualizing Religious Evolution: Toward a General Theory of Macro-Institutional Change." *Social Evolution and History* 12(2).

———. 2013b. "Political Evolution, Entrepreneurship, and Autonomy: Causes and Consequences of an "Axial" Moment." *Research in Political Sociology* 21: 3-29.

———. 2013c. "Teaching Sociological Theory for a New Century: Contending with the *Time Crunch*." *The American Sociologist* 44(2):132–54.

———. Unpublished. "Explaining the Emergence of Religio-Cultural Entrepreneurs: The Case of the Axial Age."

Abrutyn, Seth, and Jonathan H. Turner. 2011. "The Old Institutionalism Meets the New Institutionalism." *Sociological Perspectives* 54(3):283–306.

Abrutyn, Seth, and Justin Van Ness. Unpublished. "Towards a General Theory of Institutional Entrepreneurs."

Abrutyn, Seth, and Kirk Lawrence. 2010. "From Chiefdoms to States: Toward an Integrative Theory of the Evolution of Polity." *Sociological Perspectives* 53(3):419–42.

Abu-Lughod, Janet L. 1989. *Before European Hegemony: The World System A.D. 1250–1350*. New York: Oxford University Press.

Adams, Robert McC. 1966. *The Evolution of Urban Society: Early Mesopotamia and PreHispanic Mexico*. Chicago: Aldine Publishing Company.

Adorno, Theodor. 1991. *The Culture Industry: Selected Essays on Mass Culture*. London: Routledge Classics.

Albertz, Rainer. 1992. *A History of Israelite Religion in the Old Testament Period: From the Beginnings to the End of the Exile*. London: SCM Press.

———. 1994. *A History of Israelite Religion in the Old Testament Period: From the Exile to the Maccabees*. London: Westminster John Knox Press.

Aldrich, Howard, and Martin Ruef. 2006. *Organizations Evolving*. London: Sage.

Alexander, Jeffrey C. 1988a. *Action and Its Environments: Toward a New Synthesis*. New York: Columbia University Press.

———. 1988b. "Durkheim's Problem and Differentiation Theory Today." Pp. 49–77 in *Action and Its Environments*. New York: Columbia University Press.

———. 1988c. "Parsons' 'Structure' in American Sociology." *Sociological Theory* 6(1):96–102.

———. 1988d. "Culture And Political Crisis: "Watergate" and Durkheimian Sociology." Pp. 187–225 in *Durkheimian Sociology: Cultural Studies*, edited by J.C. Alexander. Cambrdge, MA: Cambridge University Press.

———. 1998. *Neofunctionalism and After*. Malden, MA: Blackwell.

———. 2003. *The Meaning of Social Life: A Cultural Sociology*. Oxford: Oxford University Press.

———. 2004. "Cultural Pragmatics: Social Performance between Ritual and Strategy." *Sociological Theory* 22(4):527–73.

———. 2006. *The Civil Sphere*. Oxford: Oxford University Press.

Alexander, Jeffrey C., and Paul Colomy. 1988. "Social Differentiation and Collective Behavior." Pp. 193–221 in *Action and Its Environments*. New York: Columbia University Press.

———(Eds.). 1990. *Differentiation Theory and Social Change: Comparative and Historical Perspectives*. New York: Columbia University Press.

Alexander, Jeffrey C., and Philip Smith. 2003. "The Discourse of American Civil Society." Pp. 121–54 in *The Meanings of Social Life: A Cultural Sociology*, edited by Jeffrey C. Alexander. Oxford: Oxford University Press.

Alford, Robert R., and Roger Friedland. 1985. *Powers of Theory: Capitalism, the State, and Democracy*. Cambridge: Cambridge University Press.

Algaze, Guillermo. 2005. *The Uruk World System: The Dynamics of Expansion of Early Mesopotamian Civilization*. Chicago: University of Chicago Press.

Almond, Gabriel A., R. Scott Appleby, and Emmanuel Sivan. 2003. *Strong Religion: The Rise of Fundamentalism Around the World*. Chicago: University of Chicago Press.

Armstrong, John A. 1961. *The Politics of Totalitarianism: The Communist Party of the Soviet Union From 1934 to the Present*. New York: Random House.

Armstrong, Karen. 2006. *The Great Transformation: The Beginnings of Our Religious Traditions*. New York: Alfred A. Knopf.

Arrighi, Giovanni. 2007. *Adam Smith in Beijing: Lineages of the Twenty-First Century*. London: Verso.

Bacon, Francis (Ed.). 1857–74. *The Works of Francis Bacon*. London.

Baldwin, David A. 1971. "Money and Power." *The Journal of Politics* 33(3):578–614.

Bales, Robert F., and Philip E. Slater. 1955. "Role Differentiation in Small, Decision Making Groups." Pp. 259–306 in *Family, Socialization and Interaction Process*, edited by Talcott Parsons and Robert F. Bales. Glencoe, IL: Free Press.

Barr, Rebecca, and Robert Dreeben. 1983. *How Schools Work*. Chicago: University of Chicago Press.

Barth, Fredrik. 1963. *The Role of Entrepreneur in Social Change in Northern Norway*. New York: Wiley.

Barton, R.F. 1919. "Ifugao Law." *University of California Publications in American Archaeology and Ethnology* 15:1–186.

Baudrillard, Jean. 1972 [1981]. *For a Critique of the Political Economy of the Sign*. St. Louis: Telos Press.

Belk, Russell W., and Melanie Wallendorf. 1990. "The Sacred Meanings of Money." *Journal of Economic Psychology* 11(1):35–67.

Bellah, Robert N. 1964. "Religious Evolution." *American Sociological Review* 29(3):358–74.

———. 2011. *Religion in Human Evolution: From the Paleolithic to the Axial Age*. Cambridge, MA: Belknap Press of Harvard University Press.

Bellah, Robert N., and Hans Joas (Eds.). 2012. *The Axial Age and Its Consequences*. Cambrdge, MA: Belknap Press of Harvard University Press.

Ben-David, Joseph. 1965. "The Scientific Role: The Conditions of its Establishment in Europe." *Minerva* 4(1):15–54.

Berger, Joseph, Bernard P. Cohen, and Morris Zelditch Jr. 1972. "Status Characteristics and Social Interaction." *American Sociological Review* 37(3):241–55.
Berger, Peter. 1969. *The Sacred Canopy: Elements of a Sociological Theory of Religion*. New York: Anchor Books.
Berger, Peter, and Thomas Luckmann. 1966. *The Social Construction of Reality: A Treatise in the Sociology of Knowledge*. New York: Anchor Books.
Berman, Harold J. 1955. "The Law of the Soviet State." *Soviet Studies* 6(3):225–37.
———. 1968. "The Soviet Legal Profession." *Harvard Law Review* 82(1):1–41.
———. 1983. *Law and Revolution: The Formation of the Western Legal Tradition*. Cambridge, MA: Harvard University Press.
———. 2003. *Law and Revolution: The Impact of the Protestant Reformations on the Western Legal Tradition*. Cambridge, MA: Harvard University Press.
Biggart, Nicole Woolsey. 1991. "Explaining Asian Economic Organization: Toward a Weberian Institutional Perspective." *Theory and Society* 20:199–232.
Black, Donald. 1976. *The Behavior of Law*. San Diego, CA: Academic Press.
———. 1998. *The Social Structure of Right and Wrong*. San Diego, CA: Academic Press.
Blau, Peter M. 1964. *Exchange and Power in Social Life*. New Brunswick, NJ: Transaction Publishers.
———. 1970. "A Formal Theory of Differentiation in Organizations." *American Sociological Review* 35(2):201–18.
———. 1977. "A Macrosociological Theory of Social Structure." *American Journal of Sociology* 83(1):26–54.
Blau, Peter M., and Otis Dudley Duncan. 1967. *The American Occupational Structure*. New York: Free Press.
Blute, Marion. 2010. *Darwinian Sociocultural Evolution: Solutions to Dilemmas in Cultural and Social Theory*. Cambridge: Cambridge University Press.
Boehm, Christopher. 1999. *Hierarchy in the Forest: The Evolution of Egalitarian Behavior*. Cambridge, MA: Harvard University Press.
Bohannan, Paul. 1980. "Law and Legal Institutions." Pp. 3–11 in *The Sociology of Law: A Social-Structural Perspective*, edited by William M. Evan. New York: The Free Press.
Boli, John, Francisco Ramirez, and John W. Meyer. 1985. "Explaining the Origins and Expansion of Mass Education." *Comparative Education Review* 29(2):145–70.
Boltanski, Luc, and Laurent Thévenot. 1991 [2006]. *On Justification: Economies of Worth*. Princeton, NJ: Princeton University Press.
Boserup, Ester. 1965. *The Conditions of Agricultural Growth: The Economics of Agrarian Change Under Population Pressure*. Chicago: Aldine Publishing.
Bourdieu, Pierre. 1977. *Outline of a Theory of Practice*. Cambridge: Cambridge University Press.
———. 1984. *Distinction: A Social Critique of the Judgment of Taste*. Cambridge, MA: Harvard University Press.
———. 1985. "The Social Space and the Genesis of Groups." *Theory and Society* 14(6):723–44.
———. 1986. "The Forms of Capital." Pp. 241–58 in *Handbook of Theory and Research for the Sociology of Education*, edited by John G. Richardson. New York: Greenwood Press.
———. 1989. "Social Space and Symbolic Power." *Sociological Theory* 7(1):14–25.
———. 1990a. *Homo Academicus*. Palo Alto, CA: Stanford University Press.
———. 1990b. *In Other Words: Essays Toward a Reflexive Sociology*. Stanford, CA: Stanford University Press.

———. 1991. *Language and Symbolic Power.* Cambrdge, MA: Harvard University Press.

———. 1992. *The Rules of Art: Genesis and Structure of the Literary Field.* Stanford, CA: Stanford University Press.

———. 1993. *The Field of Cultural Production: Essays on Art and Literature.* New York: Columbia University Press.

———. 1996. *The State Nobility: Elite Schools in the Field of Power.* Stanford, CA: Stanford University Press.

Braudel, Fernand. 1979–84. *Civilization and Capitalism: 15th–18th Century.* New York: Harper & Row.

Bredemeier, Harry C. 1962. "Law as an Integrative Mechanism." Pp. 73–90 in *Law and Sociology: Exploratory Essays*, edited by William M. Evan. New York: Free Press.

Brint, Steven, and Seth Abrutyn. 2009. "Moral-Values Politics: The Emergence of an Electoral System." Pp. 105–40 in *Evangelicals and Democracy in America*, edited by Steven Brint and Jean Reith Schroedel. New York: Russell Sage

Burgess, Ernest Watson, and Harvey James Locke. 1945. *The Family: From Institution to Companionship.* New York: American Book Company.

Burke, Peter J. 1991. "Identity Processes and Social Stress." *American Sociological Review* 56(6):836–49.

Burke, Peter J., and Donald C. Reitzes. 1981. "The Link Between Identities and Role Performance." *Social Psychology Quarterly* 44(2):83–92.

Burke, Peter J., and Jan E. Stets. 1999. "Trust and Commitment Through Self-Verification." *Social Psychology Quarterly* 62(4):347–66.

Burke, Peter J., and Judy C. Tully. 1977. "The Measurement of Role Identity." *Social Forces* 55(4):881–97.

Burke, Peter J., and Michael M. Harrod. 2005. "Too Much of a Good Thing?" *Social Psychology Quarterly* 68:359–74.

Burt, Ronald S. 1992. *Structural Holes: The Social Structure of Competition.* Cambridge, MA: Harvard University Press.

———. 2004. "Structural Holes and Good Ideas." *American Journal of Sociology* 110(2):349–99.

Calhoun, Craig. 1993. "Habitus, Field, and Capital: The Question of Historical Specificity." Pp. 61–88 in *Bourdieu: Critical Perspectives*, edited by Craig Calhoun, Edward LiPuma, and Moishe Postone. Chicago: University of Chicago Press.

Carlson, Robert G. 1990. "Banana Beer, Reciprocity, and Ancestor Propitiation among the Haya of Bukoba, Tanzania." *Ethnology* 29(4):297–311.

Carneiro, Robert L. 1970. "A Theory of the Origin of the State." *Science* 169(3947):733–38.

———. 1978. "Political Expansion as an Expression of the Principle of Competitive Exclusion." Pp. 205–24 in *Origins of the State: The Anthropology of Political Evolution*, edited by Ronald Cohen and Elman R. Service. Philadelphia: Institute for the Study of Humans Issues.

Chadwick, Henry. 1967. *The Early Church.* London: Penguin Books.

Chandler, Tertius. 1976. *Godly Kings and Early Ethics.* Hicksville, NY: Exposition Press.

Chang, Kwang-chih. 1983. *Art, Myth, and Ritual: The Path to Political Authority in Ancient China.* Cambridge, MA: Harvard University Press.

———. 1986. *The Archaeology of Ancient China.* New Haven, CT: Yale University Press.

Chase-Dunn, Christopher, and Thomas D. Hall. 1997. *Rise and Demise: Comparing World-Systems.* Boulder, CO: Westview Press.

Chaves, Mark. 2004. *Congregations in America*. Cambridge, MA: Harvard University Press.

Chirot, Daniel. 1985. "The Rise of the West." *American Sociological Review* 58(2):181–95.

Clagett, Marshall, Gaines Post, and Robert Reynolds (Eds.). 1966. *Twelfth-Century Europe and the Foundations of Modern Society*. Madison: University of Wisconsin Press.

Cohen, Mark N. 1977. *The Food Crisis in Prehistory: Overpopulation and the Origins of Agriculture*. New Haven, CT: Yale University Press.

Coleman, James S. 1970. "Political Money." *The American Political Science Review* 64(4):1074–87.

———. 1988. "Free Riders and Zealots: The Role of Social Networks." *Sociological Theory* 6(1):52–57.

Collins, Randall. 1975. *Conflict Sociology: Towards an Explanatory Science*. New York: Academic Press.

———. 1979. *The Credential Society: An Historical Sociology of Education and Stratification*. New York: Academic Press.

———. 1981a. "Long-Term Social Change and the Territorial Power of States." Pp. 71–108 in *Sociology Since Midcentury*. New York: Free Press.

———. 1981b. "Three Faces of Cruelty: Toward a Comparative Sociology of Violence." Pp. 133–60 in *Sociology Since Mid-Century*. New York: Academic Press.

———. 1988. "The Durkheimian Tradition in Conflict Sociology." Pp. 107–28 in *Durkheimian Sociology: Cultural Studies*, edited by J.C. Alexander. Cambrdge, MA: Cambridge University Press.

———. 1990. "Market Dynamics as the Engine of Historical Change." *Sociological Theory* 8(2):111–35.

———. 1997. "An Asian Route to Capitalism: Religious Economy and the Origins of Self-Transforming Growth in Japan." *American Sociological Review* 62(6):843–65.

———. 2000a. "Comparative and Historical Patterns of Education." Pp. 213–39 in *Handbook of the Sociology of Education*, edited by Maureen T. Hallinan. New York: Kluwer Academic/Plenum Publishers.

———. 2000b. "Situational Stratification: A Micro-Macro Theory of Inequality." *Sociological Theory* 18(1):17–43.

———. 2004. *Interaction Ritual Chains*. Princeton, NJ: Princeton University Press.

Colomy, Paul. 1985. "Uneven Structural Differentiation: Toward a Comparative Approach." Pp. 131–56 in *Neofunctionalism*, edited by Jeffrey C. Alexander. Beverly Hills, CA: Sage.

———. 1990a. "Strategic Groups and Political Differentiation in the Antebellum United States." Pp. 222–64 in *Differentiation Theory and Social Change: Comparative and Historical Perspectives*, edited by Jeffrey C. Alexander and Paul Colomy. New York: Columbia University Press.

———. 1990b. "Uneven Differentiation and Incomplete Institutionalization: Political Change and Continuity in the Early American Nation." Pp. 119–63 in *Differentiation Theory and Social Change: Comparative and Historical Perspectives*, edited by Jeffrey C. Alexander and Paul Colomy. New York: Columbia University Press.

———. 1998. "Neofunctionalism and Neoinstitutionalism: Human Agency and Interest in Institutional Change." *Sociological Forum* 13(2):265–300.

Colomy, Paul, and Gary Rhoades. 1994. "Toward a Micro Corrective of Structural Differentiation Theory." *Sociological Perspectives* 37(4):547–83.

Colomy, Paul, and Martin Kertzmann. 1995. "Projects and Institution Building: Judge Ben B. Lindsey and the Juvenile Court Movement." *Social Problems* 42(2):191–215.

Cook, Karen S., Coye Cheshire, and Alexandra Gerbasi. 2006. "Power, Dependence, and Social Exchange." Pp. 194–216 in *Contemporary Social Psychological Theories*, edited by Peter J. Burke. Stanford, CA: Stanford University Press.

Cookson Jr., Peter W., and Caroline Hodges Persell. 1987. *Preparing For Power: America's Elite Boarding Schools*. New York: Basic Books.

D'Aunno, Thomas, Melissa Succi, and Jeffrey A. Alexander. 2000. "The Role of Institutional and Market Forces in Divergent Organizational Change." *Administrative Science Quaterly* 45(5):679–703.

Dahrendorf, Ralf. 1959. "Toward a Theory of Social Conflict." *The Journal of Conflict Resolution* 2(2):170–83.

Dayan, Daniel and Elihu Katz. 1988. "Articulating Consensus: The Ritual and Rhetoric of Media Events." Pp. 161–86 in *Durkheimian Sociology*, edited by J.C. Alexander. Cambridge: Cambridge University Press.

Diamond, Jared. 2004. *Collapse: How Societies Choose to Fail or Succeed*. London: Viking Adult.

DiMaggio, Paul. 1988. "Interest and Agency in Institutional Theory." Pp. 3–22 in *Institutional Patterns and Organizations*, edited by Lynne G. Zucker. Cambridge, MA: Ballinger.

——— 1991. "Constructing an Organizational Field as a Professional Project: U.S. Art Museums, 1920–1940." Pp. 267–92 in *The New Institutionalism in Organizational Analysis*, edited by Walter W. Powell and Paul DiMaggio. Chicago: University of Chicago Press.

DiMaggio, Paul, and Walter W. Powell. 1983. "The Iron Cage Revisited: Institutional Isomorphism and Collective Rationality in Organizational Fields." *American Sociological Review* 48(2):147–60.

Dobbin, Frank, and John R. Sutton. 1998. "The Strength of a Weak State: The Rights Revolution and the Rise of Human Resources Management Divisions." *American Journal of Sociology* 104(2):441–76.

Durkheim, Emile. 1893. *The Division of Labor in Society*. New York: The Free Press.

———. 1895 [1982]. *The Rules of Sociological Method and Selected Texts on Sociology and Its Method*. New York: Free Press.

———. 1912. *The Elementary Forms of Religious Life*. New York: Free Press.

———. 1921. "La Famille Conjugale." *Revue Philosophique de la France et de l'Etranger* 91:1–14.

Earle, Timothy. 1991. *Chiefdoms: Power, Economy, and Ideology*. Cambridge: Cambridge University Press.

———. 2002. *Bronze Age Economics: The Beginnings of Political Economies*. Boulder, CO: Westview Press.

Easterlin, Richard A. 1987. *Birth and Fortune: The Impact of Numbers on Personal Welfare*. Chicago: University of Chicago Press.

———. 2003. "Explaining Happiness." *Proceedings of the National Academy of Sciences of the United States of America* 100(19):11176–83.

Edelman, Lauren B., and Mark C. Suchman. 1997. "The Legal Environments of Organizations." *Annual Review of Sociology* 23:479–515.

Eidheim, Harald. 1963. "Entrepreneurship in Politics." Pp. 70–82 in *The Role of Entrepreneur in Social Change in Northern Norway*, edited by F. Barth. New York: Wiley.

Eisenstadt, S.N. 1962. "Religious Organizations and Political Process in Centralized Empires." *The Journal of Asian Studies* 21(3):271–94.

———. 1963. *The Political System of Empires: The Rise and Fall of the Historical Bureaucratic Societies*. New York: Free Press.

———. 1964a. "Institutionalization and Change." *American Sociological Review* 29(2):235–47.

———. 1964b. "Social Change, Differentiation and Evolution." *American Sociological Review* 29(3):375–86.

———(Ed.). 1965a. *Essays on Comparative Institutions*. New York: John Wiley & Sons.

———. 1965b. "Political Orientations of Bureaucracies in Centralized Empires." Pp. 216–50 in *Essays in Comparative Institutions*, edited by S.N. Eisenstadt. New York: John Wiley & Sons.

———. 1971a. *Social Differentiation and Stratification*. Glenview, IL: Scott, Foresman and Company.

———. 1971b. "Some Reflections on the Significance of Max Weber's Sociology of Religions for the Analysis of non-European Modernity." *Archives de sociologie des religions* 32:29–25.

———. 1977. "Sociological Theory and an Analysis of the Dynamics of Civilizations and of Revolutions." *Daedalus* 106(4):59–78.

———. 1980. "Cultural Orientations, Institutional Entrepreneurs, and Social Change: Comparative Analysis of Traditional Civilizations." *American Journal of Sociology* 85(4):840–69.

———. 1982. "The Axial Age: The Emergence of Transcendental Visions and the Rise of Clerics." *European Journal of Sociology* 23(2):294–314.

———. 1984. "Heterodoxies and Dynamics of Civilizations." *American Philosophical Society* 128(2):104–13.

———. 1986a. "The Axial Age Breakthroughs." Pp. 1–25 in *The Origins and Diversity of Axial Age Civilizations*, edited by S. N. Eisenstadt. Albany: State University of New York Press.

———(Ed.). 1986b. *The Origins and Diversity of Axial Age Civilizations*. Albany: State University of New York Press.

———. 1987. "Macrosociology and Sociological Theory: Some New Directions." *Contemporary Sociology* 16(5):602–9.

———. 1989. "Max Weber on Western Christianity and the Weberian Approach to Civilizational Dynamics." *Canadian Journal of Sociology* 14(2):203–23.

———. 1990. "Modes of Structural Differentiations, Elite Structures, and Cultural Visions." Pp. 20–51 in *Differentiation Theory and Social Change: Comparative and Historical Perspectives*, edited by Jeffrey C. Alexander and Paul Colomy. New York: Columbia University Press.

———. 2000. "Multiple Modernities." *Daedalus* 129(1):1–29.

Eisenstadt, S. N., and Louis Roniger. 1980. "Patron-Client Relations as a Model of Structuring Social Exchange." *Comparative Studies in Society and History* 22(1):42–77.

Eisenstadt, S. N., M. Abitol, and N. Chazan. 1987. "Cultural Premises, Political Structures and Dynamics." *International Political Science Review* 8(4):291–306.

Eisenstadt, S. N., and Miriam Curelaru. 1976. *The Form of Sociology: Paradigms and Crises*. New York: John Wiley.

Ekeh, Peter P. 1974. *Social Exchange Theory: The Two Traditions*. Cambridge, MA: Harvard University Press.

Eliade, Mircea. 1978. *A History of Religious Ideas: From the Stone Age to the Eleusinian Mysteries*. Chicago: University of Chicago Press.

Elkana, Yehuda. 1986. "The Emergence of Second-Order Thinking in Classical Greece." Pp. 40– 64 in *The Origins and Diversity of Axial Age Civilizations*, edited by S. N. Eisenstadt. Albany: State University of New York Press.

Emirbayer, Mustafa, and Ann Mische. 1998. "What Is Agency?" *American Journal of Sociology* 103:962–1023.
Endres, Anthony M., and Christine R. Woods. 2006. "Modern Theories of Entrepreneurial Behavior: A Comparison and Appraisal." *Small Business Economics* 26(2):189–202.
Evan, William M. 1980. "Law as an Instrument of Social Change." Pp. 554–62 in *The Sociolog of Law: A Social-Structural Perspective*, edited by William M. Evan. New York: The Free Press.
Fagan, Brian. 2004. *The Long Summer: How Climate Changed Civilization.* New York: Basic Books.
Finke, Roger, and Rodney Stark. 1988. "Religious Economies and Sacred Canopies: Religious Mobilization in American Cities, 1906." *American Sociological Review* 53(1):41–9.
Flannery, Kent V. 1972. "The Cultural Evolution of Civilizations." *Annual Review of Ecology and Systematics* 3:399–426.
Fligstein, Neil. 1996. "Markets As Politics: A Political-Cultural Approach to Market Institutions." *American Sociological Review* 61(4):656–73.
Fligstein, Neil, and Doug McAdam. 2011. "Toward a General Theory of Strategic Action Fields." *Sociological Theory* 29(1):1–27.
———. 2012. *A Theory of Fields*. New York: Oxford University Press.
Foucault, Michel. 1988. *Madness and Civilization: A History of Insanity in the Age of Reason.* New York: Vintage Books.
———. 1995. *Discipline and Punishment: The Birth of the Prison.* New York: Vintage Books.
Fowler, James H., and Nicholas A. Christakis. 2008. "Dynamic Spread of Happiness in a Large Social Network: Longitudinal Analysis Over the 20 Years in the Framingham Heart Study." *British Medical Journal* 337:a2338. doi:10.1136/bmj.a2338.
Fox, Robin. 1967. *Kinship and Marriage: An Anthropological Perspective.* London: Cambridge University Press.
Frankfort, Henri. 1948. *Kingship and the Gods.* Chicago: University of Chicago Press.
Freidson, Eliot. 1994. *Professions Reborn: Theory, Prophecy, and Policy.* Chicago: University of Chicago Press.
Fried, Morton H. 1967. *The Evolution of Political Society.* New York: Random House.
Friedland, Roger, and Robert R. Alford. 1991. "Bringing Society Back In: Symbols, Practices, and Institutional Contradictions." Pp. 232–66 in *The New Institutionalism in Organizational Analysis*, edited by Walter W. Powell and Paul J. DiMaggio. Chicago: University of Chicago Press.
Freidson, Eliot. 1962. "Dilemmas in Doctor-Patient Relationships." Pp. 207–24 in *Human Behavior and Social Processes*, edited by Arnold M. Rose. Boston: Houghton Mifflin Company.
Froese, Paul. 2009. *The Plot to Kill God: Findings from the Soviet Experiment in Secularization.* Berkeley: University of California Press.
Fuchs, Stephen. 1989. "On the Microfoundations of Macrosociology: A Critique of Macrosociological Reductionism." *Sociological Perspectives* 32(2):169–82.
Garfinkel, Harold. 1964. "Studies of the Routine Grounds of Everyday Activities." *Social Problems* 11(3):225–50.
Gat, Azar. 2006. *War in Human Civilization.* Oxford: Oxford University Press.
Gaukroger, Stephen. 2006. *The Emergence of Scientific Culture: Science and the Shaping of Modernity, 1210–1685.* Oxford: Oxford University Press.
Gaworek, N. H. 1977. "Education, Ideology, and Politics: History in Soviet Primary and Secondary Schools." *The History Teacher* 11(1):55–74.

Geertz, Clifford. 1966. "Religion as a Cultural System." In *Anthropological Approaches to the Study of Religion*, edited by Michael Banton. London: Tavistock Publications.

Gerth, Hans, and C. Wright Mills. 1953. *Character and Social Structure: The Psychology of Social Institutions*. New York: Harcourt, Brace & World.

Giddens, Anthony. 1975. *Positivism and Sociology*. London: Heinemann.

———. 1984. *The Constitution of Society*. Berkeley: University of California Press.

Gies, Frances, and Joseph Gies. 1986. *Marriage and the Family in the Middle Ages*. New York: Perennial Library.

Gillmore, Mary Rogers. 1987. "Implications of General versus Restricted Exchange." Pp. 170–87 in *Social Exchange Theory*, edited by Karen S. Cook. Newbury Park, CA: Sage.

Gluckman, Max. 1965. *Politics, Law and Ritual In Tribal Society*. Chicago: Aldine.

Goffman, Erving. 1959. *The Presentation of Self in Everyday Life*. New York: Anchor Books.

———. 1961. *Asylums: Essays on the Social Situation of Mental Patients and Other Inmates*. Garden City, NY: Anchor Books.

———. 1963a. *Behavior in Public Places: Notes on the Social Organization of Gatherings*. New York: Free Press.

———. 1963b. *Stigma: Notes on the Management of Spoiled Identity*. Englewood Cliffs, NJ: Prentice-Hall, Inc.

———. 1967. *Interaction Ritual: Essays on Face-to-Face Behavior*. New York: Pantheon Books.

———. 1971. *Relations in Public*. New York: Harper and Row.

———. 1974. *Frame Analysis*. New York: Harper & Row.

———. 1981. *Forms of Talk*. Philadelphia: University of Pennsylvania Press.

Goody, Jack. 1998. *Food and Love: A Cultural History of East and West*. London: Verso.

———. 2000. *The European Family: An Historico-Anthropological Essay*. Boston: Blackwell Publishers.

Gospic, Katarina, Erik Mohlin, Peter Fransson, Pedrag Petrovic, Magnus Johannesson, and Martin Ingvar. 2011. "Limbic Justice—Amygdala Involvement in Immediate Rejection in the Ultimatum Game." *PLos Biol* 9(5):e1001054. doi:10.1371/journal.pbio.54.

Grafton, Anthony, and Robert B. Townsend. 2008. "The Parlous Paths of the Profession." In *Perspectives on History*. http://www.historians.org/perspectives/issues/2008/0810/0810pro1.cfm.

Granovetter, Mark S. 1985. "Economic Action and Social Structure: The Problem of Embeddedness." *American Journal of Sociology* 91(3):481–510.

Gratian. 1582 [1993]. *The Treatise on Laws with the Ordinary Gloss*. Washington, DC: Catholic University of America Press.

Greenwood, Royston, Christine Oliver, Roy Suddaby, and Kerstin Sahlin. 2008. *The SAGE Handbook of Organizational Institutionalism*. Los Angeles, CA: Sage.

Habermas, Jurgen. 1985. *The Theory of Communicative Action*. 2 vols. Boston: Beacon Press.

Hall, John A. 1985. *Powers and Liberties: The Causes and Consequences of the Rise of the West*. London: Penguin Books.

Hall, John R. 2003. "Religion and Violence: Social Processes in Comparative Perspective." Pp. 359–84 in *Handbook of the Sociology of Religion*, edited by Michele Dillon. Cambridge: Cambridge University Press.

Hamilton, Gary G., and Nicole Woolsey Biggart. 1988. "Market, Culture, and Authority: A Comparative Analysis of Management and Organization in the Far East." *American Journal of Sociology* 94(Supplement):52–94.

Hannan, Michael T., and John Freeman. 1977. "The Population Ecology of Organizations." *American Journal of Sociology* 82(5):929–64.

Hardy, Cynthia, and Steve Maguire. 2008. *Institutional Entrepreneurship*. Thousand Oaks, CA: Sage.

Hawley, Amos H. 1944. "Ecology and Human Ecology." *Social Forces* 22(4):398–405.

———. 1986. *Human Ecology: A Theoretical Essay*. Chicago: University of Chicago Press.

Hechter, Michael. 1987. *Principles of Group Solidarity*. Berkeley: University of California Press.

Henrich, Joseph. 2001. "Cultural Transmission and the Diffusion of Innovations: Adoption Dynamics Indicate That Biased Cultural Transmission is the Predominate Force of Behavioral Change." *American Anthropologist* 103(4):992–1013.

Henrich, Joseph, and F. Gil-White. 2001. "The Evolution of Prestige." *Evolution and Human Behavior* 22(3):165–96.

Hoebel, E. Adamson. 1973. *The Law of Primitive Man*. New York: Antheneum.

Homans, George C. 1950. *The Human Group*. New York: Harcourt, Brace & World.

Hsu, Cho-Yun. 1986. "Historical Conditions of the Emergence and Crystallization of the Confucian System." Pp. 306–25 in *The Origins and Diversity of Axial Age Civilizations*, edited by S.N. Eisenstadt. Albany: State University of New York Press.

Hughes, Everett C. 1942. "The Study of Social Institutions." *Social Forces* 20(3):307–10.

Irons, Peter. 1999. *A People's History of the Supreme Court: The Men and Women Whose Cases and Decisions Have Shaped Our Constitution*. New York: Penguin Books.

Jacobsen, Thorkild. 1963. "Ancient Mesopotamian Religion: The Central Concerns." *Proceedings of the American Philosophical Society* 107(6):473–84.

Jaspers, Karl. 1953. *The Origin and Goal of History*. London: Routledge & Kegan Paul.

Jellenbach, C. 1945. *Church, State, and Christian Society at the Time of the Investiture Conflict*. Oxford: Oxford University Press.

Johnson, Allen W., and Timothy Earle. 2000. *The Evolution of Human Societies: From Foraging Groups to Agrarian State*. Stanford, CA: Stanford University Press.

Joyce, Rosemary A. 2000. "High Culture, Mesoamerican Civilization, and the Classic Maya Tradition." Pp. 64–76 in *Order, Legitimacy, and Wealth in Ancient States*, edited by Janet Richards and Mary Van Buren. Cambridge: Cambridge University Press.

Keay, John. 2000. *India: A History*. New York: Grove Press.

Knorr-Cetina, Karin. 1981. "The Micro-Sociological Challenge of Macro-Sociology: Toward a Reconstruction of Social Theory and Methodology." Pp. 1–46 in *Advances in Social Theory and Methodology: Toward an Integration of Micro- and Macro-Sociologies*, edited by Karin Knorr-Cetina and Aaron Vincent Cicourel. Boston: Routledge and Kegan Paul.

Kraatz, Matthew S., and Edward J. Zajac. 1996. "Exploring the Limits of the New Institutionalism: The Causes and Consequences of Illegitimate Organizational Change." *American Sociological Review* 61(5):812–36.

Kramer, Samuel Noah. 1963. *The Sumerians: Their History, Culture, and Character*. Chicago: University of Chicago Press.

Kunkel, Wolfgang. 1966. *An Introduction to Roman Legal and Constitutional History*. Oxford: Oxford University Press.

La Valle, Davide. 1994. "Social Exchange and Social System: A Parsonian Approach." *Sociological Perspectives* 37(4):585–610.
Lawler, Edward J. 1992. "Affective Attachments to Nested Groups: Choice-Process Theory." *American Sociological Review* 57(3):327–39.
———. 2001. "An Affect Theory of Social Exchange." *American Journal of Sociology* 107(2):321–52.
———. 2006. "The Affect Theory of Social Exchange." Pp. 248–67 in *Contemporary Social Psychological Theories*, edited by Peter J. Burke. Stanford: Stanford University Press.
Lawler, Edward J., Shane Thye, and Jeongkoo Yoon. 2009. *Social Commitments in a Depersonalized World*. New York: Russell Sage.
Leca, Bernard, and Philippe Naccache. 2006. "A Critical Realist Approach to Institutional Entrepreneurship." *Organization* 13(5):627–51.
Lechner, Frank L. 1990. "Fundamentalism and Sociocultural Revitalization: On the Logic of Dedifferentiation." Pp. 88–118 in *Differentiation Theory and Social Change: Comparative and Historical Perspectives*, edited by Jeffrey C. Alexander and Paul Colomy. New York: Columbia University Press.
Lee, Richard. 1979. *The !Kung San*. Cambridge: Cambridge University Press.
Leifer, Eric. 1998. *Making the Majors: The Transformation of Team Sports in America*. Cambrdge, MA: Harvard University Press.
Lenski, Gerhard. 1966. *Power and Privilege: A Theory of Social Stratification*. New York: McGraw-Hill.
———. 1970. *Human Societies: A Macro-Level Introduction to Sociology*. New York: McGraw-Hill.
———. 2005. *Ecological-Evolutionary Theory*. Boulder: Paradigm.
Levi-Strauss, Claude. 1969. *The Elementary Structures of Kinship*. Boston: Beacon Press.
Levy, D., and M. Scully. 2007. "The Institutional Entrepreneur as Modern Prince: The Strategic Face of Power in Contested Fields." *Organization Studies* 28(7):971–91.
Lindberg, David C. 2007. *The Beginnings of Western Science: The European Scientific Tradition in Philosophical, Religious, and Institutional Context, Prehistory to A.D. 1450*. Chicago: University of Chicago Press.
Lipinski, Edward. 1979. *State and Temple Economy in the Ancient Near East*. Leuven, Belgium: Department Orientalistiek.
Liverani, Mario (Ed.). 1993. *Akkad: The First World Empire*. Padova: Sargon.
———. 2005. *Israel's History and the History of Israel*. London: Equinox.
———. 2006. *Uruk: The First City*. London: Equinox.
Lloyd, Dennis. 1964. *The Idea of Law*. Baltimore: Penguin Books.
Locke, John. 1690 [2007]. *An Essay Concerning Human Understanding*: Pomona Press.
Lopez, Robert S. 1971. *The Commercial Revolution of the Middle Ages, 950–1350*. Englewood Cliffs, NJ: Prentice-Hall.
Lounsbury, Michael. 2007. "A Tale of Two Cities: Competing Logics and Practice Variation in the Professionalizing of Mutual Funds." *Academy of Management Journal* 50:289–307.
Luhmann, Niklas. 1976. "Generalized Media and the Problem of Contingency." Pp. 507–32 in *Explorations in General Theory in Social Science: Essays in Honor of Talcott Parsons*, edited by Jan J. Loubser, Rainer Baum, Andrew Effrat, and Victor Meyer Lidz. New York: Free Press.
———. 1979. *Trust and Power*. Chichester, England: John Wiley & Sons.
———. 1982. *The Differentiation of Society*. New York: Columbia University Press.
———. 1995. *Social Systems*. Stanford, CA: Stanford University Press.

———. 1998. *Love as Passion: The Codification of Intimacy*. Stanford, CA: Stanford University Press.
———. 2000a. *Art as a Social System*. Stanford, CA: Stanford University Press.
———. 2000b. *The Reality of Mass Media: Cultural Memory in the Present*. Stanford, CA: Stanford University Press.
———. 2004. *Law as a Social System*. Oxford: Oxford University Press.
———. 2008. *Risk: A Sociological Theory*. New Brunswick, NJ: Aldine.
———. 2010. *Love: A Sketch*. Cambridge: Polity Press.
———. 2012. *Theory of Society*. Stanford, CA: Stanford University Press.
———. 2013. *A Systems Theory of Religion*. Stanford, CA: Stanford University Press.
Malinowski, Bronislaw. 1922. *Argonauts of the Western Pacific: An Account of Native Enterprise and Adventure in the Archipelagoes of Melanesian New Guinea*. London: G. Routledge.
———. 1959. *Crime and Custom in Savage Society*. Paterson, NJ: Littlefield, Adams, and Co. Mann, Michael. 1986. *The Sources of Social Power: A History of Power from the Beginning to A.D. 1760*. Cambridge: Cambridge University Press.
Marcuse, Herbert. 1964. *One-Dimensional Man*. Boston: Beacon Press.
Marquis, Christopher, and Michael Lounsbury. 2007. "Vive la Resistance: Competing Logics and the Conslidation of U.S. Banking." *Academy of Management Journal* 50:799–820.
Marsden, George M. 1990. *Religion and American Culture*. Fort Worth, TX: Harcourt Brace College.
Marx, Karl. 1845–6 [1972]. "The German Ideology." Pp. 146–202 in *The Marx-Engels Reader*, edited by Robert C. Tucker. New York: W.W. Norton & Company.
———. 1867 [1990]. *Capital, Volume 1: A Critique of Political Economy*. London: Penguin Classics.
Maryanski, Alexandra, and Jonathan H. Turner. 1992. *The Social Cage: Human Nature and the Evolution of Society*. Stanford, CA: Stanford University Press.
Mauss, Marcel. 1967. *The Gift: Forms and Functions of Exchange in Archaic Societies*. New York: W. W. Norton.
Maynard Smith, John, and Eörs Szathmary. 1995. *The Major Transitions in Evolution*. Oxford: W. H. Freeman and Company.
McNeill, William H. 1976. *Plagues and Peoples*. Garden City, NY: Anchor Press.
———. 1982. *The Pursuit of Power: Technology, Armed Force, and Society Since AD 1000*. Chicago: University of Chicago Press.
McPherson, J. Miller. 1983. "An Ecology of Affiliation." *American Sociological Review* 48(4):519–32.
———. 1988. "A Theory of Voluntary Organizations." Pp. 42–76 in *Community Organizations: Studies in Resource Mobilization and Exchange*, edited by C. Milofsky. Oxford: Oxford University Press.
McPherson, J. Miller, and James R. Ranger-Moore. 1991. "Evolution on a Dancing Landscape: Organizations and Networks in Dynamic Blau Space." *Social Forces* 70(1):19–42.
Meyer, John W. 1987. "The World Polity and the Authority of the Nation-State." Pp. 41–70 in *Institutional Structure: Constituting State, Society and the Individual*, edited by George
M. Thomas, John W. Meyer, Francisco Ramirez, and John Boli. Newbury Park, CA: Sage.
Meyer, John W., and Brian Rowan. 1977. "Institutionalized Organizations: Formal Structure as Myth and Ceremony." *American Journal of Sociology* 83(2):340–63.

Meyer, John W., Joane Nagel, and Conrad W. Snyder Jr. 1993. "The Expansion of Mass Education in Botswana: Local and World Society Perspectives." *Comparative Education Review* 37(4):454–75.

Michalowski, Piotr. 1993. "Memory and Deed: The Historiography of the Political Expansion of the Akkad State." Pp. 69–90 in *Akkad: The First World Empire*, edited by Mario Liverani. Padova, Italy: Sargon.

Michels, Robert. 1911 [1962]. *Political Parties: A Sociological Study of the Oligarchical Tendencies of Modern Democracy.* New York: Free Press.

Mills, C. Wright. 1959. *The Power Elite.* New York: Oxford University Press.

Montesquieu, Charles de Secondat, Baron de. 1750 [2002]. *The Spirit of Laws.* Amherst, NY: Prometheus Books.

Mundey, Peter, Hilary Davidson, and Patricia Snell Herzog. 2011. "Making Money Sacred: How Two Church Cultures Translate Mundane Money into Distinct Sacralized Forms of Giving." *Journal for the Scientific Study of Religion* 72(3):303–26.

Nee, Victor. 2005. "The New Institutionalisms in Economics and Sociology." Pp. 49–74 in *The Handbook of Economic Sociology*, edited by Neil J. Smelser and Richard Swedberg. Princeton, NJ: Princeton University Press.

Nissen, Hans J. 1988. *The Early History of the Ancient Near East, 9000–2000 B.C.* Chicago: University of Chicago Press.

Nolan, Patrick, and Gerhard Lenski. 2009. *Human Societies: An Introduction to Macrosociology.* Boulder, CO: Paradigm.

North, Douglass C. 1990. *Institutions, Institutional Change, and Economic Performance.* Cambridge: Cambridge University Press.

———. 2005. "Capitalism and Economic Growth." Pp. 41–52 in *The Economic Sociology of Capitalism*, edited by Victor Nee and Richard Swedberg. Princeton, NJ: Princeton University Press.

Oprisko, Robert. 2012. "Superpowers: The America Academic Elite." In *Georgetown Public Policy Review.* http://gppreview.com/2012/12/03/superpowers-the-american-academic-elite/.

Ouchi, William G. 1980. "Markets, Bureaucracies, and Clans." *Administrative Science Quarterly* 25(1):129–41.

Paige, Jeffery M. 1974. "Kinship and Polity in Stateless Societies." *American Journal of Sociology* 80(2):301–20.

Paine, Robert. 1963. "Entrepreneurial Activity without its Profits." Pp. 33–56 in *The Role of Entrepreneur in Social Change in Northern Norway*, edited by F. Barth. New York: Wiley.

Pareto, Vilfredo. 1965. *Vilfredo Pareto: Selections from his Treatise.* New York: Thomas Y. Cromwell Company.

Parsons, Talcott. 1951. *The Social System.* Glencoe, Ill.,: Free Press.

———. 1963a. "On the Concept of Influence." *Public Opinion Quarterly* 27(1):37–62.

———. 1963b. "On the Concept of Political Power." *Proceedings of the American Philosophical Society* 107(3):232–62.

———. 1964a. "Evolutionary Universals in Society." *American Sociological Review* 29(3):339–57.

———. 1964b. *Social Structure and Personality.* London: Free Press.

———. 1966. *Societies: Evolutionary and Comparative Perspectives.* Englewood Cliffs, NJ: Prentice-Hall.

———. 1968. "On the Concept of Value-Commitments." *Sociological Inquiry* 38(2):135–60.

———. 1971. *The System of Modern Societies.* Englewood Cliffs, NJ: Prentice-Hall.

———. 1973. "The Cognitive Complex: Knowledge, Rationality, Learning, Competence, Intelligence." Pp. 33–89 in *The American University*, edited by Talcott Parsons and Gerald Platt. Cambridge, MA: Harvard University Press.

———. 1990. "Prolegomena to a Theory of Social Institutions." *American Sociological Review* 55(3):319–33.

Parsons, Talcott, and Edward A. Shils (Eds.). 1951. *Toward a General Theory of Action*. New York: Harper & Row.

Parsons, Talcott, and Neil J. Smelser. 1956. *Economy and Society: A Study in the Integration of Economic and Social Theory*. New York: Free Press.

Polanyi, Karl. 1957. "The Economy as Instituted Process." Pp. 243–69 in *Trade and Market in the Early Empires: Economies in History and Theory*, edited by Karl Polanyi, Conrad M. Arensberg, and Harry W. Pearson. Glencoe, IL: Free Press.

Postgate, J. N. 1977. *The First Empires*. Oxford: Elsevier-Phaidon.

Potts, D. T. 1997. *Mesopotamian Civilization: The Material Foundations*. Ithaca, NY: Cornell University Press.

Powell, Walter W. 1999. "Neither Market Nor Hierarchy: Network Forms of Organizations." *Research in Organizational Behavior* 12:295–336.

Powell, Walter W., and Paul J. DiMaggio. 1991. *The New Institutionalism in Organizational Analysis*. Chicago: The University of Chicago Press.

Proctor, Darby, Rebecca A. Williamson, Frans De Waal, and Sarah F. Bronson. 2013. "Chimpanzees Play the Ultimatum Game." In *Proceedings of the National Academy of Sciences of the United States of America*. Radcliffe-Brown, A.R. 1965. *Structure and Function in Primitive Society*. New York: Free Press.

Radin, Paul. 1937 [1957]. *Primitive Religion: Its Nature and Origin*. New York: Dover.

Rao, Hayagreeva. 1998. "Caveat Emptor: The Construction of Nonprofit Consumer Watchdog Organizations." *American Journal of Sociology* 103(4):916–61.

Rashdall, Hastings (Ed.). 1936. *The Universities of Europe in the Middle Ages: Salerno-Bologna-Paris*. Oxford: Oxford University Press.

Redfield, Robert. 1967. "Primitive Law." Pp. 3–25 in *Law and Warfare: Studies in the Anthropology of Conflict*, edited by Paul Bohannan. Garden City, NY: The Natural History Press.

Reed, Isaac Ariail. 2011. *Interpretation and Social Knowedge: On the Use of Theory in the Human Sciences*. Chicago: University of Chicago Press.

———. 2013. "Charimatic Performance: A Study of Bacon's Rebellion." *American Journal of Cultural Sociology* 1(2):254–87.

Richards, Janet, and Mary Van Buren (Eds.). 2000. *Order, Legitimacy, and Wealth in Ancient States*. Cambridge: Cambridge University Press.

Richerson, Peter, and Robert Boyd. 2005. *Not by Genes Alone: How Culture Transformed Human Evolution*. Chicago: University of Chicago Press.

Ridgeway, Cecilia L. 1991. "The Social Construction of Status Values: Gender and Other Nominal Characteristics." *Social Forces* 70:367–86.

———. 2001. "Inequality, Status, and the Construction of Status Beliefs." In *The Handbook of Sociological Theory*, edited by J. H. Turner. New York: Kluwer/Plenum.

———. 2006. "Status Construction Theory." Pp. 301–23 in *Contemporary Social Psychological Theories*, edited by Peter J. Burke. Stanford, CA: Stanford University Press.

Robinson, Dawn T., and Lynn Smith-Lovin. 2006. "Affect Control Theory." Pp. 137–64 in *Contemporary Social Psychological Theories*, edited by Peter J. Burke. Stanford, CA: Stanford University Press.

Rueschemeyer, Dietrich. 1977. "Structural Differentiation, Efficiency, and Power." *American Journal of Sociology* 83(1):1–25.

———. 1986. *Power and the Division of Labour*. Stanford, CA: Stanford University Press.

Sahlins, Marshall. 1960. "Evolution: General and Specific." Pp. 12–44 in *Evolution and Culture*, edited by Marshall D. Sahlins and Elman R. Service. Ann Arbor: University of Michigan Press.

———. 1972. *Stone Age Economics*. New York: Aldine.
Sanderson, Stephen K. 1999. *Social Transformations: A General Theory of Historical Development*. Lanham, MD: Rowman & Littlefield.
———. 2001. *The Evolution of Human Sociality: A Darwinian Conflict Perspective*. Lanham, MD: Rowman & Littlefield.
———. 2007. *Evolutionism and Its Critics: Deconstructing and Reconstructing an Evolutionary Interpretation of Human Society*. Boulder, CO: Paradigm.
Sartre, Jean-Paul. 1968. *Search for a Method*. New York: Alfred Knopf.
Saussure, Ferdinand de. 1959. *Course in General Linguistics*. New York: McGraw-Hill.
Schmandt-Besserat, Denise. 1992. *Before Writing: From Counting to Cuneiform*. Austin: University of Texas Press.
Schutz, Alfred. 1967. *Phenomenology of the Social World*. Evanston, IL: Northwestern University Press.
Schwartz, Benjamin I. 1975. "The Age of Transcendence." *Daedalus* 104(2):1–7.
Scott, James C. 1998. *Seeing Like a State: How Certain Schemes to Improve the Human Condition Have Failed*. New Haven, CT: Yale University Press.
Scott, W. Richard. 2001. *Institutions and Organizations*. Thousand Oaks, CA: Sage.
———. 2008. "Approaching Adulthood: The Maturing of Institutional Theory." *Theory and Society* 37:427–42.
Scott, W. Richard, and John W. Meyer. 1983. "The Organization of Societal Sectors." In *Organizational Environments: Ritual and Rationality*, edited by J. W. Meyer and W. R. Scott. Beverly Hills, CA: Sage.
Service, Elman R. 1962. *Primitive Social Organization: An Evolutionary Perspective*. New York: Random House.
———. 1971. *Profiles in Ethnology*. New York: Harper & Row.
———. 1975. *Origins of the State and Civilization: The Process of Cultural Evolution*. New York: W.W. Norton & Company.
———. 1978. "Classical and Modern Theories of the Origins of Government." Pp. 21–34 in *Origins of the State: The Anthropology of Political Evolution*, edited by Ronald Cohen and Elman R. Service. Philadelphia: Institute for the Study of Humans Issues.
Sharot, Stephen. 2001. *A Comparative Sociology of World Religions: Virtuosos, Priests, and Popular Religion*. New York: New York University Press.
Shils, Edward A. 1975. *Center and Periphery: Essays in Macrosociology*. Chicago: University of Chicago Press.
Shott, Susan. 1979. "Emotion and Social Life: A Symbolic Interactionist Analysis." *American Journal of Sociology* 84(6):1317–34.
Sigerist, Henry E. 1951–61. *A History of Medicine*. 2 vols. Oxford: Oxford University Press.
Simmel, Georg. 1907. *The Philosophy of Money*. Boston: Routledge & Kegan Paul.
———. 1908 [1955]. *Conflict and the Web of Group-Affiliations*. New York: Macmillan.
Singer, Amy. 2008. *Charity in Islamic Societies*. New York: Cambridge University Press.
Skocpol, Theda. 1979. *States and Social Revolutions: A Comparative Analysis of France, Russia, and China*. Cambridge: Cambridge University Press.
Smith, Christian S., Michael O. Emerson, and Patricia Snell. 2008. *Passing the Plate: Why American Christians Don't Give Away More Money*. New York: Oxford University Press.
Snow, David A., and Sarah A. Soule. 2010. *A Primer on Social Movements*. New York: W. W. Horton & Company.

Southern, R. W. 1953. *The Making of the Middle Ages*. New Haven, CT: Yale University Press.

———. 1970. *Western Society and the Church in the Middle Ages*. London: Penguin Books.

Spencer, Herbert. 1897. *The Principles of Sociology*. New York: Appleton.

Spiro, Melford E. 1966. "Religion: Problems of Definition and Explanation." Pp. 85–126 in *Anthropological Approaches to the Study of Religion*, edited by Michael Banton. London: Tavistock Publications.

Stark, Rodney. 1999. "Micro Foundations of Religion: A Revised Theory." *Sociological Theory* 17(3):265–89.

———. 2006. *Cities of God: The Real Story of How Christianity Became an Urban Movement and Conquered Rome*. New York: Harper Collins.

———. 2007. *Discovering God: The Origins of the Great Religions and the Evolution of Belief*. New York: HarperOne.

Stark, Rodney, and William Sims Bainbridge. 1996. *A Theory of Religion*. New Brunswick, NJ: Rutgers University Press.

Starr, Paul. 1982. *The Social Transformation of American Medicine: The Rise of the Sovereign Profession and the Making of a Vast Industry*. New York: Basic Books.

Stein, Gil, and Mitchell S. Rothman (Eds.). 1994. *Chiefdoms and Early States in the Near East: The Organizational Dynamics of Complexity*. Madison, WI: Prehistory Press.

Stets, Jan E. 2005. "Examining Emotions in Identity Theory." *Social Psychology Quarterly* 68:39–56.

———. 2006. "Identity Theory." In *Contemporary Social Psychological Theories*, edited by P. J. Burke. Stanford, CA: Stanford University Press.

Stets, Jan E., Michael J. Carter, Michael M. Harrod, Christine Cerven, and Seth Abrutyn. 2008. "The Moral Identity, Moral Emotions, and the Normative Order." Pp. 227–52 in *Social Structure and Emotion*, edited by Dawn T. Robinson and Jody Clay-Warner. San Diego: Elsevier

Stets, Jan E., and Michael M. Harrod. 2004. "Verification Across Multiple Identities: The Role of Status." *Social Psychology Quarterly* 67:155–71.

Steward, Julian. 1955 [1972]. *Theory of Culture Change*. Champaign: University of Illinois Press.

Stone, Julius. 1965. *Human Law and Human Justice*. Stanford, CA: Stanford University Press.

Stone, Linda. 2004. "Has The World Turned? Kinship and Family in the Contemporary American Soap Opera." In *Kinship and Family: An Anthropological Reader*, edited by Robert Parkin and Linda Stone: Blackwell.

Stryker, Sheldon. 1980. *Symbolic Interactionism: A Social Structural Version*. Menlo Park, CA: The Benjamin Cummings Publishing Company.

Summers-Effler, Erika. 2004. "Defensive Strategies: The Formation and Social Implications of Patterened Self-Destructive Behavior." *Advances in Group Processes* 21:309–25.

Sumner, William Graham, and Albert G. Keller. 1927. *The Science of Society*. 4 vols. New Haven, CT: Yale University Press.

Sutton, John. 1984. "Organizational Autonomy and Professional Norms in Science: A Case Study of the Lawrence Livermore Laboratory." *Social Studies of Science* 14(2):197–224.

Sutton, John, Frank Dobbin, John W. Meyer, and W. Richard Scott. 1994. "The Legalization of the Workplace." *American Journal of Sociology* 99(4):944–71.

Swanson, Guy E. 1966. *The Birth of the Gods: The Origin of Primitive Beliefs*. Ann Arbor: University of Michigan Press.

Swartz, David. 1997. *Culture and Power: The Sociology of Pierre Bourdieu*. Chicago: University of Chicago.

Swedberg, Richard. 1995. "Markets as Social Structure." Pp. 255–82 in *The Handbook of Economic Sociology*, edited by Neil J. Smelser and Richard Swedberg.

———. 1998. *Max Weber and the Idea of Economic Sociology*. Princeton, NJ: Princeton University Press.

Swidler, Ann. 1986. "Culture in Action: Symbols and Strategies." *American Sociological Review* 51(2):273–86.

Taagepera, Rein. 1978. "Size and Duration of Empires: Growth-Decline Curves, 3000 to 600 B.C." *Social Science Research* 7:180–96.

———. 1979. "Size and Duration of Empires: Growth-Decline Curves, 600 B.C. to 600 A.D." *Social Science History* 3(3–4):115–38.

Tainter, Joseph A. 1988. *The Collapse of Complex Societies*. Cambridge: Cambridge University Press.

Thapar, Romila. 1975. "Ethics, Religion, and Social Protest in the First Millennium B.C. in Northern India." *Daedalus* 104(2):119–32.

——— 2004. *Early India: From the Origins to AD 1300*. Berkeley: University of California Press.

Thomas, George M., John W. Meyer, Francisco O. Ramirez, and John Boli. 1987. *Institutional Structure: Constituting State, Society, and the Individual*. Newbury Park, CA: Sage.

Thornton, Patricia H., and William Ocasio. 2008. "Institutional Logics." Pp. 99–129 in *The SAGE Handbook of Organizational Institutionalism*, edited by R. Greenwood, C. Oliver, K. Sahlin-Andersson, and R. Suddaby. Thousand Oaks, CA: Sage.

Thornton, Patricia H., William Ocasio, and Michael Lounsbury. 2012. *The Institutional Logics Perspective: A New Approach to Culture, Structure, and Process*. New York: Oxford University Press.

Turk, Austin T. 1976. "Law as a Weapon in Social Conflict." *Social Problems* 23(3):276–91.

Turner, Jonathan H. 1980. "Legal System Evolution: An Analytical Model." In *The Sociology of Law: A Social-Structural Perspective*, edited by William M. Evan. New York: The Free Press.

———. 1984a. "Durkheim's and Spencer's Principles of Social Organization: A Theoretical Note." *Sociological Perspectives* 27(1):21–32.

——— 1984b. *Societal Stratification: A Theoretical Analysis*. New York: Columbia University Press.

———. 1985. *Herbert Spencer: A Renewed Appreciation*. Beverly Hills, CA: Sage.

———. 1995. *Macrodynamics: Toward a Theory on the Organization of Human Populations*. New Brunswick, NJ: Rutgers University Press.

———. 1997. *The Institutional Order: Economy, Kinship, Religion, Polity, Law, and Education in Evolutionary and Comparative Perspective*. New York: Addison Wesley Longman, Inc.

———. 2003. *Human Institutions: A Theory of Societal Evolution*. Lanham: Bowman & Littlefield.

———. 2004. "Toward a General Theory of the Economy." *Sociological Theory* 22(2):229–46.

———. 2010a. *Theoretical Principles of Sociology, Volume 1: Macrodynamics*. New York: Springer.

———. 2010b. *Theoretical Principles of Sociology, Volume 2: Microdynamics*. New York: Springer.

———. 2010c. "The Stratification of Emotions: Some Preliminary Generalizations." *Sociological Inquiry* 80:165–75.

———. 2011. *Theoretical Principles of Sociology, Volume 3: Mesodynamics*. New York: Springer.
———. 2012. "The Structural Bases of Resource Distribution." Pp. 161–77 in *Handbook of Social Resource Theory*, edited by K. Törnblom and A. Kazemi. New York: Springer.
Turner, Jonathan H., and Alexandra Maryanski. 2008. "The Limitations of Evolutionary Theory From Biology." *Sociologica* 3:1–22.
Turner, Jonathan H., and Jan E. Stets. 2005. *The Sociology of Emotions*. Cambridge: Cambridge University Press.
Turner, Jonathan H., and Robert A. Hanneman. 1984. "Some Theoretical Principles of Societal Stratification." *Sociological Theory* 2(1):1–22.
———. 2009. *On the Origins of Societies by Natural Selection*. Boulder, CO: Paradigm.
Turner, Ralph H. 1976. "The Real Self: From Institution to Impulse." *American Journal of Sociology* 81(5):989–1016.
———. 1978. "The Role and the Person." *American Journal of Sociology* 84(1):1–23.
———. 2001. "Role Theory." In *The Handbook of Sociological Theory*, edited by Jonathan H. Turner. New York: Kluwer Academic/Plenum Publishers.
Turner, Terence S. 1968. "Parsons' Concept of Generalized Media of Social Interaction and Its Relevance for Social Anthropology." *Sociological Inquiry* 38(2):121–34.
Tylor, Edward. 1878 [2008]. *Researches into the Early History of Mankind and the Development of Civilization*. London: Kessinger.
Ullmann, Walter. 1975. *Law and Politics in the Middle Ages: An Introduction to the Sources of Medieval Political Ideas*. London: The Sources of History.
Unger, Roberto M. 1976. *Law In Modern Society: Towards a Criticism of Social Theory*. New York: Free Press.
van de Mieroop, Marc. 2004. *A History of the Ancient Near East, ca. 3000–323 BC*. Malden, MA: Blackwell.
Vandenberghe, Frédéric. 2007. "Avatars of the Collective: A Realist Theory of Collective Subjectivities." *Sociological Theory* 25(4):295–324.
Veblen, Thorstein. 1899 [1998]. *The Theory of the Leisure Class*. Amherst, NY: Prometheus Books.
Verkamp, Bernard J. 1991. "Concerning the Evolution of Religion." *The Journal of Religion* 71(4):538–57.
Wallace, Anthony F.C. 1956. "Revitalization Movements." *American Anthropologist* 58(2):264–81.
———. 1966. *Religion: An Anthropological View*. New York: Random House.
Wallerstein, Immanuel. 1974. *The Modern World-System: Capitalist Agriculture and the Origins of the European World-Economy in the Sixteenth Century*. New York: Academic Press.
Weber, Max. 1920 [2002]. *The Protestant Ethic and the "Spirit" of Capitalism and Other Writings*. New York: Penguin Books.
———. 1917–19 [1952]. *Ancient Judaism*. New York: Free Press.
———. 1922. *The Sociology of Religion*. Boston: Beacon Press.
——— 1927 [2002]. *General Economic History*. New Brunswick, NJ: Transaction Publishers.
———. 1946a. "The 'Rationalization' of Education and Training." Pp. 240–44 in *From Max Weber: Essays in Sociology*, edited by H. Gerth and C.W. Mills. Cambridge: Oxford University Press.
———. 1946b. "Science as a Vocation." Pp. 129–56 in *From Max Weber: Essays in Sociology*, edited by H. Gerth and C.W. Mills. New York: Oxford University Press.

———. 1946c. "The Social Psychology of World Religions." Pp. 267–301 in *From Max Weber: Essays in Sociology*, edited by H. Gerth and C. W. Mills. New York: Oxford University Press.

———. 1967. *Max Weber on Law in Economy and Society.* New York: Simon and Schuster.

———. 1968. *Max Weber on Charisma and Institution Building.* Chicago: University of Chicago Press.

———. 1978. *Economy and Society: An Outline of Interpretive Sociology.* Berkeley: University of California Press.

Weiss, Harvey. 1986. *The Origins of Cities in Dry-Farming Syria and Mesopotamia in the Third Millennium B.C.* Guilford, CT: Four Quarters.

Weiss, Harvey, M.-A. Courty, W. Wetterstrom, F. Guichard, L. Senior, R. Meadow, and A. Curnow. 1993. "The Genesis and Collapse of Third Millennium North Mesopotamian Civilization." *Science* 261(5124):995–1004.

Werron, Tobias. 2010. "World Sport and Its Public: On Historical Relations of Modern Sport and the Media." Pp. 33–60 in *Observing Sport: System-Theoretical Approaches to Sport as a Social Phenomenon*, edited by U. Wagner, R. Storm, and J. Hoberman. Schorndorf, Germany: Hofmann.

White, Harrison C. 1992. *Identity and Control: A Structural Theory of Social Action.* Princeton, NJ: Princeton University Press.

Wilson, David Sloan. 2002. *Darwin's Cathedral: Evolution, Religion, and the Nature of Society.* Chicago: University of Chicago Press.

Wood, Thomas E. 2012. *How the Catholic Church Built Western Civilization.* Washington, DC: Regnery.

Yoffee, Norman. 2000. "Law Courts and the Mediation of Social Conflict in Ancient Mesopotamia." Pp. 46–63 in *Order, Legitimacy, and Wealth in Ancient States*, edited by Janet Richards and Mary Van Buren. Cambridge: Cambridge University Press.

———. 2005. *Myths of the Archaic State: Evolution of the Earliest Cities, States, and Civilizations.* Cambridge: Cambridge University Press.

Yoffee, Norman, and George L. Cowgill. 1988. *The Collapse of Ancient States and Civilizations.* Tucson: University of Arizona Press.

Zelizer, Viviana. 1997. *The Social Meaning of Money: Pin Money, Paychecks, Poor Relief, and Other Currencies.* Princeton, NJ: Princeton University Press.

———. 2013. *Economic Lives: How Culture Shapes the Economy.* Princeton: Princeton University Press.

# Index

www.ingramcontent.com/pod-product-compliance
Lightning Source LLC
Chambersburg PA
CBHW050425280326
41932CB00013BA/1995

*9781138639676*